WORLD HERITAGE

World Heritage: Concepts, Management and Conservation presents an insight into discussions and debates surrounding the UNESCO World Heritage List, and the properties on it.

Since its creation 50 years ago, the World Heritage Convention has been lauded as one of the most successful international expressions of cooperation, while at the same time being widely criticised as producing an overly commercialised and globalised sense of heritage. Offering an in-depth discussion of both sides of the debate, this book explores these issues by discussing the following topics:

- How the World Heritage Convention was conceived and how it is operationalised;
- How the World Heritage concept is currently being used and misused;
- The benefits of inscription – perceived and actual existential threats faced by World Heritage Site managers including climate change, urban development, overtourism, military action and natural disaster;
- The future of World Heritage as an instrument for conservation and economic development.

Case studies from a global range of World Heritage Sites are included throughout, to showcase some of the successes and also missuses of World Heritage status.

This book will be of pivotal interest to students and scholars in the fields of tourism, heritage, archaeology, natural resource management and development studies.

Simon C. Woodward is a Geographer by training and Principal Lecturer in the School of Events, Tourism and Hospitality Management at Leeds Beckett University where he teaches on both the undergraduate and postgraduate tourism management programmes, specialising in cultural and heritage tourism; destination development and business management. Prior to joining the University in 2008, he spent 20 years as a full-time management consultant to the global heritage tourism sector, working in many developed and emerging destinations in the Middle East; East, West and Southern Africa and in Western Europe, including the UK. Simon has a particular interest in developing and managing community-based heritage.

Louise Cooke is Senior Lecturer in Conservation in the Department of Archaeology at University of York, with interests in sustainability, historic buildings, archaeological sites and cultural landscapes. She has undertaken fieldwork in Central Asia and the Middle East and has a wide-ranging portfolio of freelance and project-based work overseas in the UEA, Peru and Turkey, as well as across the UK. She joined the Archaeology Department in York in 2016, further developing connections and research with South Asia. Louise has a particular interest in creative responses to heritage management and conservation in a changing climate.

WORLD HERITAGE

Concepts, Management and Conservation

Simon C. Woodward and Louise Cooke

Routledge
Taylor & Francis Group

LONDON AND NEW YORK

Cover image: © Nigel Eve / Getty Images

First published 2023
by Routledge
4 Park Square, Milton Park, Abingdon, Oxon OX14 4RN

and by Routledge
605 Third Avenue, New York, NY 10158

Routledge is an imprint of the Taylor & Francis Group, an informa business

© 2023 Simon C. Woodward and Louise Cooke

British Library Cataloguing-in-Publication Data
A catalogue record for this book is available from the British Library

ISBN: 978-0-367-49166-6 (hbk)
ISBN: 978-0-367-49164-2 (pbk)
ISBN: 978-1-003-04485-7 (ebk)

DOI: 10.4324/9781003044857

Typeset in Bembo
by Taylor & Francis Books

This book is dedicated to the memories of Muriel Amy Woodward (1927–2017) and William Barry Woodward (1929–2020)

CONTENTS

ILLUSTRATIONS

Figures

Tables

Boxes

ACKNOWLEDGEMENTS

Simon wishes to thank the following for their support over the course of my career with World Heritage: Dr Christopher Young, for giving me my first professional contract to write a WHS Management Plan; The Very Reverend Michael Sadgrove, for involving me in the management of my home town Cathedral and local World Heritage Site in Durham City; Geoff DeVito, for involving me in Seabourn Cruise's UNESCO World Heritage conversationalist programme; HRH Prince Sultan bin Salman, Dr Ali Ghabban and Mardy Al-Khamaly for enabling me to access the astonishing archaeological and cultural heritage of Hegra (al-Hijr) in Saudi Arabia; Robert Piaskowski of the Muncipality of Krakow; Uta Mense, Dr Aylin Orbaşli and all colleagues past and present at the ASH Consulting Group, PLB Consulting Ltd, Keios Development Consulting and Leeds Beckett University, particularly Lisa Gorton, Lucy McCombes and Dr Davina Stanford. Finally, I cannot sufficiently express my gratitude to my wife Hilary for the friendship, love, patience and unstinting support she has shown since we first met in 1971, the year before the World Heritage Convention was signed!

Louise wishes to thank the following for their support: Tim Williams who opened my eyes to World Heritage through projects in the Middle East and Central Asia; the late John Hurd who enabled some of my other visits through work in a short period of consultancy for the Global Heritage Fund; my colleagues at the University of York, particularly Dr Gill Chitty and Professor Nicky Milner, who encouraged me to develop my World Heritage teaching and have enabled me to take part in other teaching and study trips to additional World Heritage properties – and to the many students who have engaged with World Heritage ideas, shared thoughts and made me think differently about the value of World Heritage. Finally Alfie – at least all of these conversations about World Heritage make you unbeatable at the Kahoot World Heritage quiz, William who took his first steps on a World Heritage Site while dodging scorpions, and Dominic who, among many other things, can always find the photos.

INTRODUCTION

'World Heritage' is often used as a shorthand reference for the list of cultural and natural heritage properties considered to be of Outstanding Universal Value as laid down and defined by the 1972 UNESCO World Heritage Convention. Since its creation, the World Heritage Convention has been lauded by some commentators as a particularly successful expression of international cooperation in the field of heritage protection and management, while others have criticised it as a neoliberal intervention that has created an overly commercialised and globalised sense of heritage.

In recent decades, the increasing internationalisation of business has broken down national barriers and has seen the spread across the globe of ubiquitous brands such as Amazon, Apple and Starbucks. At the same time global communities have also emerged, linked through social-media platforms such as Facebook, Instagram and TikTok. Has World Heritage become just another global brand, marking out certain locations as internationally relevant and then celebrated and/or disparaged by key-board warriors who may not even have had first-hand experience of the particular property they are commenting on?

Increased global wealth, generous leave entitlements for more and more workers, and the relatively low cost of travel has resulted in the exponential growth of international tourism. Up until the COVID-19 pandemic of 2020/21, it was one of the fastest growing industries in the world with the UNWTO reporting 1.5 billion international trips in 2019[1]. The growth of tourism in both industrialised and developing states has produced economic and employment benefits throughout the so-called tourism value chain in every destination, from construction to agriculture and from hospitality through to heritage. Moreover, there is an increasingly strong relationship between World Heritage and tourism with many lists of 'must see' destinations including some of the world's most iconic cultural and natural heritage sites. While one can question whether this is incidental or accidental, it is not hard to identify a relationship between the two concepts of tourism and World Heritage.

DOI: 10.4324/9781003044857-1

What is evident is that the World Heritage list today can represent different ideas to different stakeholders: a list of exceptional and high profile cultural and natural sites that are vulnerable to misuse and destruction if not protected and managed appropriately; important agents for regional and local development; or merely a directory of iconic, desirable, 'must see', 'Instagrammable' tourist destinations. These facets of the phenomenon of World Heritage are all somewhat removed from the ideals of the 1972 Convention, which saw World Heritage Sites as exemplars of their kind, with an intangible value that transcends national boundaries and that should be looked after for the sake of future generations.

Some 50 years after the World Heritage Convention there is increasing debate and scholarship on its purpose and impact, with academics and practitioners alike considering the role of the Convention in popularising and commercialising heritage, the difficulties of identifying exactly what is meant by 'outstanding universal value', and the complexities of negotiating and implementing the conservation concepts of authenticity and integrity. This book seeks to build on these debates by exploring the ways in which the World Heritage Convention was conceived and how the concept and brand of World Heritage has been generated and promoted over time. Through a series of central themes we explore how World Heritage operates today, discussing how the concept is being used (and misused) and how it provides a perspective on the great societal and environmental challenges of the 21st century.

In all of the criticisms of World Heritage as a brand and as a concept the authors admit to their own contradictions. When we read a guide book for a destination we worry about 'missing' World Heritage properties – we 'check' the World Heritage website (we both suffer from fear of missing out world heritage - FOMOWH). When we talk about those visits, we foreground the destination's name: 'the World Heritage Site of Sagrada Familia'; 'our closest World Heritage Site is Studley Royal and Fountains Abbey'. This professional engagement and critique of World Heritage is contrasted when talking to friends, family and colleagues, who may not share this passion.

As lecturers in different disciplines, teaching in two different universities in the north of England, we have both become aware of the need for a more popular and more accessible approach to World Heritage studies that answers some of the misconceptions around the process. For example, the successful nomination of a property does not change its legal protection (which remains that from the State party), nor does it provide extra funding for conservation and site protection. Rather, these benefits can emerge through protection, marketing, development and commercialisation of a property and its heritage. The varied awareness of the World Heritage brand and its use in promoting tourism is always an interesting starting point in discussions with our students – undergraduate and postgraduate – who come from many parts of the world and who bring their own understandings to the table.

In shaping this book we have sought to provide the reader with both an academic and a practitioner's perspective on World Heritage with the intention of presenting a nuanced understanding of how the original intentions behind the

1972 Convention have shifted over time and created an environment where the appeal of securing World Heritage Site status remains strong, while at the same time the implications of that status bring considerable obligations and challenges to the authorities, organisations and communities associated with each site.

The first part of the book provides a conceptual and historical introduction to World Heritage: Chapter 1 identifies the origins of World Heritage as a reaction to destruction after the 2nd World War and the growing awareness of the potential for future loss of cultural heritage properties as a result of post-war reconstruction and redevelopment. It also explores the parallel moves towards protecting natural landscapes either for their scenic beauty or ecological importance. Chapter 2 considers the operation of the World Heritage Convention and explores some of the emerging trends in inscription that reflect the increased politicisation of World Heritage, a theme explored in more detail in Chapter 3 which looks at the politics that are played out through and on World Heritage properties, as representing important places from which we can learn from the past, and as places that are potentially vulnerable to destruction and loss.

The second part considers more pragmatic issues around the protection and management of properties on the World Heritage List. Chapter 4 considers Disaster Risk Management and examines the ways in which properties must engage with concepts of risk preparedness through planning and management approaches, with Chapter 5 exploring some of the pressures associated with urbanisation and development. Chapter 6 considers climate change as it relates to World Heritage properties and how the 'list' of World Heritage properties provides a useful lens through which these vital, contemporary issues can be focused upon. The challenges faced by marine heritage sites and protected areas are explored in Chapter 7 – although representing only around 5% of the properties on the list they face some of the most severe pressures from development and climate change.

Benefits of World Heritage Site inscription are addressed in Chapter 8 which explores how local communities and tourists engage with properties on the list, as well as the instrumental, catalytic developmental role that more and more properties are being charged with delivering. Strategies for managing tourism pressures at natural and cultural sites are addressed in Chapter 9 and the interpretation and presentation of World Heritage is covered in Chapter 10.

The final part looks at current practices surrounding World Heritage: Chapter 11 reflects on how World Heritage is being used to tackle some of the UN's Sustainable Development Goals, and in Chapter 12 we finally reflect on how best to respond to the range of challenges and opportunities heritage faces as we move through the 21st century and fully come to terms with the Anthropocene.

Throughout the text are case studies selected and prepared to offer a framework for debate about how representative the World Heritage List is - the opposite of representative is the idea of canonical: the commonly-held belief that it's only the best or the biggest or the oldest or the most important sites which are captured on the World Heritage List. The case studies help to demonstrate that in fact over the last 50 years conscious efforts have been made to move away from inscribing just the iconic monuments from past cultures and civilisations towards a more inclusive approach that recognises other forms of heritage as being just as worthy of being considered to be of 'Outstanding Universal Value'. In particular, we consider how recent initiatives relating to representation have moved the World Heritage debate forward to a situation where UNESCO and others have effectively invented multiple World Heritages that may or may not always relate to local, regional or national heritage.

The case studies also give an insight into some of the pressures that are placed on sites that might be threatened by over-tourism, urban development or other aspects of 21st century life, and demonstrate how site managers and others are seeking to protect those values central to a property's inscription. They are not by any means intended to provide a comprehensive insight into how all World Heritage Sites are managed, but rather they offer an insight into the activities involved in ensuring a property's Outstanding Universal Value – the very reason for its inscription – are protected and maintained so that there is less risk of this iconic brand status being lost.

The original idea for this book sprang from a discussion the two authors had in Summer 2017 after the AGM of the Landscape Research Centre, an archaeological charity that we are both connected with and that seeks to promote greater public awareness of, and engagement with, the cultural landscape of Ryedale, North Yorkshire. Some of the ideas for this book, particularly around the idea of 'inventing World Heritage' were tested through an undergraduate course developed and taught at the University of York in Autumn 2017 and 2018 while our insights into the conservation and management challenges at World Heritage Properties, and the strategies and tools for tackling these, have built up over many years through our consultancy work in the field, in destinations as far apart as Bethlehem and The Gambia, Turkmenistan and Peru. The impact of the COVID-19 pandemic not only on our personal and working lives, but on the international heritage community as a whole, helped reshape our initial ideas into the final product you see here today which offers, we hope, an informative and critical perspective on this thing we call World Heritage.

Note

1   https://www.unwto.org/world-tourism-barometer-n18-january-2020 Accessed 29/10/21

1

THE INVENTION OF WORLD HERITAGE

1.1 A brief history of heritage protection in the 19th century

The international conservation movement has much earlier origins than the key focus of this book, which is the late 20th and early 21st centuries. Indeed, some would argue that the reason monuments survive through prehistory onwards represents a form of awareness of the 'past' (Gosden, 1994). But the formalised evolution of the international conservation movement developed from the 19th century onwards, when widespread concern with the past and its management developed as a reaction to losses apparent from the rapid changes to both urban and rural landscapes brought about through the Industrial Revolution. During the latter part of the 19th century in particular, people became increasingly aware of, yet more disconnected from, their past. As a result, debates emerged about how and in what ways the past – as represented by landscapes, historic buildings and cities – should be looked after.

This growing awareness of the scale of loss led to considerable public debate surrounding the 'correct' approach to the use and conservation of aspects of the past in many parts of the world. For instance, in the Western United States, the Scottish–American naturalist John Muir spent much of the 1880s and 1890s actively pressing for the protection from all development of what he saw as the pristine landscapes and habitats of the Sierra Nevada mountain range, while in Europe art critic John Ruskin, British architects Augustus Pugin and George Gilbert Scott and French architect Eugène Viollet-le-Duc engaged in fierce debate about how best to protect and preserve historic buildings.

For some, Ruskin's position can be simplified to be considered 'anti restoration', not least because his polemical writings argued for retaining the 'truth' and 'life' of buildings – the idea that a building's information and documentary value were the significant aspects that should be valued and protected from ill-planned restoration

DOI: 10.4324/9781003044857-2

and reconstruction (Jokilehto, 1999; Glendinning, 2013). Ruskin's argument was directly opposed to the ideas of Viollet-le-Duc Gilbert Scott and Pugin, whose practice and theories argued for greater restoration, reinvention and intervention. These latter three are particularly noted as their restoration is now represented on a number of World Heritage properties – le Duc at Carcassonne and Notre Dame, Gilbert Scott at Durham and Canterbury Cathedral and Pugin at the Palace of Westminster).

Ruskin's arguments did however influence the ideas of William Morris and Philip Webb, whose Society for the Protection of Ancient Buildings (SPAB) was founded in Bloomsbury, London, in 1877. SPAB's manifesto stated that each building had a life, formed of the changes that had occurred through its life, and that both destruction and restoration could strip this life out of a building. The early campaigns of SPAB focused principally on ecclesiastical buildings in the UK, but SPAB eventually took these debates outside of the UK, campaigning, for instance, against the proposed restoration work at St Mark's, Venice in 1879 (SPAB, 2019). These controversial debates on the 'correct' approach to historic building use and conservation that were first aired almost 150 years ago still remain an ongoing feature with conservation in general and, as we will see later, within contemporary debates about World Heritage.

And even away from the salons of London and Paris, colonial ideas of protection and conservation of archaeological sites and monuments imposed a western-European approach around the world. For example, the Archaeological Survey of India, established in 1861 under British Rule, imposed particular approaches to conservation that favoured the archaeological, monumental and physical (tangible heritage) over more representative types of heritage (such as the vernacular architecture of everyday houses) and emphasised the need to conserve historical structures rather than traditions, performance and cultural practices (intangible heritage). These distinctions between tangible and intangible heritage are still obvious when one considers the types of properties that were inscribed on the World Heritage list until relatively recently, and indeed are reinforced by the operation of two separate World Heritage lists by UNESCO: the 1972 Convention Concerning the Protection of World Cultural and Natural Heritage (which is the focus of this book), and the 2003 Convention for the Safeguarding of the Intangible Cultural Heritage.

1.2 Cultural heritage protection in the 20th century

The early years of the 20th century saw a number of international efforts in historic building conservation. In 1904 the Sixth International Congress of Architects was held in Madrid, Spain with delegates from Europe, Russia, USA and Mexico reflecting on the 'The Preservation and Restoration of Architectural Monuments' (Madrid Conference, 1904). A lot of the debate at that congress focused on concerns about how best to conserve historical, technical and aesthetic values, and one outcome of the event was a recommendation that every nation should establish a society for the preservation of historical and artistic monuments.

Twentieth-century efforts in conservation were heavily influenced by the two World Wars and the international movements that developed in their wake. For example, the First International Congress of Architects and Technicians of Historic Monuments was held in Athens in 1931.The conference was organised by the International Museums Office through the League of Nations. This was important in introducing a number of conservation approaches, promoting the idea of a common heritage shared across nation boundaries, suggesting that the conservation of this shared heritage should be a priority for action, and arguing that nation states should 'collaborate with each other on an ever-increasing scale and in a more concrete manner with a view to furthering the preservation of artistic and historic monuments' (Athens Charter, 1931) and that each should publish a heritage inventory. The hosting of the conference in Athens, a city faced with the enormous conservation challenges of its many Classical Greek archaeological sites which functioned as iconic examples of standing, monumental tangible heritage, would also impact on the types of heritage that would later be recognised through the World Heritage Convention as having Outstanding Universal Value.

During the Second World War international efforts in conservation took a different path, with an emphasis both on the protection of moveable cultural property on the one hand (through the work of the Allies Monuments, Fine Arts, and Archives programme), and the deliberate targeting of historic cities in Europe through the Lübeck and Baedeker bombing raids of 1942. Immediately after the Second World War damaged historic cities, archaeological sites and historic buildings were at the forefront of thinking about appropriate methods of post-war reconstruction. For example, in the UK 'salvage lists' detailed whether or not a building should be demolished if it was bomb-damaged. These lists were later formalised through the Town and Country Planning Acts of 1944 and 1947, forming the Heritage Protection List for England.

It is evident that the widespread destruction of built heritage in many parts of the world during the six years of conflict between 1939 and 1945 had a significant impact on the creation of an international conservation movement which saw heritage protection as a potentially useful tool for international diplomacy. UNESCO (the United Nations Educational, Scientific and Cultural Organization) was formed in 1945 and the preamble to the organisation's constitution states: 'Since wars begin in the minds of men and women, it is in the minds of men and women that the defences of peace must be constructed' (Preamble, UNESCO Constitution, n.d.). The constitution goes on to define the purpose of the organisation as being

> to contribute to peace and security by promoting collaboration among nations through education, science and culture in order to further universal respect for justice, for the rule of law and for the human rights and fundamental freedoms which are affirmed for the peoples of the world, without distinction of race, sex, language or religion, by the Charter of the United Nations.
>
> *(Article 1, UNESCO Constitution, n.d.)*

The emphasis on collaborative efforts to celebrate and protect culture, which includes heritage, reinforces the importance that this aspect of human achievement was being accorded as a tool for promoting greater understanding of the past and its value in helping us understand the present and perhaps even shape the future.

Through the organisation's protocols, the Director-General of UNESCO is charged to implement all programmes approved by the General Conference. British Biologist Julian Huxley was the first Director-General, running it from 1946 to 1948 and later becoming one of the founders of the World Wildlife Fund (now the Worldwide Fund for Nature), while Audrey Azoulay, a French politician, is the current (2022) and the second female Director-General of the organisation. UNESCO's overarching objectives have evolved over the seven decades or so of its existence to reflect changing societal needs and include: attaining quality education for all and lifelong learning; mobilising science, knowledge and policy for sustainable development; addressing emerging social and ethical challenges; fostering cultural diversity, intercultural dialogue, and a culture of peace; and building inclusive knowledge societies through information and communication (UNESCO, 2010).

UNESCO spent its first few years in a temporary location before opening its headquarters in Paris in 1958 in a building that deliberately represents the focus and interest of the optimistic, post-war Internationalist agenda. UNESCO's headquarters is a modernist, international building featuring work from three architects of different nationalities: Marcel Breuer of the United States; Pier Luigi Nervi of Italy and Bernard Zehrfuss of France. The building speaks of the confidence of the international community in the post-war years in coming together, optimistically solving problems through cooperation, communication and culture. It was within this international mix of agents and actors with considerable social capital that cultural and natural heritage started to become a clear and defining area of UNESCO's work.

The early iterations of the World Heritage movement supported through UNESCO were responding to reactive trends, principally in response to an awareness of the scale of wartime losses and to concerns about the challenges of post-war recovery and reconstruction, as well as a response to increasing alarm in some quarters at the scale of loss and destruction associated with urban development in the 1950s. The World Heritage movement is considered by most to have been a modern, international and idealistic movement, but one that was also reactive, a mirror of the wider concerns of the international conservation movement.

The cultural heritage 'moment' for UNESCO came to the forefront through the campaign to safeguard threatened archaeological sites in Egypt. The Nubia Campaign (1960–71) is generally recognised as the first collaborative international rescue effort led by UNESCO to rescue cultural heritage sites. UNESCO launched an international campaign and the high-profile coverage of the case resulted in the collection of US$80 million ($565 million today[1]) to 'save' the Abu Simbel temples in the Nile Valley that were being threatened by the construction of the Aswan High Dam (Hassan, 2007; Betts, 2015). Eventually the decision was made to move the temples in order to 'save' them from inundation, with the entire site being carefully cut into large blocks dismantled, lifted and reassembled in a new location 65 metres higher and 200 metres back from the river where it remains today.

It is significant that international teams worked together on the Nubia Campaign – in all, more than 25 countries were involved (Betts 2015). The success of the capital works was the subject of a widespread media campaign which further caught the international imagination. For instance, the project featured on the front cover of *Time* magazine, with iconic black-and-white photography showing the ancient, massive stone work meticulously cut up, wrapped and tied up, shifted by cranes and moved across the Nubian landscape. What the Nubia Campaign showed was that the international community *could* come together and *could* work together to protect heritage considered vulnerable and at risk. It was a project conceived of at an optimistic time, when technology was seen to be capable of resolving grand societal problems. Other international cultural heritage campaigns followed in Venice (Italy), Mohenjadaro (Pakistan) and Borobodur (Indonesia).

BOX 1.1 CASE STUDY 1.1: INTERNATIONAL CONSERVATION CONCERNS IN VENICE.

From the time of the Renaissance in the 15th century, Western European culture celebrated its classical inheritance and as a result artists, poets and travellers were drawn to Venice as part of the Grand Tour, a lengthy trip taken largely by young men to explore the cultural sites of ancient Greece and Rome as well as more contemporary destinations. Venice in particular embodied ideas of monumental, architectural and grand heritage that came to dominate Western European approaches to heritage.

The British art critic and writer John Ruskin visited Venice for the first time in 1835 and returned several times throughout his life, making his last visit in 1878. His admiration for both individual buildings and for the city as a whole was tempered by what he saw being done in the name of conservation. Ruskin's *The Stones of Venice* was published in three volumes from 1851 to 1853, and in it Ruskin objected to the restoration approach adopted in the city, arguing that presenting buildings in a 'pristine' condition was inappropriate and that restoration is 'a lie from beginning to end'.

Later, in 1879 SPAB launched their first international campaign to voice protest over the planned restoration of St Mark's, Venice. This included letter writing, reports and investigations and the collection of 2,000 signatures in opposition to the planned works. Venice had thus become an arena for debating broader philosophical questions of heritage and conservation, and in 1879 *The Times* reported that Venice was the 'pride and possession of the whole world', in effect foregrounding the ideas of outstanding universal value that are central to the concepts of the World Heritage movement today.

Venice continued to provide focus for international debate on approaches to conservation throughout the 20th century and beyond. For instance, in 1966, prior to the formalisation of the World Heritage Convention, UNESCO launched an international campaign in response to devastating floods in the city. The Director-General of UNESCO at the time, appealed to all, stating: 'Each one of us knows himself to be a member of the family of Man. How then could any one of us remain indifferent to the fate of these most precious jewels of our common human heritage?' (Maheu, 1967).

Venice was listed as a World Heritage Property in 1987. The property (its full name is 'Venice and its Lagoon') was unusually listed associated with all six cultural criteria, which perhaps reflects the exceptional international status of the city and its continued influence in architecture, conservation and art.

In the 2020s Venice continues to provide a focus for debate on how best to protect, conserve and manage a historic city. There have been debates, for instance, around how to combat overtourism in the principal public spaces; how to resolve the negative impacts on local communities caused by the loss of residential accommodation to Airbnb units; whether or not large cruise ships should be allowed to sail through the heart of the city; and on the best approaches protecting the city itself from potentially catastrophic rising sea levels associated with climate change. All of these challenges must be viewed through the lens of the city's World Heritage status which clearly sets out those 'values' that should be protected.

1.3 Protecting natural heritage in the 20th century

Parallel to the late 19th century interest in protecting and celebrating the rich architectural and built heritage of Europe was a growing awareness of the importance of preserving parts of the natural world. The impetus for establishing national parks and other forms of protected areas in countries such as the United States, Canada and Australia was a recognition that rapidly growing European colonisers were exploiting resources at an unsustainable rate through activities such as agriculture, timber production, mining, fishing and urbanisation (Newsome et al., 2002). The world's first National Park, Yellowstone, was established in western USA in 1872 followed by Banff Hot Springs (Canada) in 1885 and Yosemite in the US in 1890. Australia's first protected area, Royal National Park, was declared in 1879. In all instances, the intention was to protect special landscapes with a view to promoting and facilitating a certain amount of recreational use.

Elsewhere in the world, other pressures on the natural environment, such as big game hunting, gave rise to legal protection for special landscapes. In South Africa, Kruger National Park was created in 1898 to demonstrate that the US model of wilderness protection could work in sub-Saharan Africa. Two decades or so later, in 1925, Virunga National Park (originally Albert National Park) was established in what was then the Belgian Congo for much the same reason (Hendee et al., 1990). As Nash (1982) notes, one should not ignore the fact that these early examples of protection for natural areas in Africa were basically another colonial imposition, and were designed to suit the needs of the colonial powers rather than the indigenous populations living there. As will be explored later, the failure to acknowledge the needs of local communities living in and around protected areas and instead to focus on natural resource conservation can still be seen today in some parts of the world.

An important step in the development of the international conservation community was the creation, in 1928, of the International Office for the Protection of Nature. Based in Brussels, the organisation pressed for countries around the globe to designate protected areas for the purposes of landscape and wildlife protection. Throughout the 1930s, until it ceased operation in 1940, it was particularly active in pressing for more protection of African flora and fauna, working through the colonial powers across the continent. Partly as a result of these efforts, more than 50% of sub-Saharan Africa's protected areas were in place by 1962. As well as seeking to protect landscapes and threatened species from overexploitation, other factors influencing the location of protected areas on the African continent during this period included watershed protection and erosion control (Burnett & Harrington, 1994).

Two conferences hosted by the Swiss League for the Protection of Nature in 1946 and 1947 eventually led to the creation of the International Union for the Protection of Nature and Natural Resources (now the International Union for the Conservation of Nature – IUCN) in 1948. The organisation had two main interests – protecting some of the renewable natural resources on which human civilisation depends but also promoting the amenity value of wilderness and other natural areas (Hendee et al., 1990). In the late 1960s IUCN took on responsibility for developing an international convention to promote international cooperation on the conservation of natural resources under the aegis of a trust for world natural heritage. This of course paralleled the work that UNESCO was undertaking in the field of cultural heritage protection, with both documents eventually being combined at a meeting in Paris in 1972 and adopted by the UNESCO General Conference as the Convention for the Protection of the World Cultural and Natural Heritage later that year.

The first international conservation treaty however, predating the World Heritage Convention by a year, was the 'Ramsar Convention on Wetlands of International Importance, especially as Waterfowl Habitat'. Named after the Iranian city where the convention was held in 1971, the Ramsar Convention helps to protect sites of representative, rare or unique wetland types and/ or that are of international importance for conserving biological diversity. As is the case with WHS status, sites named on the Ramsar list do not have any additional legal protection though the recognition can provide additional support when lobbying against development threats (Hendee et al., 1990). It is interesting to note that in 2016, some 97 sites appeared both on the World Heritage list and the Ramsar list, almost 50% of all natural World Heritage Sites at that time.

While Europe, Africa and North America had seen major efforts towards the creation of protected areas in the first decades of the 20th century, elsewhere, however, the pace was slower. In North Africa and the Middle East, China, Central America and the Caribbean, more than 50% of the area protected was designated only in the 1980s and early 1990s (McNeely, 1994).

In short, the principal motives for declaring protected natural areas emerged from late 19th-century concerns about saving 'wilderness' from anthropogenic disturbance (including game hunting), moving on to an interest in protecting watersheds and combating erosion and finally through to safeguarding biological diversity. As regards wildlife, popular conservation movements that commenced with a focus on specific, often iconic, species were followed by campaigns and organisations that recognised the importance of protecting the habitats they relied on.

1.4 The World Heritage Convention

Alongside the high-profile reactive conservation projects in places such as Abu Simbel and Borobudur was a growing public and professional awareness of the rate and scale of loss of landscapes, buildings and species. Professionals in a wide range of disciplines, including scientists with a primary focus on natural heritage and architects, archaeologists and others with an interest in cultural heritage, were campaigning for international protection and for the establishment of a 'list' of important sites and places, as an extended and contemporary 'Wonders of the World'. There were complex negotiations with both cultural and natural heritage experts pushing for their own interests (see, for instance, Cameron & Rossler, 2016) and these international efforts were finally formalised through the Convention Concerning the Protection of World Cultural and Natural Heritage, which was adopted by the General Conference of UNESCO in Paris on 16 November 1972.

The World Heritage Convention introduced the idea of Outstanding Universal Value (OUV) which is defined as cultural and/or natural significance which is 'so exceptional as to transcend national boundaries and to be of common importance for present and future generations of all humanity' (Operational Guidelines for the Implementation of the World Heritage Convention, para. 49). To some interest groups, the coming together of both cultural and natural heritage was a compromise, but the legacy of thinking about 'cultural' and 'natural' heritage as very separate categories is itself a product of the binary western mindset and this binary classification of natural and cultural heritage added complications to the early stages of the identification, management and conservation of World Heritage properties, and which has only partly been resolved through the introduction in 1992 of an additional category of cultural landscapes representing the 'combined works of nature and of man' (UNESCO Cultural Landscapes, n.d.) (see Section 1.5.4 below).

Following on from the World Heritage Convention being agreed in 1972, the first 12 World Heritage Cultural Properties were listed in 1978, including four natural sites and eight cultural sites. States Parties who are signatories to the Convention are able to nominate new sites for inclusion every year, with applications being peer reviewed and approved or rejected at the annual meeting of the World Heritage Committee. Since the original 12 properties were inscribed in 1978, a further 1,145 properties have been added to the World Heritage List with three properties subsequently being delisted, meaning that at the time this book went to press in summer 2022, there were 1,154 World Heritage Sites (897 cultural, 218 natural and 39 mixed) across territories governed by 167 different States Parties.

As indicated above, the intervening years since the World Heritage Convention was signed have seen continued evolution of the original recording and evaluation processes that were created to support implementation of the initial Convention and these amendments are reflected and defined in the World Heritage Operational Guidelines. The current (2021) Operational Guidelines for the World Heritage Convention defines cultural heritage in a number of different groups:

- **monuments**: architectural works, works of monumental sculpture and painting, elements or structures of an archaeological nature, inscriptions, cave dwellings and combinations of features, which are of Outstanding Universal Value from the point of view of history, art or science;
- **groups of buildings:** groups of separate or connected buildings which, because of their architecture, their homogeneity or their place in the landscape, are of Outstanding Universal Value from the point of view of history, art or science;
- **sites:** works of man or the combined works of nature and of man, and areas including archaeological sites which are of Outstanding Universal Value from the historical, aesthetic, ethnological or anthropological points of view.

Definitions of the different types of natural heritage properties are as follows:

- **natural features** consisting of physical and biological formations or groups of such formations, which are of Outstanding Universal Value from the aesthetic or scientific point of view;
- **geological and physiographical formations and precisely delineated areas** which constitute the habitat of threatened species of animals and plants of Outstanding Universal Value from the point of view of science or conservation;
- **natural sites or precisely delineated natural areas** of Outstanding Universal Value from the point of view of science, conservation or natural beauty.

In order to be successful in nomination to the World Heritage List, properties must be considered to be of Outstanding Universal Value and they must also meet at least one out of the ten selection criteria as defined within the Operational Guidelines. The first six selection criteria refer principally to cultural heritage sites and the final four to natural heritage sites (these were renumbered 1–10 in 2003, rather than separate numbering for cultural and natural heritage sites). The criteria are:

  i to represent a masterpiece of human creative genius;
  ii to exhibit an important interchange of human values, over a span of time or within a cultural area of the world, on developments in architecture or technology, monumental arts, town-planning or landscape design;

iii to bear a unique or at least exceptional testimony to a cultural tradition or to a civilization which is living or which has disappeared;

iv to be an outstanding example of a type of building, architectural or technological ensemble or landscape which illustrates (a) significant stage(s) in human history;

v to be an outstanding example of a traditional human settlement, land-use, or sea-use which is representative of a culture (or cultures), or human interaction with the environment especially when it has become vulnerable under the impact of irreversible change;

vi to be directly or tangibly associated with events or living traditions, with ideas, or with beliefs, with artistic and literary works of outstanding universal significance. (The Committee considers that this criterion should preferably be used in conjunction with other criteria);

vii to contain superlative natural phenomena or areas of exceptional natural beauty and aesthetic importance;

viii to be outstanding examples representing major stages of earth's history, including the record of life, significant on-going geological processes in the development of landforms, or significant geomorphic or physiographic features;

ix to be outstanding examples representing significant on-going ecological and biological processes in the evolution and development of terrestrial, fresh water, coastal and marine ecosystems and communities of plants and animals;

x to contain the most important and significant natural habitats for in-situ conservation of biological diversity, including those containing threatened species of outstanding universal value from the point of view of science or conservation.

1.5 Filling the gaps

1.5.1 Redefining 'heritage' to be more internationally inclusive

Charters have become a symbol of the international conservation movement, particularly in the built heritage, architectural and archaeological sectors. Charters (not quite legal documents and often the product of conferences) typically feature lists of clauses and sub-clauses and statements of perceived importance written in semi-legal / semi-polemical language. However, the language used in such charters can be open to multiple interpretations and translations. For example, the word 'conservation' is commonly used in the UK, while in the USA the alternative phrase 'historic preservation' is used. Similarly, the English word 'heritage' and French word 'patrimoine' both have nuanced meanings and do not have a straightforward and equivalent translations into other languages. At the same time, similar complexity has emerged around definitions of authenticity and integrity which are both key factors to consider when a site is being proposed for World Heritage Site status. This means that despite attempts to define an international agenda for World Heritage through the notion of Outstanding Universal Value, the implications and meaning associated with global heritage are more subjective than was perhaps first anticipated in the optimistic post-war years of the 1950s and 1960s. This is demonstrated through the apparent inconsistencies and imbalances which have developed within the World Heritage process in the five decades since the Convention was signed.

Eight of the first 12 cultural sites listed on the World Heritage List in 1978 were cultural properties: **Aachen Cathedral** in Germany; the **City of Quito** in Ecuador; the **Historic Centre of Krakow** in Poland; the **Island of Goree** in Senegal; **L'Anse aux Meadows National Historic Site** in Canada; **Mesa Verde National Park** in the USA; the **Rock-hewn Churches of Lalibela** in Ethiopia; and the **Wieliczka and Bochnia Royal Salt Mines** in Poland. These first cultural properties were focused largely on reflecting the original Criterion (iii): 'typically representative of ancient civilisations', an approach to considering what is 'heritage' that can be criticised as reflecting a Eurocentric view of the past, which privileges monumental, built heritage. These sorts of cultural sites quickly began to dominate the World Heritage List in the first years of its operation at the expense of other types of heritage and natural sites and it was not long before debates commenced on the ideas of representativeness, with commentators starting to question the way in which World Heritage was apparently being defined almost exclusively in Eurocentric terms and expressing concern that this was influencing broader understandings of heritage that favoured and valued certain types of building and urban form over others.

The late Henry Cleere, an internationally renowned archaeologist who was very much involved in the World Heritage process for many decades, reflected on and researched this issue in his role as World Heritage Co-ordinator for ICOMOS (International Council on Monuments and Sites). In 2000 he established that of the 630 World Heritage Sites on the list at that time, some 55% were in European countries and that these generally spoke to what has been termed the 'grand heritage narrative', with a higher proportion being cathedrals, castles and palaces. At the time, Cleere argued that universality could only be applied to the very earliest phases of human cultural development or globalised culture of the late 20th century, stating universality is 'deeply rooted in the European tradition, combining historical and aesthetic parameters that derive from classical philosophy' (Cleere, 2001, p. 24, cited in Smith, 2006, p. 99). He was thus supporting the growing contention that the World Heritage list was not in fact representative of the full panoply of heritage and cultural assets around the world.

The reasons for the gaps in the World Heritage List related to the nomination process itself and to the way properties were identified, assessed and evaluated. But the nature of 'representation' was particularly complex given the diversity and range of cultural heritage. For example, it was not always easy to negotiate a resolution to ideas of Outstanding Universal Value in cultures where concepts of conservation vary and where significance can be found in non-material aspects of heritage, or even where ideas of 'universality' value are contested.

In 1994 UNESCO responded to these criticisms and an Expert Meeting was convened to consider a new global strategy for World Heritage and to plan a series of thematic studies to inform the creation of a more representative list that filled in perceived gaps in the properties inscribed as World Heritage. The delegates at that meeting noted that:

> In 1972 the idea of cultural heritage had been to a very large extent embodied in and confined to architectural monuments. Since that time, however, the history of art and architecture, archaeology, anthropology and ethnology no longer concentrated on single monuments in isolation but rather on considering cultural groupings that were complex and multidimensional, which demonstrated in spatial terms the social structures, ways of life, beliefs, systems of knowledge, and representations of different past and present cultures in the entire world.
>
> *(UNESCO, 1994)*

The acknowledgement of the underrepresentation of the diversity of global heritage within the World Heritage list resulted in an evolution of approaches and to the development of new initiatives for World Heritage inscription. The Global Strategy introduced in 1994 sought to address the discernible gaps and imbalances on the World Heritage List, noting for instance that:

- Historic towns and religious buildings were over-represented in relation to other types of property;
- Christianity was over-represented in relation to other religions and beliefs;
- Historical periods were overrepresented in relation to prehistory and the 20th century.

1.5.2 A Global Strategy to 'level-up' the list

At the time the Global Strategy was launched, there were 410 properties on the list, of which 304 were cultural sites and only 90 were natural and 16 mixed. The vast majority of World Heritage Sites at that time were located in developed regions of the world, notably in Europe.

One response was to change the language used to categorise heritage, to make it more reflective of understandings of heritage in other (non-European) cultural traditions. There was also a conscious attempt to rethink the criteria through which Outstanding Universal Value could be defined, for example by updating the criteria and clarifying the language that was used in both the English and French versions of the convention text and moving in general towards a more comprehensive, diverse and inclusive understanding of the wealth of human cultures. Specific amendments included:

- removing the idea of a unique artistic achievement from Criterion (i);
- re-examining Criterion (ii) in order to better reflect the interaction of cultures, instead of the approach used in the first two decades of the Convention which suggested that cultural influences occurred in only one direction;

- Criterion (iii) removed the phrase 'which has disappeared' on the basis that this excluded living cultures;
- in Criterion (v) the phrase 'especially when it has become vulnerable under the impact of irreversible change' was removed on the basis that this was seen to have favoured cultures that had disappeared;
- stressing that the interpretation of Criterion (vi), which covers living events and traditions, ideas and beliefs, should become less restrictive when considering their outstanding universal significance.

Targeted geographical initiatives and thematic approaches were also introduced to help move the list of inscribed properties from a monumental and static view of heritage to one that was more comprehensive and diversified. Particular attention was paid to progressing nominations for properties from the Pacific region and from Africa while thematic approaches covered, for example, nomadism and migration, industrial technology, water management, routes for people and goods, traditional settlements and their environments (UNESCO, 1994). The impacts of these approaches can be seen in the widening range of heritage reflected through different chronologies and time periods identified as representing World Heritage. Table 1.1 below summarises the properties inscribed on the list each decade since 1978 (including the three properties now delisted) against the three core categories and demonstrates that cultural heritage properties have in fact increased their presence on the list as time has gone on, in terms of the overall proportion of World Heritage Sites while there has been a falling-off in terms of the number of natural sites inscribed.

Turning to a selection of different types of property (Table 1.2) the emergence in the last two decades of cultural landscapes as a resource considered worthy of inscription is very evident, as is the decline over the last decade in particular of natural properties such as forests and marine or coastal sites – again, this ties in with the idea that once the landmark natural heritage sites and ecosystems had been inscribed in the first two decades or so of the World Heritage programme, the natural environment gave way to cultural heritage concerns.

TABLE 1.1 Listings per decade, 1970s–2020s, by category of property.

Decade	Cultural		Natural		Mixed		Total
	n	%	n	%	n	%	n
1970s	42	74%	12	21%	3	5%	57
1980s	191	73%	58	22%	13	5%	262
1990s	246	79%	56	18%	8	3%	310
2000s	210	80%	50	19%	3	1%	263
2010s	181	78%	38	16%	12	5%	231
2020s	29	85%	5	15%	0	0%	34
Total properties inscribed	899	78%	219	19%	39	3%	1,157

Source: Authors' own summary, based on UNESCO statistics.

TABLE 1.2 Listings per decade, 1970s–2020s, by type of property.

Decade	Forests		Marine & Coastal		Cities		Cultural Landscapes		Total
	n	%	n	%	n	%	N	%	n
1970s	5	23%	3	14%	14	64%	0	0%	22
1980s	33	25%	8	6%	87	67%	2	2%	130
1990s	33	18%	19	10%	114	62%	17	9%	183
2000s	19	13%	12	8%	71	47%	49	32%	151
2010s	0	0%	8	10%	27	33%	46	57%	81
2020s	0	0%	0	0%	8	57%	6	43%	14
Total properties inscribed	90	15%	50	9%	321	55%	120	21%	581

Source: Authors' own summary, based on UNESCO statistics.

Having reflected on those issues, UNESCO endeavoured to address the geographical range of World Heritage by encouraging and supporting work in different regions. For example, regional expert meetings and regional studies were set up with initiatives in sub-Saharan Africa, in the Pacific and Arab regions, in Southeast Asia and in Central Asia. The number of countries who signed the World Heritage Convention grew from 139 to 178 in the first ten years after the launch of the Global Strategy (and at the time of writing is 194) and of that list, 27 States Parties to the World Heritage Convention have no World Heritage Properties. Concurrent with this Global Strategy of reaching out and identifying heritage sites around the world that might be suitable for World Heritage listing, UNESCO also introduced a limitation on the number of properties that any State Party could nominate to the list in any nomination cycle, though this could be one natural site and one cultural site (and is influenced by the way in which the nomination process has become so politicised as well). By the 2000s the number of sites successfully being listed from Europe and North America became more balanced with sites from Asia and the Pacific – though both these regions still dominate the other regions with Africa, Arab states and Latin America and the Caribbean still very much underrepresented. Of course, by 2022 the impact of those early years of the operation of the World Heritage Convention cannot be undone, as cumulatively Europe and North America are still dominating the total number of sites on the World Heritage List.

1.5.3 Acknowledging intangible heritage

Further acknowledgement of the need to tackle the restrictive interpretation of universal heritage and the subsequent lack of diversity inherent in the 1972 Convention came when UNESCO adopted the separate Convention for the Safeguarding of Intangible Cultural Heritage in 2003. This particular Convention is complementary to other international instruments dealing with cultural heritage, with its purpose to safeguard the practices, representations, expressions, knowledge and skills that communities, groups and in some cases individuals recognise as parts of their cultural heritage. It thus provides a valuable addition to the portfolio of protective and celebratory measures aimed at global heritage.

For example, the **Old Towns of Djenne** in the Mopti region of Mali were inscribed on the list in 1988 principally because of the outstanding nature of their earthen architecture. To ensure the longevity and survival of the city's remarkable built heritage, maintenance and its associated social practices are key. The statement of authenticity for the site reflects on the importance of the transmission of construction techniques from generation to generation through the Barey Corporation (the Masons Guild). This again indicates the complexities around a binary approach to heritage, given that the statement of authenticity for this cultural World Heritage Site is dependent on intangible cultural heritage.

1.5.4 Introducing cultural landscapes

As we have seen above, the complexity of incorporating intangible heritage within the World Heritage process reflected the way in which heritage was initially defined as a binary construct: cultural or natural. However, the evolution of the World Heritage process took another step forward in 1992 when the UNESCO formally recognised the intertwining of tangible and intangible heritage (alongside cultural and natural heritage) through the concept of Cultural Landscapes, which reflect the 'combined works of nature and of man' (UNESCO Cultural Landscapes, n.d.). **Tongariro National Park** in New Zealand was inscribed as the first World Heritage cultural landscape in 1993, having originally been listed in 1990 as a natural site because of its important geological and ecological value. However, the revised nomination recognised the enormous cultural and religious significance of the mountains at the heart of the property for the Maori people, for whom they symbolise the spiritual links between this community and the natural environment.

Perhaps one of the most well-known examples of a World Heritage cultural landscape is **Uluru–Kata Tjuṯa National Park** in Australia's Northern Territory. The property was first inscribed on the World Heritage List in 1987 under the original criteria (ii) and (iii) for natural properties and was listed as Uluru (Ayers Rock – Mount Olga) National Park, foregrounding the name given to it at the time Australia was colonised. The original nomination documentation submitted to UNESCO did note that there was a clear relationship between cultural and natural heritage and it was thus nominated as both a cultural and a natural property. However, at the time the evaluation of the nomination was carried out by advisors from IUCN and as a result it was only inscribed on the World Heritage List for its natural values. Reporting on the outcome of the application of the Eleventh Session of the World Heritage Committee at which this decision was made, UNESCO placed on record its understanding that the property was more than just of natural heritage interest, noting 'The Committee commended the Australian authorities on the manner in which the management of this property gave an appropriate blend of the cultural and natural characteristics of this property'.[2] Following on from the implementation of the Cultural Landscape initiative the site's position on the list was reviewed with ICOMOS undertaking the evaluation and revising the criteria against which the Outstanding Universal Value of the property was recognised so that both natural and cultural values are reflected.

Cultural landscapes are therefore another example of the World Heritage process responding to the challenge of the simplistic binary oppositions within heritage that were built into the original 1972 Convention. One can thus see the evolution of the concept of World Heritage from a starting point of something which was either cultural or natural and which excluded intangible heritage, to the situation today in which cultural landscapes represent both cultural and natural heritage, and the intertwining of tangible and intangible heritage.

The **English Lake District** was successfully inscribed as a World Heritage Site in 2017, as a cultural landscape nominated under cultural criteria (v) and (vi). In the past there had been a series of unsuccessful nominations for the Lake District, in 1986 as a mixed site and in 1989 as a cultural site. The successful nomination of the English Lake District as a cultural landscape made its case on the value of the interwoven relationship between people and the landscape as shown through farming traditions and practises, and the embedded nature of those farming traditions in shaping the landscape. But the longer history of applications for World Heritage status provides a useful example of the political motivation of some States Parties, desperate to secure World Heritage status for a particular property and content to make repeated nominations which reflect an ongoing 'reimagining' of a place in line with the evolving narrative of Outstanding Universal Value.

The eventual inscription of the Lake District as a World Heritage Site generated considerable debate about the relationship between Outstanding Universal Value on one hand, and local needs on the other. Some suggested that one benefit of inscription was that local residents would be better placed to appreciate their own heritage because it had been identified as internationally significant and, moreover, that World Heritage status would stimulate additional tourism and hence bring new revenue generation and employment opportunities (Heritage Alliance, 2017). However, others have argued that the concept of cultural landscape that is now encapsulated within the Lake District World Heritage Site is in fact a pretend, 'fairytale' rural economy (Monbiot, 2017) and that the pastoral practices which have shaped the landscape celebrated with World Heritage status, and which are needed to sustain that same cultural landscape, may well put a brake on future debates about rewilding, natural regeneration and environmental benefits of carbon capture which some argue will be needed to overcome the impacts of overgrazing on the hillsides of this iconic landscape.

There is still work to do in terms of making the World Heritage List representative of the world's heritage. What we are now seeing are much more creative ways to think about the central notion of outstanding universal value. One example is through serial nominations and we will see examples of these in subsequent chapters.

1.6 Summing up

As of February 2022, 194 state parties were signatories to the 1972 Convention and there are 1,154 inscribed properties from 167 state parties on the World Heritage list, meaning that there are 27 States Parties that are signatory to the Convention but which don't (yet) have a World Heritage property within their territorial borders. Of the current set of inscribed properties, 897 (78%) are cultural heritage sites, 218 (19%) are natural World Heritage Sites and 39 (3%) are mixed, reflecting both cultural and natural values. Three properties formerly on the list have been delisted, the most recent being Liverpool – Maritime Mercantile City which lost its World Heritage status at the 44th session of the World Heritage Committee hosted in Fuzhou, China, in July 2021. There are currently 52 properties on the list of World Heritage in Danger.

As we have explored in this first chapter, to become a World Heritage property the inherent significance or value of that site needs to be more than just of national interest – it needs to reflect what has become known as Outstanding Universal Value (OUV). We have also shown that interpretations of this idea have evolved over the last 50 years as the thinking about what really is 'World Heritage' has been negotiated and renegotiated to reflect changing assumptions and aspirations about what should be on the list. The fact that the concept of OUV is so contested reflects the politics behind recognition and in retrospect it is easy to see how the original idea in the 1972 Convention, of a system of recognition that transcends national boundaries and which highlights sites deemed to be of common importance to both present and future generations, could in fact be so complex.

This complexity is central to all discussions of World Heritage and it is useful to reflect on the fact that the conventional understanding of World Heritage has tended to create a 'fixed' approach to heritage values which underestimates the ways in which heritage is mutable. As we have sought to demonstrate here, heritage values and significance fluctuate over time. Moreover, how one person thinks about a place may well be different to the way another person thinks about the same location because of their different backgrounds, beliefs and understandings. Magnifying these mutable factors over areas, countries and indeed the whole world, it is perhaps inevitable that tensions about what heritage is sit at the heart of World Heritage critics and scholarship. What is clear, however, is that the central tenet of the 1972 World Heritage Convention – namely that there should be a tool for identifying, protecting and celebrating some of the world's most outstanding places – remains as valid today as it was 50 years ago.

In the following chapter, we examine in more detail the implementation of the World Heritage Convention in order to shed light on the processes of nomination, evaluation and inscription and to demonstrate the implications of listing for successful properties.

Notes

1 https://www.officialdata.org/us/inflation/1970?amount=80000000 (accessed 12 December 2021).
2 United Nations Educational, Scientific and Cultural Organization Convention Concerning the Protection of the World Cultural and Natural Heritage. Report of the World Heritage Committee. Eleventh Session. SC-87/CONF.005/9 (UNESCO Headquarters, 7–11 December 1987). Paris, 20 January 1988.

References

Athens Charter. 1931. https://www.icomos.org/en/167-the-athens-charter-for-the-restoration-of-historic-monuments (accessed 7 January 2022).

Betts, P. 2015. The warden of World Heritage: UNESCO and the rescue of the Nubian Monuments. *Past & Present*, 226, 100–125.

Burnett, G. W. & Harrington, L. M. B. 1994. Early National Park adoption in sub-Saharan Africa. *Society & Natural Resources*, 7 (2), 155–168.

Cameron, C. & Rossler, M. 2016. *Many Voices, One Vision: The Early Years of the World Heritage Convention*. London: Routledge.

Cleere, H 2001. The uneasy bedfellows: universality and cultural heritage. In: R Layton, P. G Stone and J Thomas, eds. *Destruction and Conservation of Cultural Property*. London: Routledge.

Glendinning, M. 2013. *The Conservation Movement: A History of Architectural Preservation*. London: Routledge.

Gosden, C. 1994. *Social Being and Time*. Oxford: Blackwell.

Hassan, F. 2007. The Aswan High Dam and the International Rescue Nubia Campaign. *African Archaeological Review*, 24, 73–94.

Hendee, J. C. Stankey, G. H. & Lucas, R. C. 1990. *Wilderness Management*. 2nd ed. Golden, CO: North America Press.

Heritage Alliance. 2017. Heritage Update 351. https://email.premmdesign.co.uk/t/View Email/r/B93C38E9CF8D373D2540EF23F30FEDED (accessed 7 January 2022).

Jokilehto, J. 1999. *A History of Architectural Conservation*. London: Butterworth-Heinemann.

Madrid Conference. 1904. https://www.getty.edu/conservation/publications_resources/research_resources/charters/charter01.html (accessed 7 January 2022).

Maheu, R. 1967. For Florence and Venice. *UNESCO Courier* 1967. https://unesdoc.unesco.org/ark:/48223/pf0000078222.locale=en (accessed 7 January 2022).

McNeely, J. 1994. Protected areas for the 21st century: Working to provide benefits to society. *Biodiversity and Conservation*, 3, 390–405. doi:10.1007/BF00057797.

Monbiot, G. 2017. Black Box. http://www.monbiot.com/2017/07/11/black-box (accessed 7 January 2022).

Nash, R. 1982. *Wilderness and the American Mind*. 3rd ed. New Haven, CT: Yale University Press.

Newsome, D. Moore, S. A. & Dowling, R. K. 2002. *Natural Area Tourism. Ecology, Impacts and Management*. Clevedon, Bristol: Channel View.

Smith, L. 2006. *The Uses of Heritage*. Abingdon: Routledge.

SPAB. 2019. The SPAB's early campaigning in Venice. https://www.spab.org.uk/news/spabs-early-campaigning-venice (accessed 7 January 2022).

UNESCO. 1994. Expert Meeting on the 'Global Strategy' and thematic studies for a representative World Heritage List. https://whc.unesco.org/archive/global94.htm (accessed 7 January 2022).

UNESCO. 2010. https://unesdoc.unesco.org/ark:/48223/pf0000188700 (accessed 7 January 2022).

UNESCO. 2021. *Operational Guidelines.* https://whc.unesco.org/en/guidelines/ (accessed 7 January 2022).

UNESCO Constitution. n.d. http://portal.unesco.org/en/ev.php-URL_ID=15244&URL_DO=DO_TOPIC&URL_SECTION=201.html (accessed 7 January 2022).

UNESCO Cultural Landscapes. n.d. https://whc.unesco.org/en/culturallandscape/ (accessed 7 January 2022).

2

IMPLEMENTING THE WORLD HERITAGE CONVENTION

2.1 Operational Guidelines

2.1.1 Who is involved?

The Operational Guidelines for the Implementation of the World Heritage Convention are regularly updated and these define the processes involved in nomination of World Heritage. The current process, summarised in the 2021 version of the Operational Guidelines, is summarised in Figure 2.1.

The organisations that are involved in the operation of the World Heritage Convention include States Parties, the World Heritage Committee of UNESCO, the World Heritage Centre in Paris and three international organisations: ICCROM (International Centre for the Study of the Preservation and Restoration of Cultural Property), ICOMOS (International Council on Monuments and Sites) and IUCN (International Union for Conservation of Nature).

States Parties are the different countries that are signatories to the Convention and who are thus able take part in the World Heritage process by preparing tentative lists of sites to be considered for World Heritage status, nominating sites for consideration for inclusion on the list and then overseeing the management of properties in their own territory that are inscribed on the World Heritage list.

The **World Heritage Committee** meets once a year and consists of representatives from 21 of the States Parties to the Convention who are elected by their General Assembly for terms of up to six years. Its role is to consider the nominations received, review periodic reviews on the state of conservation at properties on the list, allocate funds to specific projects associated with conservation challenges at key sites, and to consider whether or not sites whose Outstanding Universal Value is being threatened, or has been materially altered

DOI: 10.4324/9781003044857-3

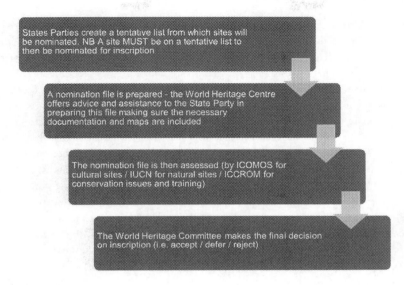

States Parties create a tentative list from which sites will be nominated. NB A site MUST be on a tentative list to then be nominated for inscription

A nomination file is prepared - the World Heritage Centre offers advice and assistance to the State Party in preparing this file making sure the necessary documentation and maps are included

The nomination file is then assessed (by ICOMOS for cultural sites / IUCN for natural sites / ICCROM for conservation issues and training)

The World Heritage Committee makes the final decision on inscription (i.e. accept / defer / reject)

FIGURE 2.1 The nomination process.

through development or other factors, should be placed on the list of Properties in Danger or in fact removed from the World Heritage list altogether.

The **UNESCO World Heritage Centre**, located in Paris, was established in 1992 and is responsible for the day-to-day management of the Convention and the administration of the World Heritage Fund. It provides advice and technical support to States Parties during the nomination process, helps to coordinate the periodic reporting programme that is so important for understanding the state of conservation at listed properties and will also help direct emergency interventions when a site is threatened. It has an important role in sharing technical advice about aspects of heritage conservation and is also engaged more generally in raising awareness of World Heritage issues among the public, targeting young people around the world in particular.

The three separate organisations involved in the evaluation of World Heritage nominations are:

- the **International Centre for the Study of the Preservation and Restoration of Cultural Property** (ICCROM);
- the **International Council of Monuments and Sites** (ICOMOS);
- the **International Union for Conservation of Nature and Natural Resources** (IUCN).

2.1.2 The process: nomination and inscription

The process involved in nomination to the World Heritage list is that States Parties create a tentative list from which sites will be nominated. A site must be on a tentative list to then be nominated for inscription. If a site is on the tentative list and is then nominated for inscription, the next process is the preparation of a nomination file. The World Heritage Centre offers advice and assistance to the State Party in preparing this file and make sure the necessary documentation and maps are included. In the early years of the World Heritage programme there was a relatively limited amount of paperwork needed to support applications but in recent years nomination documents have become extremely substantial, containing a wealth of technical information that supports the nomination and that allows UNESCO and its advisers to make a critical assessment of whether or not the nominated property meets the necessary standard for inclusion on the list – does it really demonstrate Outstanding Universal Value and meet the relevant criteria specified for the type of property (cultural, natural or mixed). As an example of the level of detail needed, the nomination file for a cultural heritage property put forward (successfully) for listing in 2021 and that was reviewed by one of the authors ran to 267 pages with a further 16 pages of maps, an Executive Summary and a 44-page Risk Assessment.

Following on from the creation of the nomination file, it will be assessed by a team of technical advisers to UNESCO. In the past ICOMOS would look at nominations for cultural sites while the IUCN reviewed natural sites. However, there is increasing collaboration between both organisations on all nominations, and particularly for nominations for mixed sites and for cultural landscapes. ICCROM's role is to review conservation issues and training proposals contained within nomination documents. The assessment process is normally in two parts: a desk-based review and a site-based assessment to examine particular issues on the ground. In recent years the advisory bodies have consulted their membership more widely for this evaluation work, permitting a greater range of perspectives on the nominations and, in effect, democratising the evaluation process more broadly than has been the case in the past (at the time of writing, ICOMOS had more than 10,500 individual members and IUCN some 1,400 members).

The various reports are coordinated and from an assessment of the nomination file, a recommendation is then put forward to the World Heritage Committee who will then make the final decision on inscription at their annual assembly. At this point they can do one of three things: they can accept the site for inscription to the World Heritage List; they can recommend deferring the site (perhaps the evaluation has shown a need for more detailed technical information about a particular conservation or management issue) or they can reject the nomination outright. It should be remembered that it is possible for a States Party to renominate a site in a future year, perhaps by 'reimagining' the OUV to fit within the emerging trends for World Heritage inscription (as happened with the Lake District nomination discussed in Chapter 1, for instance). This reimagining and realignment of tentative World Heritage properties is something that become more evident in recent years and can be seen as part of the political gamesmanship around the World Heritage process.

2.1.3 Defining the boundaries

A key consideration in identifying a possible World Heritage Site is the definition of the site's boundary. This boundary is drawn up to incorporate all the attributes that convey the property's Outstanding Universal Value and to ensure the integrity and/or authenticity of the property. Because the site boundary is about reflecting the attributes that support the statement of the property's OUV, it is sometimes the case that the site boundary as drawn on a map is not necessarily what one might consider to be the obvious boundary around the place in question and there are many instances, such as at **Borobudur Temple Compounds** in Indonesia[1] or the **Ancient and Primeval Beech Forests of the Carpathian and Other Regions of Europe**,[2] where boundary revisions have been requested to either include additional land of significance, or to subsequently exclude part of a property that no longer meets the relevant quality standards.

The other feature of a World Heritage Site is the buffer zone, which is an area outside the site boundary, effectively surrounding the nominated property and generally given complementary legal or restrictions placed on its use and on possible future development to give an added layer of protection to the property. Many buffer zones have been identified because they provide the immediate setting of the nominated property, and might offer important views into or out of the World Heritage Site.

The World Heritage property was inscribed in 1986 as a cultural site called **Studley Royal Park including the Ruins of Fountains Abbey**. The site boundary covers the area of ruins of Fountains Abbey and also the designed landscape area around Studley Royal (see Plate 2.1). In contrast, the site buffer zone is much more extensive as the views from the designed landscape that stretch out beyond Ripon and through to the hillside on the other side of the valley are seen as central to the OUV of the property.

The buffer zone for a World Heritage Site is functionally important as support for the property and its protection, and again, as with the site boundary, the buffer zone may not always appear to be really obvious to the lay person. When preparing, reviewing and updating a World Heritage Management plan (see below) it thus is important to focus on the attributes and the Outstanding Universal Value of the property in question to really understand why a certain site has the boundaries and buffer zones it has.

PLATE 2.1 Studley Royal Park including the Ruins of Fountains Abbey, Yorkshire, UK. Source: Photograph by Louise Cooke.

2.1.4 The management plan

If a property is inscribed to the World Heritage List, site managers and local authorities will work towards managing, monitoring and preserving the property through the use of a management plan. A management plan should represent a thorough and shared understanding of the property and vision for its future, drawn up and agreed by all stakeholders. It will include a prioritised list of interventions around conservation and the promotion of public engagement with the property as well as proposals for monitoring the condition of the site and for responding to particular issues that may arise over the period of the plan (which is typically for five years). The management plan should also record what resources will be needed to implement the anticipated protection and management measures, allocation of necessary resources, identify sources of support and also consider capacity building issues so that future plans are able to build on the foundations of the current plan.

Overall, the management plan should be an accountable, transparent description of how the management system functions for a particular World Heritage property, an approach that mirrors best practice in the conservation management process for any kind of site. These are now a requirement for all inscribed sites, though management plans have been requested only from candidate sites entering the nomination process in the early 2000s. This means that many early World Heritage Sites were nominated without a management plan, an oversight that has sometimes placed them at a disadvantage for instance when addressing pressures associated with tourism at the property, responding to the potential impacts of climate change on the site and its surroundings, and around disaster risk preparedness.

2.1.5 Monitoring the state of conservation

Following on from the management plan, the State Party has an obligation to regularly prepare State of Conservation Reports (about the state of conservation and the various protection measures put in place at their sites) and Periodic Reports (on the application of the World Heritage Convention and state of conservation of properties on a regional rolling basis every six years). These two reports allow the World Heritage Committee to assess conditions both regionally and at individual properties, and thus to decide on the necessity of adopting specific measures to resolve recurrent problems at specific sites, across sites of a similar nature or in the same part of the world and more generally on the implementation of the World Heritage Convention.

If a site is considered to be under a particular threat, say because of armed conflict, environmental challenges or planned urban development, and the severity of the threat is such that its Outstanding Universal Value is threatened, the World Heritage Committee may place it on the separate list of World Heritage in Danger, or even delist it altogether. The list of World Heritage in Danger is updated on an annual basis and following the 44th session of the World Heritage Committee in July 2021, there were 52 properties listed on it – 36 cultural properties and 16 natural sites. Properties on the List in Danger are predominantly in the Middle East (exclusively cultural sites, generally threatened by armed conflict) and Africa (largely natural sites, susceptible to a range of pressures). Placing a property on the List in Danger is used principally as a lever to encourage the relevant States Party and its partners to tackle whatever is threatening the site. As indicated previously, on occasion the World Heritage Centre is able to provide support to States Parties in identifying how best to resolve the challenges faced at a property and there have been many positive outcomes over time, to the extent that since 1988 more than 40 properties have been removed from the list because the conservation problem or the management problem has now been successfully resolved. The first one site removed from the List in Danger was the **Djoudj National Bird Sanctuary** in Senegal, a wetland that was threatened by the damming of waters upstream, and the most recent, **Salonga National Park** in the Democratic Republic of Congo which was removed from the list in 2021 as a result of reduction in the threat of poaching and illegal encroachments into the protected area.

There are occasions, however, when the situation becomes untenable and a site is removed completely from the World Heritage List. To date, only three World Heritage Sites have been delisted:

- the **Arabian Oryx Sanctuary** in Oman, removed from the World Heritage list in 2007 largely because of the Omani government's decision to reduce the size of the protected area by 90% to facilitate hydrocarbon exploitation in the area, though the decision was strengthened by the fact that the population of the Arabian Oryx (*Oryx leucoryx*) had dwindled in just a decade from around 450 animals to 65, with only four breeding pairs;
- **Dresden Elbe Valley** in Germany which was delisted in 2009 because of plans to construct a four-lane bridge across the river in the buffer zone of the site, a move that was generally supported by the local community, who it appears were not too concerned about the loss of status;
- **Liverpool – Maritime Mercantile City** in the UK which lost its status as a World Heritage Site at the 44th Session of the Committee in 2021 following years of concern about the impact on the site and its buffer zone of the major 'Liverpool Waters' property development as well as other, smaller developments within the site.

As is the case with the initial listing process, politics is also involved in the listing of sites on the list of World Heritage in Danger, and in the delisting process as we will we explore below.

2.1.6 Understanding the relationship between inscription and other designations

World Heritage properties might also be covered by other designations; for example, cultural sites in the UK might also be designated as a listed building or a scheduled ancient monument, and these existing designations might cover all of the elements of the World Heritage property. So, the heritage significance of the site might be considered as being reflected, at least in part, by other heritage designations. Crucially, it is important to understand that recognition of a site as World Heritage by UNESCO does not in itself bring additional protection or management controls; it is expected that the States Party will have those heritage protection policies already in place.

2.2 Emerging trends in inscription

In this section we consider a number of recent trends in the types of sites that have been inscribed on the World Heritage List as UNESCO and others have sought to respond to some of the criticisms made against it regarding issues like representativeness of different cultures. Three key themes we look at below are transboundary properties, serial nominations and transnational serial nominations.

2.2.1 Transboundary properties

Transboundary World Heritage properties are single properties that cross one or more national boundaries, of which there are 43 at the time of writing. An example is the **Curonian Spit** cultural landscape, an elongated 98 km long and 0.4–4 km wide sand dune peninsula in the Baltic which was inscribed as a World Heritage property for both Lithuania and the Russian Federation in 2000. In other words, the creation of a transboundary property acknowledges modern geographical boundaries but recognises there was a time when these boundaries did not exist.

2.2.2 Serial nominations

A more recent trend is that of serial nominations, which consists of two or more sites that are physically disconnected. So, a single World Heritage Site may contain a series of cultural and or natural properties in different geographical locations, provided that they are related because they belong to the same historical cultural group, or are characteristic of the same geological or geomorphological formation, the same biogeographical province or the same ecosystem type. As the case study of the **Pearling, Testimony of an Island Economy** World Heritage Site in Bahrain demonstrates, sometimes the 'critical mass' of Outstanding Universal Value is provided by there being multiple locations associated with the heritage in question.

BOX 2.1 CASE STUDY 2.1: PEARLING, TESTIMONY OF AN ISLAND ECONOMY, BAHRAIN.

Bahrain is now one of the most densely populated countries in the world and the number of inhabitants has risen ever since the discovery of the first oil well in 1932 and the subsequent development of the oil industry and increased demand for the workforce. From antiquity until the 1930s, Bahrain's pearling activities, the collection and trade of natural pearls, has been significant – this is shown through historic documents, through heritage structures and through the abundance and quality of the pearl beds as well.

The World Heritage Site consists of 17 historic buildings in Muharraq City, three offshore oyster beds, part of the seashore and the Qal'at Bu Mahir Fortress on the southern tip of Muharraq Island from where boats used to set off for the oyster beds. This makes for quite a complex series of site boundaries and site buffer zones. The justification for this as a serial property is that when combined together, these different elements convey a complete understanding of the cultural tradition of pearling and the related human system established in a single product economy. In total there are 15 components – the three oyster beds as maritime properties, the seashore sites on the southern tip of the island, 11 urban properties, of which there are 17 different architectural structures. In terms of categories of cultural property as set out in the World Heritage Convention, it is a serial site that consists of four sites, nine monuments and two groups of buildings.

When the nomination document was originally submitted in 2010, it was proposed to be nominated in two cultural criteria, criterion iii and criteria iv. However, when successfully inscribed on the World Heritage List in 2012 it was only Criterion (iii): 'to bear a unique or at least exceptional testimony to a cultural tradition or to a civilization which is living or which has disappeared'.

The evidence put forward by the States Party against criterion iv stated that pearling and the testimony it brought forth on and around Muharraq Island is an

> outstanding example of traditional sea use and human interaction with the environment, which shaped the economic system and cultural identity of an island society. The oyster beds and the architectural testimony of this socio-cultural and economic system are representative of a tradition that became vulnerable and has been gradually abandoned in the 1930s. The collapse of the international natural pearl market value, in the face of the global economic crisis and the introduction of large-scale cultivation of pearls, has irreversibly impacted the system's viability and vitality.
>
> *(ICOMOS, 2011)*

'The ICOMOS evaluation of the nomination argued that that although criterion iv was justified by the States Party, on review ICOMOS considered that the same argument put forward by Bahrain could be applied to other places in the Gulf region; that there are few tangible remains associated with the sea-harvesting traditions and that the majority of the nominated property is an architectural testimony that reflects the trading of pearls rather than the sea use. As such, it was considered that this criterion had not been justified (ICOMOS, 2011). The final outcome for Bahrain was the successful nomination of this site even though it was listed against just one criterion rather than the two originally proposed in the nomination document.

2.2.3 Transnational serial nominations

Transnational serial nominations have become a central theme of recent World Heritage inscriptions and indeed in some cases, existing World Heritage properties have been re-imagined as transnational serial properties. For example, the **Frontiers of the Roman Empire** World Heritage property in the UK and Germany was originally inscribed on the World Heritage list in 1987 as just a UK World Heritage Property, 'Hadrian's Wall'. The property has since been extended in 2005 and 2008 to include the Roman defences in Germany (the Limes) and also the Antonine Wall in Scotland. Further sites in Austria, Germany and Slovakia were inscribed as a separate World Heritage Property in 2021, **Frontiers of the Roman Empire – The Danube Limes (Western Segment)**.

Through serial properties we can see both political uses of heritage but also heritage contributing to international dialogue between countries. Another example of a complex transboundary serial World Heritage property is the **Silk Roads: the Routes Network of Chang'an–Tianshan Corridor**, which links properties in China, Kazakhstan and Kyrgyzstan. The property was successfully listed in 2014 and comprises 33 archaeological sites across the three countries, with the justification for OUV being focused on criteria (ii), (iii), (v) and (vi). The language used to justify the World Heritage inscription relates to the diversity of human activity along this trade route over a period of more than two millennia, and celebrates the fact that these trade routes, as well as acting as conduits for goods and people, also facilitated the flow of ideas, beliefs and technological innovations including ideas related to architecture and town planning which subsequently shaped the urban spaces and lives of all those who lived in the Chang'an-Tianshan Corridor since the emergence of long-distance trade in the 2nd century BC.

Another complex example of a transboundary serial World Heritage property is the **Qhapaq Ñan, Andean Road System** that links together individual sites in Argentina, Bolivia, Chile, Colombia, Ecuador and Peru. Like the Silk Road, the Qhapaq Ñan was another complex network of trade and defensive routes that covered 30,000 km^2, ranging across diverse landscapes covering rainforest, fertile valleys, desert, as well as the Andes themselves. The World Heritage property includes 273 component sites over an area of more than 6,000 km^2. The individual components within the nomination were selected to highlight the social, political, architectural and engineering achievements of the network, along with the infrastructure for trade, accommodation and storage and religious significance. It was successfully inscribed against four of the cultural criteria, (ii), (iii), (iv) and (vi). The history of nomination is also interesting as well: because there are 314 separate components in the property, the submission document by itself was 2,765 pages long and the nomination dossier was submitted recommending that this network had Outstanding Universal Value under all six criteria for a cultural heritage property.

An even more complex and fascinating transnational World Heritage property is **The Architectural Work of Le Corbusier, an Outstanding Contribution to the Modern Movement** which was added to the list in 2016. This comprises a series of 17 properties located across three continents in seven countries: Argentina, Belgium, France, Germany, India, Japan and Switzerland. The nomination linked together these Corbusier buildings because they are considered as representative of the new architectural language associated with the modern movement, and the period of half a century in which Corbusier developed his ideas. The property was nominated against three cultural criteria: (i), (ii) and (vi). What is interesting and really quite different to many other transnational cultural World Heritage Sites is the fact that the assets listed in the nomination documentation are both 'of the place' in which they are located but also not necessarily 'of that place'. This relates to the way in which Corbusier worked: he designed a building which, as far as he was concerned, could be situated in different contexts. For example, there is a city museum of one design in Japan and another, of exactly the same design in Switzerland and another identical one in India (which is not part of the World Heritage inscription). In this instance, the inclusion on the World Heritage List of these different buildings celebrates the way in which the modern architectural movement translated its ideas to different countries, in some way reflecting that initial phase of enthusiasm for internationalism that is deeply embedded in the work of UNESCO and in the original ambitions of the World Heritage movement, as we considered in Chapter 1.

Finally, in a self-referential context that some may find amusing, it should also be noted that the history of conservation thinking and practice is itself represented in the World Heritage List through Viollet-le-Duc's restoration work at Carcassonne, inscribed in 1997 on account of the lengthy period of restoration work undertaken in the 19th century that, as we indicated in Chapter 1, had a major influence on the development of conservation theory.

2.3 The politicisation of decision making

It should be borne in mind that there is a political dimension around every World Heritage Committee meeting and the decisions that are made. How the World Heritage Committee responds to the recommendations of the advisory bodies ICCROM, ICOMOS and IUCN has been increasingly subject to insightful research by commentators such as the archaeologist Lynn Meskell of the University of Pennsylvania, the ethnologist Christoph Brumann from the Max Planck Institute for Social Anthropology in Halle, Germany and the American lawyer Elizabeth Betsy Keough,[3] all of whom have identified concerns with the politicisation of the whole process of nomination, evaluation and decision making for cultural heritage properties in particular. This is not surprising as cultural World Heritage properties (including cultural landscapes) embody national identities and politics which are then integrated into statements of Outstanding Universal Value that celebrate particular memories and interpretations of the past.

One of the central criticisms of the World Heritage process has been the increasingly political nature of decision making, as evidenced by the fact that the recommendations by IUCN and ICOMOS to the World Heritage Committee about whether or not a site should be inscribed are not always supported by its members. For instance, a comparison of the Recommendations by IUCN and ICOMOS to the 42nd session of the World Heritage Committee in 2018 with the outcomes of the World Heritage Committee (see Table 2.1) gives insight into these disparities (with sites recommended for referral for deferral becoming inscribed) and how criteria proposed for inscription by the state party are deselected through the evaluation and discussion of the relative merits of the property. In other cases (as with the example of the **English Lake District** seen earlier) sites may be repeatedly put forward for eventual inscription in subsequent World Heritage Committee meetings.

In some cases, major concerns about threats to a property being considered for inscription appear to have been either not listened to or ignored. For example, **Göbekli Tepe**, an early Neolithic site in Turkey, was confirmed at the 2018 meeting as a cultural World Heritage Site, yet the recommendation from ICOMOS for Göbekli Tepe was that it should be simultaneously listed as a World Heritage Site and put on the list of World Heritage in Danger. This call for it to be put on the list of properties in danger reflected concerns about encroaching urban development and the proposed construction of a railway line in part of the buffer zone. Rather than upset the Turkish authorities by putting the site immediately on the list in danger, the Committee instead made five broad recommendations for the States Party to attend to within a year of inscription, to demonstrate that the site's integrity and values could be protected.

The values identified for, and celebrated at, some World Heritage properties can be particularly complex and the statements of significance prepared for the sites can become fertile ground for dispute between different States Parties. In the case of dark heritage sites (in other words, sites associated with war, genocide and disaster) these values and the sites to which they refer to are already complex – they are spaces where we encounter issues of memory and contested memory, and in some instances are already difficult for us as individuals to acknowledge and to engage with. If we locate this personal discomfort within the broader international deliberations of Outstanding Universal Value it is not surprising that dark heritage is particularly complex within the World Heritage context. By interrogating the minutes of the World Heritage Committee meetings, we can get insight into the politics of World Heritage and the politics associated with these complex dark heritage properties.

As an example, the **Hiroshima Peace Memorial (Genbaku Dome)** (the only structure left standing in the area of the city where the first atomic bomb exploded on 6 August 1945) was inscribed as a World Heritage property in 1996 against the cultural Criterion (vi), which at the time was defined as 'be directly or tangibly associated with events or living traditions, with ideas, or with beliefs, with artistic and literary works of outstanding universal significance'. The ICOMOS evaluation for this site states that it is exceptional to nominate a site under just one criterion, and indeed UNESCO documentation specifies that it considers that Criterion (vi) should justify inclusion in the List only in exceptional circumstances or in conjunction with other criteria. However, there is no comparable building anywhere in the world, and the evaluation document clearly states that the overriding

TABLE 2.1 Comparison of the Recommendations by IUCN and ICOMOS to the 42nd session of the World Heritage Committee in 2018 (WHC/18/42.COM/8B) with the outcomes of the World Heritage Committee (note: table does not include those already withdrawn or postponed).

Site Name and Location	Criteria Proposed by State Party	Recommendation by IUCN and ICOMOS	Outcome 2018
Cultural sites			
Belgium / Netherlands Colonies of Benevolence	(iii) (v) (vi)	Deferral	Deferred (Inscribed 2021 Criteria (ii) (iv))
China Historic Monuments and Sites of Ancient Quanzhou (Zayton)	(ii) (iii) (vi)	Not recommended for inscription	Not inscribed in 2018 (Inscribed 2021 as: Quanzhou: Emporium of the World in Song-Yuan China Criteria (iv))
Czechia Žatec – the Town of Hops	(ii) (iii) (iv)	Deferral	Deferred and as of 2021 remains on tentative list
Denmark Aasivissuit – Nipisat. Inuit Hunting Ground between Ice and Sea	(iii) (v)	Inscribe	Inscribed Criteria (v)
France Historic Urban Ensemble of Nîmes	(ii) (iv)	Deferral	Deferred and as of 2021 remains on tentative list
Germany Archaeological Border complex of Hedeby and the Danevirke	Criteria: (iii) (iv)	Inscribe	Inscribed (iii) (iv)
Germany Naumburg Cathedral	(i) (ii) (iv)	Previously referred back to state party	Inscribed Criteria (i) (ii)
India Victorian Gothic and Art Deco Ensembles of Mumbai	Criteria: (ii) (iv)	Inscribe	Inscribed (ii) (iv)
Indonesia Age of Trade: Old Town of Jakarta (formerly Old Batavia) and 4 Outlying Islands (Onrust, Kelor, Cipir and Bidadari)	(ii) (iii) (iv) (v)	Not recommended for inscription	Deferred and as of 2021 remains on tentative list
Iran Sassanid Archaeological Landscape of Fars Region	(i) (ii) (iii) (iv) (v)	Deferral	Inscribed Criteria (ii) (iii) (v)
Italy Ivrea, industrial city of the 20th century	(ii) (iv) (vi)	Referral	Inscribed Criteria (iv)
Italy Le Colline del Prosecco di Conegliano a Valdobbiadene	(iv) (v)	Not recommended for inscription	Not inscribed 2018 (Inscribed 2019 Criteria (v))
Japan Hidden Christian Sites in the Nagasaki Region	Criteria: (iii)	Inscribe	Inscribed Criteria (iii)

Site Name and Location	Criteria Proposed by State Party	Recommendation by IUCN and ICOMOS	Outcome 2018
Kenya Thimlich Ohinga Archaeological Site	(iii) (iv) (v)	Previously referred back to state party	Inscribed Criteria (iii) (iv) (v)
Oman Ancient City of Qalhat	(iii) (v) (vi)	Referral	Inscribed Criteria (ii) (iii)
Republic of Korea Sansa, Buddhist Mountain Monasteries in Korea	(iii) (iv)	Inscribe	Inscribed Criteria (iii)
Romania Roşia Montană Mining Landscape	(ii) (iii) (iv) (vi)	Inscribe	Withdrawn in 2018. Inscribed in 2021 Criteria (ii) (iii) (iv)
Saudi Arabia Al-Ahsa Oasis, an Evolving Cultural Landscape	(iii) (iv) (v)	Not recommended for inscription	Inscribed Criteria (iii) (iv) (v)
Spain Caliphate City of Medina Azahara	Criteria: (iii) (iv)	Inscribe	Inscribed Criteria (iii) (iv)
Turkey Göbekli Tepe	(i) (ii) (iii) (iv)	Inscribe and simultaneously add to list of World Heritage In Danger	Inscribed Criteria (i) (ii) (iv) Not added to list of World Heritage In Danger
Natural sites			
China Fanjingshan	Criteria (vii) (ix) (x)	Recommended for referral	Inscribed Criteria (x)
France Chaîne des Puys – Limagne fault tectonic arena	Criteria (viii)	Previously referred back to state party	Inscribed Criteria (viii)
Iran: Arasbaran Protected Area	(ix) (x)	Not recommended for inscription	Not inscribed and as of 2021 remains on tentative list
Russian Federation: Bikin River Valley	(x)	Recommended for referral	This extension to the Russian Federation: Central Sikhote-Alin property was approved in 2018
South Africa Barberton Makhonjwa Mountains	(viii)	Recommended for referral	Inscribed Criteria (viii)
Mixed Sites			
Columbia Chiribiquete National Park – 'The Maloca of the Jaguar'	(iii) (viii) (ix) (x)	Recommended for inscription	Inscribed Criteria (iii) (ix) (x)
Canada Pimachiowin Aki	(iii) (vi) (ix)	Recommended for inscription	Inscribed Criteria (iii) (vi) (ix)
Mexico Tehuacán-Cuicatlán Valley: originary habitat of Mesoamerica	(iii) (iv) (vi) (x)	Previously referred back to state party	Inscribed Criteria (iv) (x)

significance of the dome lies in what it represents. The building has no aesthetic or architectural significance per se. Rather, its mute remains symbolise on the one hand the ultimate in human destruction and the power of the atomic bomb while on the other hand the structure's remains communicate a message of hope for a world peace and the elimination of all nuclear weapons (Beazley, 2010).

Ways in which the nomination of the Genbaku Dome was considered as complex from a political perspective can be illustrated by the responses to the listing of the site that came from two other States Parties, China and the USA. China expressed reservations during the final approval process because from its viewpoint it was other Asian countries and peoples who suffered the greatest loss in life and property during the Second World War and that Japan was the main aggressor in the region (one should remember that Japan invaded China in 1937 and that hostilities did not cease until 1945).

Meanwhile the USA issued a statement disassociating itself from the final decision to inscribe the Genbaku Dome on the World Heritage List, stating that

> The United States and Japan are close friends and allies. We cooperate on security, diplomatic, international, in economic affairs around the world. Our two countries are tied by deep personal friendships through many Americans and Japanese. Even so, the United States cannot support its friend in this inscription. The United States is concerned about the lack of historical perspective in the nomination of Genbaku Dome. The events antecedent to the United States' use of atomic weapons to end World War II are key to understanding the tragedy of Hiroshima. Any examination of the period leading up to 1945 should be placed in the appropriate historical context.[4]

Interestingly, this appears to call into question the actual terminology used to frame statements about the property's Outstanding Universal Value, confirming the widespread belief that all heritage is effectively political. The American statement went on to note that the United States believed the inscription of war sites outside the scope of the Convention and it urged the committee to address the question of suitability of war sites for the World Heritage List. Of itself this statement contradicts a number of the tentative list properties currently proposed by States Parties, for example sites associated with the **Battlefield of Waterloo** (Belgium), **The Walk of Peace from the Alps to the Adriatic – Heritage of the First World War** (Slovenia) and feed through to complex discussions about the nature of Outstanding Universal Value with regards to dark heritage and the view from ICOMOS and IUCN (2018) 'that a cautious approach should be taken for sites associated with negative memories' with regard to the proposed World Heritage property **Funerary and Memorial Sites of the First World War** (Belgium, France).

2.4 Conclusion

Overall, the diversity and representativeness of World Heritage as evidenced by the structure and content of the List is changing. One can see that changes to the definition of Outstanding Universal Value and the conceptualising of sites that emerged out of the 1994 Global Review has shifted thinking about World Heritage from its original position as a status or marker allocated to denote an individual site within a particular nation state to a more inclusive understanding that allows properties to spread across national boundaries and that brings together in serial nominations properties with a shared past. This move away from simply marking a site to considering the wider context within which it originally developed, but also how it functions today, connects through to the central role that the World Heritage movement could play in addressing the UN's Sustainable Development Goals (SDGs), a theme we explore in more detail in Chapter 11. In other words, the evolution of the concept of World Heritage and the way that it is being operationalised means that properties on the list should no longer be seen just as exemplars of Outstanding Universal Value, but rather as agents to support social and economic development and as laboratories to explore adaption to the challenges of climate change.

This 'mission creep' of the World Heritage List support the arguments made by Cameron & Rossler (2016) who contended that the World Heritage Convention contributes to an extraordinary international dialogue on heritage matters and that the associated policy and site-specific decisions have affected the way that heritage values have been perceived and conservation strategies formulated over time. The debates over gaps or omissions from the list have helped to foster a new understanding of heritage theory and practice. Nonetheless, this optimism must be balanced as there remain flaws in the listing process as well as insufficient funds to support a robust programme of international cooperation that will help protect our World Heritage properties from the threats of urbanisation, mass tourism and environmental damage. Moreover, the blatant politicisation of the decision-making process suggests that we should continue to be critical of different areas of World Heritage practice by reflecting on what might be the different agendas of the experts and the professionals involved in the nomination, inscription and management process, as well as questioning the real intentions of the members of the World Heritage Committee itself.

Notes

1 See https://whc.unesco.org/en/soc/2739 (accessed 4 February 2022).
2 See https://wilderness-society.org/unesco-world-heritage-site-renomination-process-in-slovakia/ (accessed 4 February 2022).
3 See, for instance, Keough, 2011; Brumann, 2018; Meskell, 2018.
4 See https://whc.unesco.org/archive/repco96x.htm#annex5 (accessed 4 February 2022).

References

Beazley, O. 2010. Politics and power: the Hiroshima Peace Memorial (Genbaku Dome) as world heritage. In: S. Labadi & C. Long, eds. *Heritage and Globalisation*. Abingdon: Routledge, 45–65.

Brumann, C. 2018. Undermining Southern Solidarity in the UNESCO World Heritage Committee. *Ethnos*, 84 (3), 1–20. doi:10.1080/00141844.2018.1471514.

Cameron, C. & Rossler, M. 2016. *Many Voices, One Vision: The Early Years of the World Heritage Convention*. London: Routledge.

ICOMOS. 2011. *Evaluations of Nominations of Cultural and Mixed Properties to the World Heritage List: ICOMOS Report for the World Heritage Committee, 35th Ordinary Session*. UNESCO, June 2011. https://whc.unesco.org/archive/2011/whc11-35com-inf.8B1e.pdf (accessed 7 January 2022).

ICOMOS & IUCN. 2018. Recommendations by IUCN and ICOMOS to the 42nd session of the World Heritage Committee in 2018 (WHC/18/42.COM/8B). https://whc.unesco.org/archive/2018/whc18-42com-8B-en.pdf (accessed 7 January 2022).

Keough, E. B. 2011. Heritage in peril. A critique of UNESCO's World Heritage Program. *Washington University Global Studies Law Review*, 10 (3), 593–615.

Meskell, L. 2018. *A Future in Ruins. UNESCO, World Heritage and the Dream of Peace*. Oxford: Oxford University Press.

UNESCO. 1997. *Report of the World Heritage Committee*. 20th Session, Merida, Yucatan, Mexico. 2–7 December 1996. Annex V. Paris: UNESCO.

3

WORLD HERITAGE AS AN INSTRUMENT OF INTERNATIONAL POLITICS

3.1 Introduction

This chapter reviews in more detail the interface of World Heritage with international politics. We start by considering the complexity of the concept of Outstanding Universal Value as it relates to so-called 'dark heritage' sites – that is, locations associated with death, disaster and suffering (Stone et al., 2018; Kennell & Powell, 2021). The concept of Outstanding Universal Value also presents complexity in that it provides a high-profile arena for both the destruction and creation of heritage. Because they can represent contested identities, World Heritage properties can be particularly vulnerable to loss at times of conflict. It is thus useful to reflect on the founding principles of UNESCO: 'since wars begin in the minds of men and women, it is in the minds of men and women that the defences of peace must be constructed' (Preamble, UNESCO Constitution, n.d.). The chapter therefore considers the ways in which politics is interwoven within the WH process with case studies drawn from Europe, the Middle-East, Asia and Africa.

3.2 Embedding complexity within World Heritage inscription

As we saw in the discussion of the **Genbaku Dome** nomination in Chapter 2, at times the political nature of heritage is embedded within the World Heritage process. For many, dark heritage sites are difficult to study, difficult to read about and difficult to engage with, and through the international lens of World Heritage they can become even more complex and difficult because of the tensions that can emerge when addressing the values and attributes associated with a difficult past, and the messages that these can send about both the positive and the less–desirable sides of human behaviour. The former prison colony of **Robben Island**, South Africa, was added to the list in 1999 with the inscription documentation stating that the prison

DOI: 10.4324/9781003044857-4

buildings 'bear eloquent witness to its sombre history' and that they 'symbolise the triumph of human spirit, of freedom and of democracy over oppression'. To the fore on the UNESCO page for the site[1] is that statement 'its buildings, particularly those of the late 20th century such as the maximum security prison for political prisoners, witness the triumph of democracy and freedom over oppression and racism'. If nothing else, that is a clear political statement repudiating the apartheid government that ruled South Africa for much of the second part of the 20th century.

Another example of debate emerged in 2020 relating to Hagia Sophia, Turkey, part of the **Historic Areas of Istanbul** World Heritage Site (see Plate 3.1). The controversy here surrounds the use of Hagia Sophia, originally built as a Christian church in the sixth century under the direction of Justinian and then repurposed as a mosque in 1453. In 1935, Ataturk secularised the building and thereafter opened it as a museum. In 1985, it was awarded World Heritage Status as a component of Historic Areas of Istanbul World Heritage Site. In 2020, the Turkish President Recep Tayyip Erdogan converted the site back into a mosque, so that formal prayers could take place although managed in such a way that the building remained open for non-Muslim visitors. The controversy here surrounds the repurposing of the building to a mosque without the prior consultation with UNESCO. The UNESCO statement that was published very soon after on Hagia Sophia notes that this:

> raises the issue of the impact of this change of status on the property's universal value. States have an obligation to ensure that modifications do not affect the Outstanding Universal Value of inscribed sites on their territories. UNESCO must be given prior notice of any such modifications, which, if necessary, are then examined by the World Heritage Committee.
>
> *(UNESCO, 2020)*

PLATE 3.1 Hagia Sophia, Istanbul. Inscribed on the World Heritage List in 1985 and converted back to religious use in 2020.
Source: Photograph by Peter Tinkler.

This example demonstrates how values change over time and how heritage is used to support the development of domestic politics – and how the entanglement with international politics through the World Heritage context can create unintended consequences.

BOX 3.1 CASE STUDY 3.1: AUSCHWITZ BIRKENAU, POLAND.

One of the most famous dark heritage sites where we encounter complex issues of memory and contested meanings is Auschwitz Birkenau, located outside the small town of Oświęcim in Southern Poland. It was inscribed as a World Heritage property in 1979, listed as part of the first wave of World Heritage properties and it presents a good example of how concepts of heritage have been developing around dark heritage sites in the intervening period.

When listed in 1979 it was inscribed as a cultural property using Criterion (vi): to be directly or tangibly associated with events or living traditions, with ideas, or with beliefs, with artistic and literary works of outstanding universal significance. Within the meaning of that particular criterion, the meaning of the site is about it being a monument to loss and to this dark chapter in human history, and as reminder of the 'martyrdom and resistance of millions of men, women and children'.[2] The statement of Outstanding Universal Value emphasises the importance of the property as tangible, physical evidence for the events that took place there.

It is important to note that the name of the World Heritage property was changed in 2007, from Auschwitz-Birkenau to 'Auschwitz Birkenau German Nazi concentration and extermination camp 1940 to 1945'. The state party (in this case Poland) were keen to change the name in order to distinguish it as representing a particular period in Poland's past associated with the German Nazi occupation.

As well as understanding the politics of inscription and naming, it is also important to consider the wider conservation and management measures that are appropriate for dark heritage sites and why it is that for most dark heritage sites, considerable importance is placed on the tangible heritage assets. So at Auschwitz Birkenau, for instance, the famous sign over one of the entrance gates that reads '*Arbeit macht frei*'; the railway lines leading into the site; the barrack blocks and the barbed wire fencing are all carefully conserved. For such sites of tragedy and suffering, the materiality of these places is significant as their retention is both a prompt for memory as well as incontrovertible evidence of past events that, in a post-truth era of global politics, some still try to deny.[3]

3.3 Mixed messages – responses to heritage destruction

All heritage encapsulates contested meanings and World Heritage Sites can be impacted in different ways as a result of conflict, principally because of the ability of any group with power over a geographical area to damage or even destroy the tangible evidence associated with a past or present culture whose legacy they dispute or do not value at all because it conflicts with their own world view. So, what is it about World Heritage status that can add to a property's vulnerability during conflict? World Heritage properties are high profile and provide an arena for demonstrable acts of destruction and concurrent acts of condemnation (demonstrated forcefully in former US President Donald Trump's January 2020 tweet threatening destruction of Iran's cultural sites – and the swift rebuttal by the then Director-General of UNESCO). This raises the idea that the threatened, or actual, destruction of World Heritage properties relates to memory being erased (remember – the materiality of historic places is often argued to be the prompt that keeps memories alive). And any international reaction to condemn such threats and actions then provides the response that the protagonists were seeking in the first instance, providing in their eyes a rationale for the destruction of these high-profile properties (Stone, 2020).

BOX 3.2 CASE STUDY 3.2: BAMIYAN VALLEY, AFGHANISTAN.

The Bamiyan Valley in Afghanistan famously highlighted the vulnerabilities of potential World Heritage properties when it was targeted for destruction by the Taliban, the ruling power in Afghanistan in the 1990s and 2000s. The relationship between the desire by UNESCO to list the Bamiyan Buddhas as a World Heritage property and the threats by the Taliban to destroy the sixth-century monumental statues, relates to a conflict between the perceived focus of the international community on cultural heritage and their perceived lack of concern about local food shortages and the impact of the sanctions that were in place on the residents of the area at the time. The situation was further complicated by the contrasting views of what constituted national heritage held by the various parties involved. These tensions between urgent day-to-day needs and wider national heritage and conservation interests became focused on a debate about the future of this high-profile site, which was already perceived of international significance prior to its World Heritage listing in 2003.

The reason for the destruction of the Bamiyan Buddhas in March 2001 has been presented by the Taliban as a necessary action to draw attention to what they perceived to be the main crisis in the area – widespread hunger in the local population. But it also revealed the complexity of international heritage diplomacy and contested notions of legitimacy in decision making. For instance, a UNESCO mission was attempted, and whilst it did not engage with the Taliban it did consult with other stakeholders inside and outside Afghanistan. These tensions culminated in the destruction of the Bamiyan Buddhas. The response from UNESCO culminated in 2003 when the **Cultural Landscape and Archaeological Remains of the Bamiyan Valley** was inscribed as a World Heritage property and simultaneously placed on the list of World Heritage in Danger.

The site's listing reflects five of the six cultural Criteria: (i), (ii), (iii), (iv) and (vi). The last criterion is particularly significant, stating the Outstanding Universal Value for the Bamiyan Buddhas relates to the way the monuments have

suffered at different times of their existence, including their deliberate destruction in 2001. This has perhaps had unintended consequences in relation to the
long debates regarding their potential reconstruction (as would fit in with
Buddhist notions of renewal embedded within conservation), and in relation to
notions of authenticity embedded within the World Heritage Convention. The
complexity is that Criterion (vi) notes the property's Outstanding Universal
Value as developing from the site's current condition and links that to this
global response to their destruction in 2001. Therefore, any reconstruction
work could be seen as impacting both the authenticity of the site, and
impacting the Outstanding Universal Value for which the site has been listed as
a World Heritage property.

As of 2022 (21 years after the initial destruction), the Cultural Landscape and
Archaeological Remains of the Bamiyan Valley remains on the list of World Heritage in Danger on the basis that there still needs to be progress in developing a
long-term conservation plan which balances concerns of conservation and
removal of the property from the List of World in Danger over reconstruction
efforts.

A contrasting approach to the Bamiyan example is found in the city of Mostar,
Bosnia and Herzegovina, which was heavily impacted during the Balkan conflict of
the 1990s. During the Croat-Bosniak war there was widespread destruction in the
historic city and the 16th-century stone bridge across the steep, narrow gorge of the
Neretva River, that had previously joined the two parts of this historic town, was
completely destroyed in November 1993 by the Croatian army. Some argue that it
was destroyed for strategic reasons (to prevent troops and supplies being moved
across the gorge) while others contend that its demolition was purely a political act
designed to destroy the symbolic significance the bridge held in serving the diverse
ethnic communities who lived in Mostar prior to the conflict (Coward, 2009).
Subsequent to that destruction, there was a long programme of reconstruction at the
bridge at Mostar and it was finally inscribed on the World Heritage list in 2005 as
The Old Bridge Area of the Old City of Mostar, associated with Criterion (vi).

Mostar presents a significant contrast to the Bamiyan Buddhas in relation to
post-conflict reconstruction, with the reconstruction of the old bridge and its surroundings being seen as a universal symbol of coexistence of communities and as a
symbol of peace and powerful cooperation. These two sites show extreme responses
to heritage impacted by conflict with both valued in very different ways as either a
symbol of reconciliation or a symbol of destruction of cultural property. Both are
World Heritage properties but both now embody very different meanings. This
highlights the role of the World Heritage process in the creation and curation of
heritage at an international level. As a whole we can see that heritage sites have different narratives and have different meanings and significances, but they are identified
by UNESCO as having particular types of Outstanding Universal Value and to some
extent, a particular set of meanings associated with a site. This can then mean that

debates around conservation and reconstruction can become complicated and generate their own conflict at local, national and international scales.

3.4 Responses to ongoing conflict

The 2010s have seen further impacts of conflict on World Heritage properties, and perhaps nowhere more obviously than in the Levant. The Syrian civil war began in 2011, when pro-democracy protests erupted in the southern city of Deraa. Protests then spread nationwide and escalated into a brutal war which drew in regional and world powers. Without wanting to diminish for a second the scale of human tragedy that has occurred in the last ten years, we focus for the purposes of this discussion on how the Syrian conflict can shed light on cultural property destruction within the context of contemporary conflict.

One of Syria's most noted archaeological sites is **Palmyra**, a cultural World Heritage property inscribed on the list in 1980 and associated with three cultural Criteria: (i), (ii) and (iv). Palmyra was one of the early sites to be added to the list, and the way that its Outstanding Universal Value was identified (basically celebrating the role that Palmyra played within the European 'Grand Tour') raises interesting discussions around representation of national heritage internationally and around decolonialism. It could also be considered how this reception of Palmyra as relating to a classical inheritance also impacted the response to the subsequent destruction.

From the earliest stages of the civil war, UNESCO had reacted to threats to the cultural property in a series of actions. For example, in 2012 the then Director-General of UNESCO appealed for the protection of Syria's cultural heritage as the conflict developed and started to escalate. Then, in 2013 a red list of Syrian antiquities at risk was launched, with the Director-General deploring the escalation of violence and the damage to World Heritage in Syria. At that point, all six of Syria's World Heritage properties were placed on the list of World Heritage in Danger. Through 2014 the UNESCO Director-General was continuing to condemn the military presence and destruction of World Heritage properties in Syria.

In the late summer of 2015 the Islamist group ISIS, who by that time were occupying the part of Homs Governate that included Palmyra, severely damaged the archaeological remains at the site, toppling columns, blowing up temples and demolishing the remains of a second-century Roman theatre. Further destruction happened until ISIS was ousted from the area in 2017. Their actions led to international outcry, with public awareness of the situation being assisted partly because of the huge amount of imagery that was broadcast by ISIS itself on various social media channels. This inevitably led to further condemnation of the destruction of cultural property at Palmyra (and elsewhere in Syria) from UNESCO who, in a formal decision recorded at the 41st Session of the World Heritage Committee held in Krakow in July 2017, urged:

> all parties associated with the situation in Syria to refrain from any action that
> would cause further damage to cultural heritage of the country and to fulfil

their obligations under international law, and in particular the United Nations Security Council Resolution 2347 of March 2017, by taking all possible measures to protect such heritage, including the halting of all damages that result from targeting World Heritage properties, sites included in the Tentative List and other cultural heritage sites.

(UNESCO, 2017)

In the last few years, some conservation work has commenced in Palmyra but this has also not been without its controversy, with UNESCO urging the state party to limit restoration works on the site's statues to emergency interventions essential to stabilise the fragile structures until the security situation improves to the extent that detailed studies and fieldwork can be undertaken safely, enabling the identification of a comprehensive strategy to be drawn up for the conservation and restoration of the site in Palmyra. This is partly a response to ongoing discussions around the possibility of rebuilding parts of the property, including the potential for 3D-printing Palmyra (Cunliffe, 2016; Kamash, 2017).

Indeed, in summer 2016 a two-thirds replica of the Arch of Triumph from Palmyra, carved from Egyptian marble and based on photographic records of the monument, was put on display in London's Trafalgar Square before being toured to other destinations including New York and Dubai.[4] This particular initiative was controversial not least because the project was undertaken by the Oxford-based Institute of Digital Archaeology who were outsiders to the site (and to Syria), and the reconstructed arch was never on display in Syria, while the crowd-sourced imagery had the potential to endanger those individuals collecting the imagery (Cunliffe, 2016; Kamash, 2017).

This recent example of how new technologies can be employed to recreate 'lost' heritage reveals significant debates on ideas of the ownership and authority in decision making on heritage sites – in particular, issues around contemporary colonialism through digital archaeology – all further complicated by the apparent international significance of World Heritage properties.

It is useful to consider that all six of Syria's World Heritage properties remain on the list of World Heritage in Danger, although it is Palmyra and (to a lesser extent) Aleppo that have received the most significant international coverage since the start of the Syrian conflict a decade ago. This overlooks heritage within the rest of the country – so in this case it could be critiqued that the international response has been one of 'cherry picking' these high-profile World Heritage properties in order to achieve its own objectives. This relates back to the idea of whether the World Heritage List is representative, but also, in the context of cultural property destruction, to the way in which particular high-profile sites seem to be targeted for both destruction and reconstruction. Thus a few iconic heritage sites become the target for specific attention in a time of conflict, with the relevant action (destruction or reconstruction) suiting the political objectives of the relevant actor. In the case of Syria, the World Heritage properties provide a particular lens on particular episodes of destruction. However, in Syria, just as in every other country in the world, the vast majority of heritage is not listed as World Heritage and any insights into loss and vulnerabilities of those non-World Heritage properties are much harder to identify, broadcast and understand because they lack the spotlight of inscription.

BOX 3.3 CASE STUDY 3.3: TIMBUKTU, MALI.

The destruction of a number of 15th- and 16th-century mausoleums and shrines in Timbuktu, Mali, together with the subsequent legal action surrounding the case, gives insight into the development of international responses to damage to cultural World Heritage Sites.

Timbuktu was inscribed as a cultural World Heritage property in 1988 associated with three cultural Criteria: (ii), (iv) and (v). Conflict broke out in northern Mali in early 2012 as several insurgent groups started a campaign for independence or greater autonomy for the region. Fourteen mausolea in Timbuktu were destroyed in early summer 2012, and in response UNESCO added the property on the list of World Heritage in Danger at its 36th Meeting of the World Heritage Committee in St Petersburg in late June/ early July 2012. Timbuktu had previously been on the list of World Heritage in Danger from 1990 until 2005, principally because of environmental changes and the impact of desertification on the site.

The example of Timbuktu is significant as it resulted in the first prosecution of cultural property destruction in the context of war crimes. Following the destruction of the mausolea an individual (Ahmed Al-Faqi Al-Mahdi) was prosecuted at the International Criminal Court (ICC).[5] The ICC ordered reparations of 2.7 million euros for the victims of the crime – in this case the community in Timbuktu – with individual compensation to victims most affected including the guardians of the site who had suffered the loss of income and the descendants of those whose mausolea were destroyed and who suffered mental harm (Moffett, 2017; Joy, 2018). In recognising that the international community in this case, represented by UNESCO and Mali, had suffered harm they were awarded a symbolic 1 euro each. In doing this, the ICC recognised a difference between the impact of this destruction on the local community and the impact of this destruction on the international community.

The case is significant as this is the very first time the ICC has demanded reparations for the destruction of cultural property. This is a strong message that perpetrators who target cultural heritage can be held to account. It also presents very significant case law in relation to concepts of local, national and international significance (and ultimately Outstanding Universal Value). UNESCO could potentially use this as precedent within the context of the 1972 World Heritage Convention, because the ICC have recognised the impact of cultural property destruction for both the local and the international community.

Subsequently the Timbuktu mausolea have been rebuilt, with the works financed partly by the Swiss government and the European Union. The reconstruction was driven by the local community but wider international politics was also being played with the way in which reconstruction was financed as another example of heritage diplomacy. There is now review of the effectiveness or otherwise of the reconstruction work in Timbuktu, which focused on the community as custodians and as skilled practitioners for repair and maintenance. However, the ownership of the reconstruction work is perhaps now seen as problematic as shown in their apparent lack of maintenance (Joffrey & Essayouti, 2020). Of course, this is all against the backdrop of ongoing conflict and upheaval in Mali as at the time of writing, although the 2013 ceasefire remains in place, there remain occasional attacks from insurgent groups.

3.5 Wider politics at play within World Heritage

When considering the role of politics within the ambit of World Heritage, it is important to consider the actual membership of UNESCO. For example, the UK joined UNESCO as a founding member from 1946 but withdrew its membership in 1985 under direction from Prime Minister Margaret Thatcher, who felt that the organisation was a barrier to the UK's desire to promote a neoliberal agenda around the world. Nonetheless, in the eight-year period before the UK re-joined UNESCO in 1997, a handful of UK properties were still able to be inscribed on the list, including **Blenheim Palace**, the **Tower of London** and the **Old and New Towns of Edinburgh**. This success at securing inscriptions even when outside the organisation could probably not be achieved today, since by leaving UNESCO a country is unable to secure representation on the Committee that evaluates applications for inscription, and is also unable to engage in the behind-the-scenes negotiations that are important in the way in which decisions are being made. Yet it still retains the responsibility of protecting and managing any World Heritage properties within its borders to the appropriate UNESCO standards. It is thus a potentially risky strategy to take if a country wishes to retain influence in the politics of global heritage.

Another example is the USA, which was also a founding member of UNESCO but withdrew membership from 1984 before rejoining in 2002. However, almost a decade later, in 2011, the USA stopped funding UNESCO when the Obama administration froze financial contributions to the organisation after it granted Palestine full membership as a state. Finally, in 2018 the USA fully withdrew from the organisation. This is particularly significant because the USA was once responsible for about 22% of UNESCO's budget (Coningham, 2017). The withdrawal in 2018 was a reaction to the listing of a Palestinian World Heritage property – **Hebron/Al-Khalil Old Town** – and in particular to the terminology used in the relevant documentation, which was seen to diminish the significance of the site (associated with the final resting place of Abraham/ Ibrahim) to the Jewish faith while emphasising its Palestinian heritage.[6] As a result of this decision, the USA and then Israel notified UNESCO of their withdrawal with the rationale for the withdrawal being cited as continuing anti-Israel bias (previous concerns had also been expressed also at references to the

Dome of the Rock in Jerusalem being made only to *al-Haram al-Sharif*, which is the Arab and Islamic name for the site).

As mentioned above, the World Heritage Site of Hebron/ Al Khalil Old Town was inscribed in July 2017 under Criteria (ii), (iv) and (vi). The centre of interest is the site of the Al Ibrahimi mosque, the Tomb of the Patriarchs whose buildings are in a compound built in the first century AD, to protect the tomb of the patriarch, Abraham Ibrahim, and his family. This place has become a site of pilgrimage for Judaism, Christianity and Islam.

At the World Heritage committee meeting in 2017, 12 countries voted in favour, three voted against and six abstained. As 12 countries voted in favour, it was inscribed and was also simultaneously placed on the List of World Heritage in Danger. Immediately upon the listing of this site, Israel announced a US$1 million cut to payments to UNESCO, stating that the money would be diverted to establish a Jewish heritage museum elsewhere.

Investigating this nomination and the evaluation in more detail, it is possible to shed more light on the controversy. ICOMOS were not able to undertake a site visit as part of their assessment, but still nominated the property and stated that it unquestionably justifies Criteria (ii), (iv) and (vi) as well as meeting the conditions of integrity and authenticity. The controversy here revolves around the fact that the evaluation was undertaken without a site visit, and thus the ICOMOS team was actually unable to fully evaluate whether the property justified some criteria, conditions of authenticity and integrity and management requirements and level of threat. Further, in the records of those meetings, they record that there is regret that Israel, as the occupying power, did not give the necessary permissions for ICOMOS to undertake the site visit. This led to additional accusations of anti-Israeli bias, through the explicit statement that Israel was an occupying power.

The phrasing and reaction to the process and decision making for this World Heritage property brings to light the way in which heritage is contested on the international stage. For example, the Israeli politician Benjamin Netanyahu tweeted that 'UNESCO has become a theatre of the absurd. Instead of preserving history, it distorts it'.[7] In summary, the Israeli and US withdrawal from UNESCO can be seen to be a backward step for global cultural cooperation (Coningham, 2017).

BOX 3.4 CASE STUDY 3.4: SITES OF JAPAN'S MEIJI INDUSTRIAL REVOLUTION: IRON AND STEEL, SHIPBUILDING AND COAL MINING.

Another very high-profile political example of World Heritage inscription causing tensions focuses on the 20th-century history of Japan and South Korea. The controversy is about the inscription in 2015 of a number of sites associated with Japan's Meiji Industrial Revolution. It is a serial property consisting of 23 elements relating to the iron and steel industry of the 19th and 20th centuries. At the heart of the controversy is the association of Japan's industrial revolution with the use of forced Korean and Chinese labourers during the country's colonial period. South Korea's culture minister Park Yang-woo condemned Japan for trying to distort historical facts, suggesting that: 'Japan has undermined the existence value of the World Heritage and trust of the international community by failing to keep its promise [. . .] History must be based on the truth. The Japanese government must be honest and respect history' (Yeon-soo, 2020).

When the site was nominated, Japan pledged to the international community that it would establish a centre to commemorate Koreans and others who were taken against their will and forced to work in inhumane working conditions. Yet, adding to the initial controversy over the World Heritage inscription, tensions have since emerged as a result of the opening of a heritage centre on Battleship Island (one of the component parts of the property) where the interpretation does not make reference to that forced labour.

As another dark heritage site it poses a range of issues; not just how to communicate difficult memories associated with conscripted/ slave labour but also, since the Battleship Island site appeared in the 2012 James Bond movie *Skyfall*, catering for a massive upswing in tourism numbers. For some, the current approach to presenting and interpreting this particular World Heritage Site exemplifies the invention of heritage by ignoring a colonial past.

3.6 Conclusion

As the various case studies in this chapter have shown, there are complex political considerations in relation to heritage at local, national and international scales. These can affect whether or not a nominated property is actually inscribed or not, and who takes part in that decision; the naming of things; how heritage values are communicated (which can lead to diplomatic tensions); and whether or not a property might be targeted for destruction (or rehabilitation) during times of conflict. It can be debated whether these issues are just too embedded with the concept of heritage to disentangle and therefore whether World Heritage is a force for good or actually something that is rather more complicated, and with unintended consequences resulting from the international perspective afforded to World Heritage properties. Nonetheless, the political dimension is ever present in heritage, for heritage-making is essentially a political act.

Notes

1 See https://whc.unesco.org/en/list/916 (accessed 27 November 2021).
2 ICOMOS recommendation letter to UNESCO, dated 7 June 1978.
3 Weaver et al., 2009.
4 See https://www.bbc.co.uk/news/uk-36070721 (accessed 27 November 2021).
5 See https://whc.unesco.org/en/news/1559/ (accessed 27 November 2021).

6   See https://www.e-ir.info/2019/02/14/why-did-the-u-s-and-israel-leave-unesco/ (accessed 27 November 2021).
7   See https://www.independent.co.uk/news/world/unesco-israel-withdraw-netanyahu-u nited-nations-trump-latest-a7997506.html (accessed 27 November 2021).

References

Coningham, R. 2017. Why the US withdrawal from UNESCO is a step backwards for global cultural cooperation. *The Conversation.* https://theconversation.com/why-the-us-withdrawa l-from-unesco-is-a-step-backwards-for-global-cultural-cooperation-85692 https://theconve rsation.com/why-the-us-withdrawal-from-unesco-is-a-step-backwards-for-global-cultural-cooperation-85692 (accessed 29 June 2022).

Coward, M. 2009. *Urbicide: The Politics of Urban Destruction.* London: Routledge.

Cunliffe, E. 2016. Should we 3D print a new Palmyra? *The Conversation.* https://theconversa tion.com/should-we-3d-print-a-new-palmyra-57014 (accessed 29 June 2022).

Joffrey, T. & Essayouti, B. 2020. *Lessons learnt from the reconstruction of the destroyed mausoleums of Timbuktu, Mali.* HERITAGE2020 (3DPast | RISK-Terra) International Conference, September 2020, Valencia, Spain. 913–920, ff10.5194/isprs-archives-XLIV-M-1–2020–913–2020ff. ffhal-02928898f.

Joy, C. 2018. The International Criminal Court and crimes against cultural heritage in Timbuktu. *Anthropology Today,* 34 (1), 15–17.

Kamash, Z. 2019. 'Postcard to Palmyra': bringing the public into debates over post-conflict reconstruction in the Middle East. *World Archaeology,* 49 (5), 608–622. doi:10.1080/ 00438243.2017.1406399.

Kennell, J. & Powell, R. 2021. Dark tourism and World Heritage Sites: a Delphi study of stakeholder perceptions of the development of dark tourism products. *Journal of Heritage Tourism,* 16 (4), 367–381.

Moffett, L. 2017. Timbuktu destruction: landmark ruling awards millions to Malians. *The Conversation:* https://theconversation.com/timbuktu-destruction-landmark-ruling-awards-millions-to-malians-82540 (accessed 29 June 2022).

Stone, P. 2020. Destroying cultural heritage is an attack on humanity's past and present – it must be prevented. https://theconversation.com/destroying-cultural-heritage-is-an-attack-on-humanitys-past-and-present-it-must-be-prevented-129412 (accessed 29 June 2022).

Stone, P. R., Hartmann R., Seaton T., Sharpley R. & White, L. Eds. 2018. *The Palgrave Handbook of Dark Tourism Studies.* London: Palgrave Macmillan.

UNESCO. 2017. Decision: 41 COM 7A.50 https://whc.unesco.org/en/decisions/6996 (accessed 29 June 2022).

UNESCO. 2020. *UNESCO statement on Hagia Sophia,* Istanbul. https://en.unesco.org/ news/unesco-statement-hagia-sophia-istanbul.

UNESCO Constitution. n.d. http://portal.unesco.org/en/ev.php-URL_ID=15244&URL_ DO=DO_TOPIC&URL_SECTION=201.html (accessed 7 January 2022).

Weaver, R. L., Delpierre, N. & Boissier, L. 2009. Holocaust denial and governmentally-declared 'truth': French and American perspectives. *Texas Tech Law Review,* 41 (2), 495–518.

Yeon-soo, K. 2020. Should UNESCO remove Japanese sites from World Heritage list? *The Korea Times.* https://www.koreatimes.co.kr/www/nation/2020/07/356_292132.html (accessed 29 June 2022).

4

MANAGING MAJOR THREATS TO CULTURAL AND NATURAL HERITAGE SITES

4.1 Introduction

As discussed in Chapter 2, every World Heritage Site is expected to have a management plan that, among other things, identifies threats to the integrity of the property which might impact on its Outstanding Universal Value and which proposes suitable protection and mitigation measures. Some threats are associated with anthropogenic activity (e.g. conflict, tourism or indirect factors such as pollutants that have been expelled into the atmosphere or watercourses as a result of industrial activity) while others are natural hazards such as geological and geomorphological processes (e.g. earthquakes, weathering). The term risk is conventionally used to refer to potential circumstances that might arise at some point in the future and compromise the 'normal' state of affairs, and for which mitigation can be planned. A risk is different from a crisis, which refers to a contemporaneous event that is characterised by ambiguity of cause, effect and means of resolution, and which necessitates immediate action to resolve it (Pearson & Clair, 1998). Both risks and crises can pose a threat to World Heritage and thus it is important to understand how managers identify and respond to such pressures.

This chapter considers the types of threats (short-, medium- and long-term) that can be anticipated for World Heritage properties (cultural and natural) and looks at how UNESCO uses the separate list of World Heritage in Danger as a tool for highlighting the need for action at properties at risk of damage or loss as a result of natural or anthropogenic factors. We look at how property managers use the Disaster Risk Management (DRM) framework in their day-to-day activities. Different management challenges are illustrated through case studies from a selection of cultural and natural World Heritage properties including the **Historic Centre of Mexico City and Xochimilco** and **Bam and its Cultural Landscape (Iran)**. Not covered in this chapter are specific issues around war and conflict (Chapter 3)

DOI: 10.4324/9781003044857-5

and the management challenges associated with visitation at cultural and natural heritage sites, which are addressed in Chapter 9.

4.2 Planning for, and responding to, natural disaster

Under the definitions of the Granada Convention of 1985 a hazard is defined as the probability of occurrence within a specific period of time of a natural phenomenon which could damage buildings or objects; risk is defined as the expected damage or loss resulting from a particular natural phenomena or combination of phenomenon; while vulnerability is a measure of the likely degree of damage or loss to a given element at risk or a set of such elements resulting from the occurrence of a natural phenomenon (Granada Convention, 1985) (it should be remembered that the Granada Convention was a Council of Europe initiative that referred to cultural heritage only). Natural disasters that might affect World Heritage properties – cultural or natural – include: seismic activity; tornadoes and typhoons; tsunami; flooding; land-, earth- and mudslides and avalanches; storms and fires. It is important to note that there are often secondary hazards which arise as a result of the primary disaster – so an earthquake may set off a landslide, which then disrupts power supplies and causes localised fires. Any management plan prepared for a World Heritage Site where there is a considered likelihood of natural disaster will identify appropriate responses that go beyond repairing or restoring whatever aspect of the property that is damaged by the disaster in question, and should also address the associated impacts on the communities and economies affected by the event in question.

The high-profile impacts of Hurricane Katrina in 2005 provided considerable insight into the need for disaster risk reduction to be people-centred rather than property-focused and that there was a need to engage all sectors of society effectively, revealing there was no point having a technical solution if people weren't involved in that solution. This followed on from the development of frameworks for reducing the risks to places from disaster that were being shaped in the early 2000s, including the framework for action from the World Conference on Disaster Reduction in Kobe, Hyogo in Japan (2005). The resulting Hyogo Framework (2005) was concerned with ensuring that disaster risk reduction is seen by governments as a national as well as local priority and that there is a way to identify, assess and monitor disaster risks and enhance early warning, and to use knowledge, innovation and education as a way to reduce the underlying risk factors and to strengthen disaster preparedness for effective response at all levels. It should be noted that the Hyogo Framework was developed not just for heritage sites at risk of disaster, but for all types of settlement, community and landscape.

The Hyogo Framework ran for ten years until 2015, and was replaced by the Sendai Framework for Disaster Risk Management, which was adopted at the Third UN World Conference on Disaster Risk Reduction, also held in Japan in Sendai. The goal of the Sendai Framework (2015) is to prevent new and reduce existing disaster risk. It contains a number of targets and priorities, essentially to understand disaster risk, to strengthen disaster risk governance, to manage disaster risk, to invest in disaster reduction for resilience, and to enhance disaster preparedness. The Sendai framework lasts until 2030 with a clear set of aspirations to reduce global disaster mortality and to reduce the number of affected people globally by natural disasters. The priorities focus action on understanding disaster risk, strengthening disaster risk governance, investing in disaster risk reduction for resilience, and in an effective response to 'build back better'.

BOX 4.1 CASE STUDY 4.1: THE HISTORIC CENTRE OF MEXICO CITY AND XOCHIMILCO.

Mexico City was impacted by earthquakes in 1985 and in 2017, with these events happening in both years on the same day, 19 September. The 2017 earthquake was measured at 7.1 on the Richter Scale while the earlier 1985 event measured 8.0 on the Richter Scale.

The Historic Centre of Mexico City and Xochomilco was inscribed as Mexico's first World Heritage property in 1987, against four cultural Criteria: (ii), (iii), (iv) and (v). The ICOMOS evaluation of the nomination acknowledged the vulnerability of the site to seismic events and to rapid urban change. The city itself is built on a former lakebed which makes it particularly vulnerable to earthquakes, even those with epicentres hundreds of kilometres away, as the soft clay on which the city stands amplifies the tremors.

The 1985 Earthquake caused substantial human and economic losses: an estimated 6,000–8,000 lives lost and US$4.1 million–8.3 billion (2012 figures) (CDMX Resilience Office, 2016); 1,847 heritage buildings damaged, including 351 historic monuments, 14 museums, and 8 archaeological areas – nearly 20% of the overall economic losses. Longer term, the Catedral Metropolitana suffered damage as a result of subsidence though a conservation scheme, *Corrección Geométrica de la Catedral* has been considered successful.

A number of seismic alert systems have been developed – The National Civil Protection System and National Centre for Disaster Prevention, and since 1985, Mexico has been credited with taking significant steps to reduce deaths, injuries and damage from earthquakes. In fact, analysis of the 2017 earthquake revealed much of the damage was to a particular group of mid-20th-century buildings impacted by particular seismic design codes (Tena-Colunga et al., 2021).

Mexico City is now held as a model of best practice in disaster risk management, having become an seismic-conscious city, using ideas of DRM within a very moderate budget and, from a heritage management perspective, understanding the vulnerabilities of the World Heritage property and identifying suitable protection measures. City-wide the focus is on people, noting vulnerabilities relating to the physical nature of its seismic position as well as social vulnerabilities due to inequalities.

This evolution in thinking around disaster risk preparedness, from being a technical solution based around specific assets or locations, to something that is much more focused on the people who live and work in different parts of the globe that are at risk of major disaster, is as important for World Heritage as much as for any other aspect of contemporary life and culture. All natural disasters can impact World Heritage Sites, and these should be considered both in the initial Management Plan preparation activities that support the nomination process and then as part of the cycle of review and updating of the Management Plan every five or so years. Disaster Risk Management involves consideration of proactive and reactive measures to safeguard heritage sites and significant amount of work has been undertaken in this area from a World Heritage perspective has in recent years, for example by Rohit Jigyasu and his colleagues at ICORP – the International Scientific Committee on Risk Preparedness, part of ICOMOS.

Paragraphs 179 and 180 of the 2021 World Heritage Operational Guidelines identify a hierarchy of threats to both cultural and natural sites with specific and immediate threats referred to as 'Ascertained Danger' and less imminent threats being referred to as 'Potential Danger'. For cultural World Heritage properties, Ascertained Danger can include the serious deterioration of materials or of the integrity of a structure, or a serious loss of historical authenticity, while for natural World Heritage properties Ascertained Danger may refer to a serious decline in the population of the particular species which supports the site's OUV, or to severe deterioration of the natural beauty or scientific value of the property. Potential Dangers cover the situation where a cultural or natural property is faced with threats which could have a negative impact on its inherent characteristics. These threats might be a weakening of legislation protecting the site, armed conflict or development pressures, or the threatening impacts of climatic, geological and other environmental factors.

One of the ways in which the World Heritage process responds to natural disasters is through the separate list of World Heritage in Danger. As discussed in Section 2.1.5, this is a list of World Heritage properties for which the current conservation status is viewed as being vulnerable, and which can include any property that is threatened by serious and specific danger. At the annual World Heritage Committee meeting, a case of urgent need may be identified for a specific property and a new entry to the separate list of World Heritage in Danger could be made. UNESCO will publicise that entry immediately (see Box 4.2). While being placed on the list of World Heritage in Danger highlights the needs of a particular World Heritage property, it doesn't automatically mean that the site will be able to raise more funding to support the management or conservation issues though it does strengthen the case for intervention and investment in remedial and preventative works.

BOX 4.2 CASE STUDY 4.2: BAM AND ITS CULTURAL LANDSCAPE, IRAN.

The ancient city of Bam is situated on the southern edge of the Iranian high plateau. Its origins can be traced back to the sixth to fourth centuries BC, though its heyday is generally stated to have been the period from the seventh to 11th century AD, when it functioned as an important stopping point on the trade routes of the Silk Roads. Life in the oasis was based on complex underground irrigation canals called *qanats* and Bam has some of the best preserved and earliest evidence of *qanats* in Iran. The *Arg-e Bam*, which is the oldest part of Bam, consists of a fortified medieval town built using a vernacular earthen building technique called *chineh,* in which layers of damp earth are built up, layered on top of each other and used in combination with mud bricks (*khesht* in Farsi).

Bam and its surrounding settlements and landscape was impacted on 26 December 2003 by an earthquake with a magnitude of 6.6. The earthquake was particularly destructive in Bam itself, with the death toll amounting to over 26,000 people and a further 30,000 injured. UNESCO's response at its July 2004 session of the World Heritage Committee was to list Bam simultaneously as a cultural World Heritage property under Criteria (ii), (iii), (iv) and (v), and to place on the World Heritage List in Danger.

In reviewing the nomination of Bam as a World Heritage property, there was discussion about both the integrity and the authenticity of the site. In terms of integrity, Bam is seen as organically growing from a relict cultural landscape, with the World Heritage property encompassing the central part of the oasis and the citadel of Bam. However, the area runs along the Bam seismic fault and indeed the epicentre of the 2003 earthquake was almost directly beneath the *Arg-e Bam* itself (Langenbach, 2005). In terms of authenticity, there was consideration of the fact that although the 2003 earthquake caused significant damage to the city, much of the loss was to modern structures and restorations and indeed the materials found at the older levels were generally well preserved. Moreover, the fact that these earlier levels had now been revealed as a result of the earthquake enabled further archaeological research on the development of the city.

After the earthquake Bam was very quick to enter the international conservation agenda, not least because Iran had just hosted a major international conservation conference with one of the conference tours having gone out to Bam just two weeks before the earthquake hit. Thus many key members of the international conservation community had first-hand knowledge of the heritage of Bam and thus perhaps felt a stronger sense of loss at the damage caused by the quake. In terms of developing tourism to the property after the earthquake, visitor-friendly measures were very quickly put in place including a temporary visitor walkway so that visits could continue and so that visitors could view both the destruction but also the recovery work that was being carried out. Although exact figures are not available, it appears that the earthquake didn't reduce the number of visitors but rather there was an uplift in visitation (Vatandoust et al., 2007).

Because Bam had been placed on the list of World Heritage in Danger at the time of its inscription, its status was reviewed annually at World Heritage Committee meetings, with discussions taking place as to whether to retain it on that list. Bam was finally removed from the List of World Heritage in Danger in 2013 on the basis that the state party had addressed all of the work that needed to be undertaken through its ongoing conservation and management planning, and as a result the state of conservation of the property was sufficient for removal from the list. The extra level of support, interest and awareness that came from being on the separate list of World Heritage in Danger had proved to be a useful tool in supporting States Parties and other international bodies in directing and supporting post-disaster recovery at Bam.

4.3 Changing approaches to disaster risk management

As we started to indicate above, over the last 20 years or so there has been a radical new approach to disaster risk management, moving from a very technical response to a response which is much more people-centred. The disaster risk management cycle embeds understanding of risk assessment, risk prevention and mitigation from the outset of the management planning process, which then helps all stakeholders prepare for the emergency. During a disaster, the appropriate emergency response procedures will be put in place, while after the event there will be an assessment of damage and treatment of damage such as repairs, restoration and retrofitting followed finally by longer-term recovery and rehabilitation. At each stage there should be a review of the outcomes of the interventions, with this cycle feeding into a final post-crisis review which informs the next round of prodromal planning.

In reality there is a merging of different responses to disaster with each event posing its own contextual complexities. For example, the **Kathmandu Valley, Nepal** was inscribed as a cultural World Heritage Site very early on in 1979. It is listed as a cultural site with its OUV developing from three cultural criteria. Nepal was impacted in 2015 by a very extensive earthquake: at 7.8 on the seismic scale it caused significant disruption and damage to the World Heritage property. At the World Heritage Committee in 2015 the damage caused by the earthquake to the property was considered as representing both ascertained and potential danger, in accordance with the Operational Guidelines and called upon the States party to initiate a reactive monitoring mission and for the international community to provide financial and technical assistance (UNESCO, 2015). Subsequent World Heritage Committee meetings (2016–2021) have focused discussion of this property on the need for an integrated recovery approach, the complexities of recovery and unintended impacts of authenticity and integrity with the threat of being placed on the World Heritage in Danger list. At the same time, the ICOMOS Scientific Committee on Risk Preparedness issued a series of videos documenting the technical responses to post-disaster recovery in the Kathmandu Valley (ICORP, n.d.), and work by Saul and Waterton (2017) has explored the response of communities and their heritage to the aftermath of the earthquake.

In terms of World Heritage in particular, the values for which the property was inscribed on the list in the first place should be the basis for all disaster risk management plans and actions, to help reduce the possibility of emergency responses and recovery activities that have unintended negative consequences for a World Heritage property. The risk analysis process should identify all of the potential risks and identify the vulnerability factors associated with those risks, and then analyse the cause and effect relationships to consider the potential impact on the heritage values. The World Heritage property significance and attributes should be in the centre of assessment of its vulnerability. A proactive example that shows the connection between the value of the World Heritage property and the Management Plan objective is Fountains Abbey in the UK, whose management plan assesses in detail all possible vulnerabilities to the property's Outstanding Universal Value, to help the management team understand, plan and mitigate the potential impact of potential disasters.

4.4 Politics of disaster

Recent scholarship by Brown et al. (2019) focuses on the ways that discussions of threats (actual and perceived) to cultural and natural heritage properties can sometimes result in complex deliberations by the World Heritage Committee. They argue that the development of diplomatic practises around heritage are being used by States Parties to ensure that their properties are only ever considered for, rather than inscribed on, the list of World Heritage in Danger because of the negative connotations that status might bring upon them. They argue recent years have seen a proliferation of sites which have been 'considered' for the list of World Heritage in Danger though not eventually inscribed, suggesting that this particular tool of the World Heritage Committee is not resolving, in any real sense, threats to properties but is actually further endangering these sites by failing to provide a mechanism for change (Brown et al., 2019).

There are also notable regional imbalances in the number of sites on the list of World Heritage in Danger – 24% of Africa's World Heritage List sites and 30% of the Arab state sites have been inscribed on the list in danger, while only 3% of Europe and North America sites and 5% of sites in the Asia and the Pacific region have been listed as in being in danger. Does that mean that actually one-third or one-quarter of all sites in Africa or the Arab states are in danger, while a very small proportion of the sites in Europe and North America or Asia are in danger? Or is this actually reflecting wider politics here? Brown et al. (2019) consider this as examples of 'technocratic techniques of prevarication' in order to stave off inscription to the list of World Heritage in Danger (as seen with the discussion of **Venice, Italy**, which was 'threatened' with being added to the list of World Heritage in Danger at World Heritage Committee meetings in 2016 and 2017).

4.5 Conclusion

Given the unprecedented changes in frequencies of a range of natural disasters influenced by the unfurling climate crisis it is no surprise this is an area of extensive academic and practice-based research, and from a wide range of disciplines. The shift from technical to people-centred approaches has also been reflected in the changing narrative surrounding disaster, with some authors, for example, Solnit (2009), making a clear case for the disruption and consequent resourcefulness caused by disaster as central to a new vision for a more resilient and collaborative society. It is certainly the case that dramatic changes and threats to a place *can* (but not always) result in an outpouring of action, and we will see in subsequent chapters how other types of change impact World Heritage properties.

References

Brown, N., Luizza, C. and Meskel, L. 2019. The politics of peril: UNESCO's List of World Heritage in Danger. *Journal of Field Archaeology*, 44 (5), 287–303.

CDMX Resilience Office. 2016. *Mexico City Resilience Strategy*. https://resilientcitiesnetwork. org/downloadable_resources/Network/Mexico-City-Resilience-Strategy-English.pdf.

Granada Convention. 1985. *Convention for the Protection of the Architectural Heritage of Europe*. https://www.coe.int/en/web/culture-and-heritage/granada-convention (accessed 8 January 2022).

Hyogo Framework. 2005. https://www.unisdr.org/2005/wcdr/intergover/official-doc/ L-docs/Hyogo-framework-for-action-english.pdf (accessed 8 January 2022).

ICORP. n.d. Reconnecting the Sacred Valley Kathmandu. http://icorp-ontheroad.com/p ilot-episode-kathmandunepal (accessed 8 January 2022).

Langenbach, R. 2005. Performance of the Earthen Arg-e-Bam (Bam Citadel) during the 2003 Bam, Iran, Earthquake. *Earthquake Spectra*, 21 (1), 345–374.

Pearson, C. & Clair, J. 1998. Reframing crisis management. *Academy of Management Review*, 23 (1), 59–76. doi:10.2307/259099.

Saul, H. & Waterton, E. 2017. Heritage and communities of compassion in the aftermath of the great earthquake, Nepal: a photographic reflection. *Journal of Community Archaeology & Heritage*, 4 (3), 142–156.

Sendai Framework. 2015. https://www.preventionweb.net/files/43291_sendaiframework fordrren.pdf (accessed 8 January 2022).

Solnit, R. 2009. *A Paradise Built in Hell*. London: Random House.

Tena-Colunga, A., Hernández-Ramírez, H., Godínez-Domínguez, E. A. et al. 2021. Mexico City during and after the September 19, 2017 earthquake: assessment of seismic resilience and ongoing recovery process. *Journal of Civil Structural Health Monitoring*, 11, 1275–1299.

UNESCO. 2015. Decision: 39 COM 7B.69. https://whc.unesco.org/en/decisions/6324 (accessed 29 June 2022).

Vatandoust, A., Taleqani, E. M. & Nejati, M. 2007. *Risk Management for the Recovery Project of Bam's Cultural Heritage in ICOMOS 2007*. Heritage at Risk: Cultural Heritage and Natural Disasters. https://www.icomos.org/images/Cultural_Heritage_and_Natural_Disa sters.pdf (accessed 4 July 2022).

5

URBANISATION AND DEVELOPMENT

5.1 Introduction

This chapter considers some of the particular conservation and management issues affecting urban World Heritage properties, of which there are more than 300 at the time of writing.[1] The transformation of the concept of World Heritage from its early origins as a reactive perspective on threatened heritage sites to a more proactive and global mission centred not just on protecting cultural property but also on promoting social and economic regeneration can be clearly understood through UNESCO's work on urban World Heritage. Urban World Heritage can be particularly complex given the range of economic development pressures that can affect a property's Outstanding Universal Values, with particular issues including heritage impact assessment, commercialisation and commodification. These issues have been addressed through the development of the Historic Urban Landscape, or HUL, approach to planning and implementing conservation and development in urban areas, and we explore the contribution of HUL as one of the core themes of this chapter.

5.2 Urban pressures

Urban studies, in terms of understanding how to plan and develop our cities in a way that meets the needs of contemporary society, is a well-established academic discipline and field of practice with a long history of study and experiment, from the Enlightenment of the 18th century through to the 20th century work of, for example, Scottish writer Sir Patrick Geddes (whose planned urban design of the **White City of Tel-Aviv** in Israel is itself a World Heritage property), Brazilian architect Oscar Niemeyer (whose new city of **Brasilia** is also itself a World Heritage property) and Sir Edwin Lutyens and Herbert Baker, whose designs for New Delhi are part of a tentative World Heritage property for India. Cities can be

DOI: 10.4324/9781003044857-6

symbols of culture, language, memory and death (among others) – and of course they are major destinations for tourism in many parts of the world.[2]

More than 50% of the world's population, about 4.4 billion people, live in cities today and 5 billion people are predicted to live in urban areas by the year 2028.[3] Most urban expansion in the next decade will take place in countries in the Global South. The United Nations (2015) estimates that the world's cities occupy just 3% of the earth's land, but account for between 60% and 80% of energy consumption and about 75% of carbon emissions. Rapid urbanisation exerts pressures on energy networks, fresh water supplies, sewage and waste disposal networks, open spaces and transport infrastructure, while at the same time-consuming large amounts of energy, contributing to greenhouse gas emissions and creating public health issues, all issues addressed in the UN's Sustainable Development Goal 11 (see Chapter 11). Cities thus have an important environmental, cultural and imaginative space in today's society, which in turn generates sustained debate around the best approaches to contemporary city planning. It is within this context that urban initiatives have emerged, particularly for heritage cities, that address the need for a more inclusive planning approach that accommodates different layers of significance and which is based around participatory approaches to planning and development.

Further impetus by UNESCO for a focus on the particular challenges facing urban World Heritage emerged from the observation that urban World Heritage properties were those that appeared to be reporting the most complex management problems in the State of Conservation Reports submitted periodically to the organisation. The 2005 Vienna Memorandum on World Heritage and Contemporary Architecture launched a programme of meetings and discussions on the subject which led to the creation of the concept of the Historic Urban Landscape (HUL), an approach that considers the historic city in its topographical and environmental context through an understanding of the broader landscape context, as well as recognising its economic and social cultural values and the fact that these are constantly evolving as society's needs change over time. We explore the importance of HUL in more detail below.

5.3 The Historic Urban Landscape

UNESCO's **Recommendation on the Historic Urban Landscape** was adopted at the 36th Session of the organisation's General Conference held in Paris in November 2011. In the words of the document summarising its contribution to changing paradigms of urban planning:

> The historic urban landscape approach moves beyond the preservation of the physical environment, and focuses on the entire human environment with all of its tangible and intangible qualities. It seeks to increase the sustainability of planning and design interventions by taking into account the existing built environment, intangible heritage, cultural diversity, socio-economic and environmental factors along with local community values.
>
> *(UNESCO, 2013, p. 5)*

The historic urban landscape must thus be understood to be the result of the historic layering of cultural and natural values; the site's topography, geomorphology, hydrology and natural features; its built environment; its historic and contemporary infrastructure, above and below ground; its open spaces and gardens; land use and patterns of spatial organisation; perceptions and visual relationships, as well as all other elements of the urban structure. Vitally, it also includes social and cultural practices alongside economic processes and the intangible dimensions of heritage as related to diversity and identity (UNESCO, 2013; UNESCO, 2016).

The primary concern of HUL is to move urban planning (and conservation) beyond just the preservation of the physical environment by instead focusing on the entire human environment with all of its tangible and intangible qualities, to increase the sustainability of planning and design interventions (UNESCO, 2013). HUL therefore embeds a way of understanding the layers within a city and understanding the relationship between past, present and future within those same layers. Through HUL, cities can be thought of as being an ecosystem, with current generations engaged in maintaining the continuation of urban life through action and planning law, working together to achieve climate resilience and to create cities that will serve the needs of all constituents, including the poor and marginalised (UNESCO, 2013; UNESCO, 2016). Within this there is the aspiration that urban conservation can be reimagined to create new forms of productivity and socio-economic development, and inspire the creation of innovative financial tools for the management of historic urban landscapes.

BOX 5.1 CASE STUDY 5.1: BORDEAUX, PORT OF THE MOON, FRANCE.

Bordeaux, France is identified as an example of better practice in terms of urban planning and the balance between change and conservation. **Bordeaux, Port of the Moon** was inscribed as a World Heritage property in 2007 against Criteria (ii) and (iv). The inscription identifies the importance of the town as a focal point for cultural exchange for more than two millennia but particularly since the 12th century CE, the outstanding urban and architectural legacy of the Age of Enlightenment including innovative classical and neoclassical trends which give it an exceptional urban and architectural unity and coherence. Also noted is the importance of the city's urban form as a representation of the influence of philosophers who wanted to make towns into melting pots of humanism, universality and culture.

One of the important aspects of the Outstanding Universal Value statement for Bordeaux is the recognition that change continues to the present time, and that successive stages of construction and development are legible in the city's urban plan. Bordeaux represents an urban and architectural ensemble and in contrast to the way in which OUV is determined for other World Heritage cities: for Bordeaux, it is about the idea of 'the city' as an organism and how that city developed and continues to develop over time, and indeed will develop in the future.

Bordeaux is considered one of the better examples of managing conservation and sustainable development through the HUL approach. This is brought together through the example of the number of listed buildings (more than any other French city apart from Paris); the Heritage Protection Plan and how that is revised; and the way in which the World Heritage property has designated and enforced a buffer zone. Supporting all of this are well-developed management structures overseeing the protection and conservation of the nominated property. This includes the sharing of responsibilities over national, regional and local governments and the fact that interventions on properties within the World Heritage Site boundary need to have support for the Ministry of Culture. There are also plans in place to ensure the management and conservation of the property to take into account preserving the historic and heritage character so they allow the controlled evolution of the historic centre, and that they unify the various planning rules and in turn contribute to the international significance of Bordeaux as a city.

As such, Bordeaux is held up as a demonstration of best practice in the adaptation of urban conservation tools in ways that take into account broader economic, social and environmental concerns and as a prime example of bringing together heritage preservation and sustainable development (Appendino, 2017).

BOX 5.2 CASE STUDY 5.2: HISTORIC CENTRE OF SHAKHRISYABZ, UZBEKISTAN.

The **Historic Centre of Shakhrisyabz, Uzbekistan** was listed as a World Heritage property in 2000 associated with two cultural Criteria (iii) and (iv) connected to its 15th-century (Timurid) architecture. The inscription of Shakhrisyabz is associated with specific focus on cultural and natural World Heritage in the Central Asian states following independence.

The Historic Centre of Shakhrisyabz was added to the List of World Heritage in Danger in 2016, in response to concerns relating to the 'State Programme for complex measures for development and reconstruction of Shakhrisyabz City (2014–2016)' (Vileikis et al., 2018) a project that was intended to improve transportation and drainage infrastructure, to restructure and improve the urban landscape, to conserve and reconstruct cultural heritage sites, and to provide hotel and residential developments within the historic centre (ICOMOS, 2016). However, UNESCO and its advisory bodies expressed concern that the redevelopment project was undertaken without an assessment of the impacts of the scheme. Following on from these concerns the redevelopment project was 'paused' but the historic centre had already been substantially impacted.

As a result of being added to the list of World Heritage in Danger a number of reactive monitoring missions (as UNESCO refers to these site visits) were undertaken in 2016, and 2019 to assess the threats to the property's

Outstanding Universal Value. The 2016 mission estimated that some 30% of the historic urban fabric (comprising city walls, historic buildings and urban archaeological stratigraphy) located within the boundaries of the World Heritage property had already been impacted (ICOMOS, 2016), while inappropriate conservation works had impacted the historic fabric and other changes the setting of the historic monuments, turning *the central area into a theme park for visitors* (ICOMOS, 2016). The 2016 mission concluded the key attributes that conveyed OUV had been lost, and that these were not recoverable. As a result of this mission the property remained on the list of World Heritage in Danger and was threatened with removal from the list altogether.

The subsequent 2019 mission was tasked with problem-solving and with identifying if a change to the World Heritage property boundary would be sufficient to avert the threat of removal, if impacts to the OUV could be mitigated and if the attributes that contribute to OUV could be recovered. The 2019 mission stressed the importance of using an inclusive approach to urban planning (making use of the HUL approach) as a means of enabling well-planned and phased developments, and the importance of people-centred approaches to planning in the historic centre (ICOMOS, 2019).

At the subsequent 2019 World Heritage Committee meeting it was agreed to allow the state party a further two years to develop options for the site (to review the boundary modification or to propose a new nomination for the property) or face removal of the property from the World Heritage List. The 2021 meeting allowed a further year to resolve the issues – taking into account work already undertaken by the States Party on a potential boundary modification and the impacts of the COVID pandemic on progressing work on these issues.

Shakhrisyabz demonstrates the complexities of managing change within an urban setting, and the fragile balancing of development and conservation planning while placing people at the centre of changes. However, as Vileikis et al. (2018) note, the results can be inconsistent – in the example of Uzbekistan this shows how a State Party can successfully engage with aspects of the HUL approach for some World Heritage properties – for example, used well on the Historic Centre of Bukhara and Itchan Kala (Khiva), while failing to engage with the concepts on other properties such as Shakhrisyabz.

BOX 5.3 CASE STUDY 5.3: LIVERPOOL MARITIME MERCANTILE CITY.

Liverpool Maritime Mercantile City was inscribed as a cultural property in 2004 associated with three cultural Criteria: (ii), (iii) and (iv). It was placed on the separate list of World Heritage in Danger in 2012, due principally to the proposed construction of Liverpool Waters, a massive redevelopment of the historic docklands north of the city centre, and was removed from the World Heritage List in 2021, only the third property to be treated so.

The listing of Liverpool as a World Heritage property was complex from the outset. Rodwell & Turner (2018) note that when ICOMOS undertook the evaluation of the inscription, they excluded the category urban landscape, which created a tension from the very beginning of the listing leading to conflicting views between the importance of development and redevelopment and the heritage significance of the site. These tensions unravelled quite rapidly following on from its inscription and were associated with a series of developments: the development of new museums in the Albert Dock area; proposals for the Liverpool Waters Development (a proposed mixed-use development with a series of tall buildings in the buffer zone) and plans for the development of a new football ground for Everton Football Club at Bramley-Moore Dock in the northern part of the World Heritage Site.

Given the scale of the planned developments and their potential to impact the World Heritage property, the State Party was asked to adopt a moratorium including a ban on new buildings within the property and its buffer zone until the local plan, which was to include a skyline or height policy, had been reviewed by the World Heritage Centre and by relevant advisory bodies. However, coming to any such decisions proved complex because of the need for the relevant Local Authorities to balance the economic and social needs of communities with heritage conservation and protection.

The listing of Liverpool on the World Heritage in Danger List provided a space within which local residents and others could reflect on the advantages and disadvantages of World Heritage listing, through a series of public events coordinated through Engage Liverpool.[4] At the same time, this brought the community face to face with the apparent abstract, political realities of international heritage diplomacy, with the Liverpool situation being perceived as 'payback' for previous decisions and action by the former UK UNESCO ambassador (Engage Liverpool Blog, 2018). For some commentators, the apparent indifference shown by local and national bodies in the Liverpool case to the threat of losing World Heritage status was at odds with the economic and cultural development motivations seen within other World Heritage nominations.[5] Nonetheless, some of the public outcry after the final decision was made for removal in 2021 reveals the complexity of negotiating between local, national and international interests in a World Heritage property. For instance, a leading (local) academic specialising in the politics of urban renewal argued that 'Liverpool has been treated unfairly in relation to other World Heritage cities and its unique urban history of development has not been recognised. It has, in fact, been treated like a monument or a museum, not a living city' (Parkinson, 2021). In particular, the decision demonstrates some of the challenges of enabling economic growth through major capital projects in a historic urban environment.

BOX 5.4 CASE STUDY 5.4: HISTORIC CITY OF AHMADABAD, INDIA.

The walled city of **Ahmadabad** was founded in the 15th century on the banks of the Sabarmati River and was the state capital of Gujarat until 1965. The Bhadra Fort was built in 1411 by Sultan Ahmed Shah, and the fort walls followed over the next 50 years. The city is described as growing through processes of consolidation and densification (Desai, 2018). The historic city is celebrated for its unique monumental architecture, its vernacular wooden buildings forming *pols* and *havelis*, and for its distinctive urban morphology. Ahmadabad was inscribed as India's first World Heritage city in 2017 against cultural Criteria (ii) and (v).

The Ahmadabad nomination developed out of the work of noted historian Professor Rabindra Vasavarda and two colleagues, Dr Jigna Desai and Kushi Shah. Production of the nomination documents was facilitated by ICOMOS who challenged ideas of 'listing' and rather started to think about the 'city', shifting from nominating 'sites' to the 'city' as a whole and highlighting the attributes of the site (pers comm, Desai). In 2010 the then Chief Minister of Gujarat, Narendra Modi, supported the nomination of Ahmadabad as a World Heritage property and although the outcome was successful, this was not without controversy. Ahmadabad had originally been nominated against three cultural Criteria: (ii), (v) and (vi). Following on from the ICOMOS evaluation, the proposal had been recommended for deferral at the 2017 World Heritage Committee meeting with the evaluation team recommending refining the nomination criteria to focus on Criteria (ii) and (v); to undertake documentation of the historic buildings (particularly the private properties), to review the site boundary and buffer zone, and to further develop a wide range of conservation management planning documents.

This was discussed at a particularly interesting World Heritage Committee session highlighting the nature of international heritage diplomacy which can be viewed online.[6] Following on from the presentation of the recommendation for deferral for Ahmadabad by ICOMOS, a statement was made to the committee by the representatives of Turkey who suggested a new draft amendment for the removal of Criterion (vi) and therefore for the overall support of the nomination. This suggestion was supported by subsequent statements by representatives from (among others) Azerbaijan, Cuba, Croatia, Kazakhstan, Vietnam, Kuwait, Zimbabwe, Tunisia, Jamaica, Lebanon and Tanzania. ICOMOS subsequently commented on the wording of the amendment from 'deferral' to 'inscription'. This is an example of what Meskell (2018) considers as the importance of taking the microphone and speaking at the World Heritage Committee, relating this to a country's level of political influence and their attempts to upgrade or change a recommendation. The statement of Outstanding Universal Value defining the criteria for nomination and statement of authenticity and integrity for Ahmadabad was subsequently adopted at the 2018 World Heritage Committee meeting.

However, the issues noted in the 2017 ICOMOS evaluation highlight the tensions relating to inscribing living cities as World Heritage properties and particularly within the context of sustainable development. The property is large, covering some 535 hectares, the length of the east–west axis is about 2 km and the length of the north-south axis is about 2.5 km. The original city walls are almost 11 km in length and include 12 original gates, two closed gates from the Sultanate period, and two gates added in the nineteenth century. The challenge is balancing the conservation needs of this extensive and varied World Heritage property with the changing needs of Ahmedabad's population of 6 million people, which include:

- ongoing efforts relating to post-disaster recovery from a 2001 earthquake;
- changes and developments in a wide range of urban infrastructures;
- population shifts resulting in changing demographics and characteristics of the population of the historic core, which have resulted in a changing relationship with the traditional buildings and for the communities traditionally using the *pols* (courtyard communities), both of which contribute to the property's Outstanding Universal Value;
- the influx of tourism as a result of the World Heritage nomination and the beginnings of gentrification through the provision of tourist accommodation and facilities;
- the decline in the availability of skills for building maintenance and repair which is particularly significant for the traditional timber-built buildings and the *pols* that they define.

While the issues are at a wide city-scale, it seems to be within small-scale community-led projects that sustainable approaches to urban planning and conservation emerge. For example, those led by Dr Jigna Desai show potential ways of meeting the demands of the World Heritage city with the conservation needs of the historic buildings through creative re-use and through student-led studio projects to better meet the changing needs of the population of the old city. However, there is more that can be done through the SDG framework, and through national initiatives, for example Ahmadabad is an Indian 'Smart City': an initiative to promote ICT to deliver high-quality services and urban environments that enhance lifestyle. Whether or not this initiative is able to meet the challenges in the old city will emerge in future years.

5.4 Concluding remarks

The Organization of World Heritage Cities was established in 1993 with the purpose of encouraging cooperation and exchange of information and expertise among member cities with regard to the management of World Heritage. At the time of writing some 250 cities from every continent belong to the organisation, which exists as a forum for discussion and research, as well as acting as an advocate for best practice in planning and conservation for historic cities. World Heritage cities are driving forward development of concepts of urban planning – embedded both with the HUL approach and within SDGs – demonstrate the complex interconnections between people, place and landscape and the necessity of understanding the relationship people have with setting, context and value as fundamental within the urban planning processes. As can be seen in the examples of Bordeaux, Shakhrisyabz, Liverpool and Ahmedabad, the intersection between heritage and urban planning and change is complex. Chapter 11 will consider further examples of work on World Heritage properties that show this interlinkage between aspirations for relating to urban planning and the SDGs.

Notes

1 See https://whc.unesco.org/en/cities/ (accessed 1 December 2021).
2 See https://www.unwto.org/urban-tourism (accessed 1 December 2021).
3 See https://www.iied.org/urbanising-world (accessed 1 December 2021).
4 See https://www.engageliverpool.com/projects/engage-with-the-unesco-whs/ (accessed 4 February 2022).
5 See https://www.savebritainsheritage.org/campaigns/item/739/PRESS-RELEASE-SAVE-re grets-loss-of-Liverpool-World-Heritage-status (accessed 4 February 2022).
6 See https://whc.unesco.org/en/sessions/41com/records/?yid=U7iYnJg7ecE&day=2017-07 -08#tU7iYnJg7ecE8018 (accessed 1 December 2021).

References

Appendino, F. 2017. *Balancing Heritage Conservation and Sustainable Development – The Case of Bordeaux*. IOP Conference Series: Materials Science and Engineering, 245 062002.
Desai, J. 2018. *Equity in Heritage Conservation: The Case of Ahmedabad, India*. London: Routledge.
Engage Liverpool Blog. 2018. News from Bahrain: Engage at UNESCO World Heritage Committee. 27 June 2018. https://www.engageliverpool.com/news/international-supp ort-for-liverpools-whs/ (accessed 3 July 2022).
ICOMOS. 2016. Report of the joint World Heritage Centre/ICOMOS Reactive Monitoring mission to the Historic Centre of Shakhrisyabz (Uzbekistan), 9 To 12 December 2016 https:// whc.unesco.org/en/list/885/documents/ (accessed 3 July 2022).
ICOMOS. 2019. Report on the joint High Level World Heritage Centre / ICOMOS Reactive Monitoring mission to the Historic Centre of Shakhrisyabz (Uzbekistan), 21–26 January 2019https://whc.unesco.org/en/list/885/documents/ (accessed 3 July 2022).
Meskell, L. 2018 *A Future in Ruins. UNESCO, World Heritage, and the Dream of Peace*. New York: Oxford University Press.
Parkinson, M. 2021. Removing Liverpool's World Heritage status is unfair but city will flourish regardless. *Liverpool Echo*, 22 July. https://www.liverpoolecho.co.uk/news/news-opinion/ removing-liverpools-world-heritage-status-21117300 (accessed 8 July 2022).
Rodwell, D. & Turner, M. 2018. Impact assessments for Urban World Heritage: European experiences under scrutiny. *Built Heritage*, 2, 58–71.
United Nations. 2015. SDG 11 Goal 11: Make cities inclusive, safe, resilient and sustainable. https://www.un.org/sustainabledevelopment/cities/ (accessed 3 July 2022).

UNESCO. 2013. New life for historic cities: the historic urban landscape approach explained. https://whc.unesco.org/en/activities/727/ (accessed 3 July 2022).

UNESCO. 2016. *The HUL Guidebook – Managing Heritage in Dynamic and Constantly Changing Urban Environments: A Practical Guide to UNESCO's Recommendation on the Historic Urban Landscape.* http://historicurbanlandscape.com/themes/196/userfiles/download/2016/6/7/wirey5prpznidqx.pdf (accessed 3 July 2022).

Vileikis, O., Voyakin, D., Utegenova, A. & Allayarov, S. 2018. Pragmatic approaches to world heritage management: along the Central Asian Silk Roads. In: S. Makuvaza, ed. *Aspects of Management Planning for Cultural World Heritage Sites.* Cham, Switerland:Springer.

6

WORLD HERITAGE AND CLIMATE CHANGE

6.1 Introduction

A recent review of the impact of climate change on World Heritage revealed that one-third of all natural sites (including 60% of World Heritage Forests) and one in six cultural heritage sites are threatened by the direct and indirect impacts of what is perhaps the greatest challenge facing society in the 21st century (UNESCO, 2021). This chapter examines not just the known but also the anticipated impacts of climate change on World Heritage properties and considers the practical adaptation and management measures needed to tackle these changes. Some sites have already faced substantial challenges because of more extreme weather events, while for others changes are likely to be incremental and possibly almost imperceptible, though nonetheless important.

6.2 What is climate change?

Climate change relates to long-term shifts in temperature and weather patterns. Indicators commonly used to demonstrate climate change include higher global land and ocean temperatures; rising sea levels; ice loss on the ice sheets of the Arctic and Antarctic and in mountain glaciers; frequency and severity changes in extreme weather such as hurricanes, heatwaves, wildfires, droughts, floods and precipitation; and cloud and vegetation cover changes.[1] Originally referred to as global warming, changes in the climate were predicted as an outcome of anthropogenic activity from at least the second half of the 20th century, when, for example, the observation of the global atmospheric carbon dioxide concentration showed changes (Le Treut et al., 2007). Recognition by multiple agencies and governments that climate change could have severe social, economic and environmental impacts around the globe led to concerted research efforts, culminating in the establishment of the Intergovernmental Panel on Climate Change (IPCC) in 1988.

DOI: 10.4324/9781003044857-7

In short, since the industrial revolution began, the concentration of CO_2 in the atmosphere has increased by around 40% as a result of the burning of fossil fuels to power homes, factories and transport – in turn causing an enhanced greenhouse effect, impacting the water cycle, atmospheric circulation and ocean currents. Latest NASA statistics[2] suggest that human activities are estimated to have increased Earth's global average temperature by about 1°C (1.8°F) since the pre-industrial period and that global average temperatures are currently increasing by 0.2°C (0.36°F) per decade. The concept of the Anthropocene as a new geological epoch shaped by human actions is now well established (Crutzen, 2002).

Despite the scientific consensus on the challenges that climate change will bring us all, global action has been slow to develop, with the UN Framework Convention on Climate Change (UNFCCC) and subsequent 1997 Kyoto Agreement that legally bound developed State Parties to goals for greenhouse gas emission reductions only coming into force in 2005. The more comprehensive Paris Climate Change Agreement of 2015 was adopted by 195 Nations, with agreement reached to reduce the amount of harmful greenhouse gas produced and increase renewable types of energy in an effort to keep global temperature increase 'well below' 2°C (3.6°F) and to try to limit it to 1.5°C.

At the time of the negotiation of the 2015 Paris Climate agreement, representations from the island nations from the Pacific stressed the significance of global efforts to reach the desired 1.5°C limit since these islands are some of the most vulnerable to climate change and change above 1.5°C would effectively be a life sentence for the islands and their populations. And from a World Heritage perspective, properties like the **Vallée de Mai Nature Reserve** or the **Aldabra Atoll**, both in the Indian Ocean, would be irreversibly damaged or even lost completely, removing a palm forest that is unchanged since prehistoric times in the case of the Vallée de Mai, and the home for more than 150,000 giant tortoises – the largest population in the world – in the case of Aldabra. And it wouldn't just be natural properties that are lost – in the Pacific Ocean, for instance, the **Nan Madol: Ceremonial Centre of Eastern Micronesia** – a complex archaeological site associated with the Saudeleur Dynasty of 1,200–1,500 CE – will also be lost.

Prepared in response to the Paris Agreement, the IPCC (2018) Report SR15 Global Warming of 1.5°C highlighted a number of climate change impacts that could be avoided by limiting global warming to 1.5°C compared to 2°C, or more. For instance, by 2100, global sea level rise would be 10 cm lower with global warming of 1.5°C compared with 2°C. The likelihood of an Arctic Ocean free of sea ice in summer would be once per century with global warming of 1.5°C, compared with at least once per decade with 2°C. Coral reefs would decline by 70–90% with global warming of 1.5°C, whereas virtually all (> 99%) would be lost with 2°C. The IPCC Report resulted in the declaration of a climate emergency by the parliaments of Wales, Scotland, the UK, Éire, Canada, France and Argentina (among others) in 2019, arguing for lower carbon emissions, with campaigners, including the Greta Thunberg-inspired school strikes for climate, arguing for a sharper, quicker transition to zero carbon.

Most recently, the world's governments, scientists, activists and lobbyists met in Glasgow, Scotland, in November 2021 at COP26. At the end of the conference, 197 parties agreed to the so-called 'Glasgow Climate Pact', with governments from around the world committing themselves to further accelerating their decarbonisation plans and, specifically, to strengthening their emissions-reduction targets for 2030 by 2022 rather than the deadline of 2025 originally agreed under the Paris agreement. Developed countries were encouraged to increase funding for adaptation initiatives in the Global South, and rules to create a framework for a global carbon market were approved, settling a problem that had plagued negotiators since 2015. The need to reduce global greenhouse-gas emissions by 45% by 2030 was formally recognised though late interventions in the negotiations by China and India meant that there was a commitment only to 'phase down' rather than 'phase out' the use of coal in power stations.[3]

Notwithstanding the mixed messages coming out of COP26, there are still moves afoot across the global cultural and heritage communities to address the challenges of climate change. For instance, in spring 2021 Europa Nostra and ICOMOS published their Heritage Green Paper (Potts, 2021), arguing that 'responding effectively to climate change is the defining task of our time' (p. 4). Once again, the impact of a 1.5° rise in global temperatures for heritage is clearly spelled out, with the report's authors arguing that it represents a threshold beyond which many cultural heritage properties may be irreversibly damaged and where there will be a significant loss of biodiversity. The report not only provides details on the impacts of global warming on heritage but also demonstrates how heritage can be used as an instrument for tackling climate change, presenting recommendations for action for both policy makers and heritage managers. For instance, there is a call towards promoting sustainable and smart travel modes (which may ultimately lead to a decline in visits to many heritage sites, with a consequent loss of visitor revenue) as well as the adoption of the concept of the circular economy with its implications for the sourcing of materials for restoration and conservation, for instance. For natural heritage, there is a clear statement that historic landscape conservation should embrace the idea of 'circular territorial metabolisms'. Also promoted are greater use of traditional land, water, agricultural and forestry management systems.

Furthering the work of Europa Nostra and ICOMOS, the Climate Heritage Network Race to Resilience Campaign was launched at COP26 in Glasgow, calling for States Parties, heritage professionals, communities and activists working together to identify and implement strategies to protect heritage sites from the worst impacts of climate change.[4] The aspiration of this movement is that all cultural actors, from the arts to heritage, should play their part by introducing and implementing culture-based strategies that enable everyone around the world not just to survive climate stresses, but to thrive in spite of them. This therefore includes those responsible for protecting, managing and facilitating public access to World Heritage Sites. It is thus important to understand what some of these impacts might be, a topic we explore below. This is important since the most recent World Heritage General Assembly in 2021 failed to adopt an updated climate change policy, despite the endorsement of the same by the World Heritage Committee. Instead, the General Assembly requested further consultation on the proposals[5] which means that in the meantime, the 194 individual States Parties signed up to the Convention, relevant Ministries, landowners, property managers, local communities and other stakeholders will need to address the climate crisis at site and policy levels.

6.3 Climate change and cultural properties

6.3.1 Impacts of climate change on cultural properties

It is evident that both cultural and natural World Heritage properties are already faced with a wide range of climate change related issues. Reimann et al. (2018) reviewed the cases of 49 cultural World Heritage Sites located in low-lying areas (less than 10 m above sea level) in the Mediterranean basin and identified 42 (85% of the total) at risk from coastal erosion and 37 (76%) at risk from flooding. Their projections are that climate change will increase flood risks by 50% by 2100 and erosion by 13%, thus compromising the future of a comparatively high number of terrestrial World Heritage properties in this part of the world alone. Most at risk are properties in the Adriatic Sea, particularly those on the coasts of Italy and Croatia.

Predicting and managing the impacts of climate change at a global scale and across the culture:nature:heritage nexus is complex. These include direct impacts from an increase in temperature, precipitation, increases in evapotranspiration, flooding, changes in groundwater etc. It is also important to consider the indirect impacts from changes in agriculture and vegetation that will impact the availability of materials, population movement, and abandonment.

The range of impacts associated with climate change is specific to different types of World Heritage property and their location. In this context UNESCO initiated research early in the 2000s (UNESCO, 2006; UNESCO, 2007a; UNESCO, 2007b) and further considered in relation to Natural Heritage (UNESCO, 2014) and tourism (UNESCO, 2016). Indications of some of the threats to cultural heritage properties associated with climate change include:

- Increased temperatures will damage fragile rock structures, particularly sandstone, in which are carved the monuments of World Heritage Sites like **Hegra Archaeological Site** (also known as al-Hijr or Madāʾ in Ṣāliḥ, in Saudi Arabia), **Petra** (Jordan) and **Writing-on-Stone / Áísínai'pi** (Canada);
- Increased evaporation will alter humidity levels and will impact sites like **Quseir Amra** (Jordan); the **Mogao Caves** (China) and the **Complex of Koguryo Tombs** (Democratic People's Republic of Korea) where murals and wall paintings will suffer from corrosion, mould and salt damage;
- Changes in freeze-thaw and ice storms, and an increase in wet frost, will speed up the erosion of rock carvings such as those in the **Ḥimā Cultural Area** of Saudi Arabia (inscribed 2021) as well as exacerbate problems of spalling on

stone and concrete buildings. This will affect many buildings in those latitudes most susceptible to rapid variations in diurnal/ nocturnal winter temperatures;

- Extreme weather phenomena will also inflict significant damage to archaeological sites and built heritage including manuscripts and artifacts contained in some of them. For instance, in July 2021 the 3,000-year-old **Yin Xu** World Heritage Site in China's Henan Province was hit by flash floods associated with extremely high rainfall;[6]
- Changes in groundwater levels may lead to subsoil instability, ground heave and subsidence, threatening the structural integrity of historic properties. For example, the **Abu Mena** World Heritage Site, the remains of a third-century Christian sanctuary outside Alexandria, Egypt, has been on the list of World Heritage in Danger for two decades already as a result of rising groundwater and the impact on building foundations. Such problems will only increase in magnitude in the future;
- Catastrophic flooding, particularly when associated with sea level rise and/or severe storms, will severely impact the integrity of many unprotected or poorly protected coastal heritage properties including sites like **Venice**; the many colonial forts and dockyards around the Caribbean and low-lying properties in the Indian and Pacific Oceans.

Climate change will also cause change, damage and loss to intangible cultural heritage. Changes in biodiversity may lead to the disappearance of vegetation and animal species with a consequent knock-on impact on cultural practices, food systems and culinary traditions as well as compromising food security in areas affected by drought. Furthermore, it is predicted that climate change impacts will result in increased migration and the movement of people globally. In many cases, this may cause significant stress in urban areas that are already heavily populated, with larger, more dense populations increasing levels of economic and social stress. Again, this may have significant negative implications for both cultural and natural heritage properties in destinations where resources are already limited.

6.3.2 Responding to these challenges

Key concepts now embedded within the discourse around climate change and World Heritage are:

- **Mitigation** – taking action to increase energy efficiency and improve sustainability;
- **Adaptation** – anticipating the adverse effects of climate change and taking appropriate action to prevent or minimise the damage they can cause;
- **Resilience** – the capacity to recover quickly from adversity.

From 2006 a requirement was introduced to include climate change within all World Heritage Site Management plans (World Heritage Centre, 2006; Philips

2014). Nonetheless, despite these good intentions there are structural limitations within the existing World Heritage process with regard to the response to climate change challenges, limited by the ways in which climate change is considered within management plans (and in particular, how current management plans do or do not draw on the ideas of mitigation, adaptation and resilience); the reporting (and misreporting) of climate change and the blunt instrument of listing World Heritage properties on the separate list of World Heritage in danger. These limitations are well demonstrated by the example of sites such as Chan Chan, Peru, which has lingered on the list of World Heritage in Danger since 1986 (see case study).

BOX 6.1 CASE STUDY 6.1: CHAN CHAN, PERU.

Peru ratified the World Heritage Convention in 1982 and **Chan Chan** was inscribed as a Cultural World Heritage property in 1986, becoming Peru's fourth World Heritage Site. Chan Chan was inscribed as a cultural site on the basis of Criteria (i) and (ii) as a 'masterpiece of town planning' and 'architectural ensemble' as the most representative city of the Chimu kingdom reaching at its most powerful in the 15th century, prior to falling to the Incas.[7] The planning of this huge city reflects a strict political and social strategy, marked by the city's division into nine 'citadels' or 'palaces' forming autonomous units.

Chan Chan's vulnerabilities come from its location and from the materials of its construction. Located on the coastal plain in northwestern Peru, Chan Chan is one of the largest earthen archaeological sites in the world, covering a huge area of 1,414.57 ha. Because of its location Chan Chan has always been impacted by the El Niño and La Niña phenomena, the cyclical wetting and drying sequence associated with the southern Pacific Ocean. It was in response to the phenomena that the site was listed on the separate list of World Heritage in Danger in 1986.

It is important not to confuse the El Niño and La Niña phenomena with climate change. However, in the case of Chan Chan the focus of the site's conservation activities since the 1980s provide the 'longer range' view of conservation that is precisely what is needed when planning for climate change. The issue at Chan Chan is how to respond to the scale of the site and its complex conservation challenges. Through this long period on the list of World Heritage in Danger the national government has sought international assistance on numerous occasions, though rarely with success. For instance, only five requests for aid were approved in the period 1987–1999), with the total amount approved being some US$118,700, equating over 30 years to just less than one cent per m^2. A depressing contrast can be found here with the estimates for the costs of the 3D printing of Palmyra's Triumphal Arch of between £100,000 (Turner, 2016) to US$2.5 million (Heathcote, 2016).

The state of conservation report for the site lists the threats for which the property is on the list of World Heritage in Danger as:

- The fragile state of conservation of earthen structures and decorated surfaces due to extreme climatic conditions (El Niño phenomenon) and other environmental factors;
- Inadequate management system in place;
- Insufficient capacity and resources for the implementation of conservation measures;
- Increase in the levels of the phreatic (groundwater) water table.

The Peruvian authorities and various other international teams have worked at Chan Chan to develop conservation solutions which include temporary measures (sand bags and shelters) that can be installed and removed in line with the El Niño / La Niña oscillation. However, the extant structures and exposed archaeology at Chan Chan are comprised of earth – mudbricks (adobe), plasters etc. – and earth architecture is uniquely impacted by water whether falling as rain, rising from water tables or coming in on moisture laden winds (Cooke, 2010). In the case of Chan Chan this water and wind is also salt laden – as they blow in from the Pacific Ocean.

In the more than 30 years that Chan Chan has been on the list of World Heritage in Danger further complexity has arisen in terms of the site's conservation management needs. This includes changes in the surrounding landscape. Satellite imagery shows the dramatic landscape change from desert-like through to irrigated farmland up to the site boundary. This means alongside the El Niño / La Niña phenomena, Chan Chan's fragile archaeology is now impacted by changes in the groundwater table as a result of changes in intensive farming practices. In the context of long-term change and threat to the Outstanding Universal Value of Chan Chan, the impact of being included on the List of World Heritage in Danger can be questioned since none of the key pressures appear to have been alleviated in all the time the site has been on the list.

At the time of writing (2022) Chan Chan remained on the list of World Heritage in Danger. Currently it is still being recommended that Chan Chan continue its efforts towards the development of a sustainable conservation plan. Given recent UNESCO announcements on how World Heritage Sites should plan to tackle the impacts of climate change, it can be anticipated that mitigation, adaptation and resilience will be considered alongside the management and conservation objectives for the site as a whole. But the scale of the site and the limited resources show the failings of the system management and conservation for vulnerable sites, and the competing demands on landscape (between heritage conservation and economic development) rather than the failings of the local and national heritage agencies' response.

6.4 Climate change and natural heritage

6.4.1 Terrestrial natural heritage

As the lead international agency involved in habitat and landscape protection and conservation, the IUCN is naturally at the forefront of identifying the likely impacts of climate change on natural heritage and on working with a wide range of stakeholders to identify appropriate solutions. Climate change impacts experienced in the past few years that have materially impacted terrestrial natural World Heritage Sites include:

- increased intensity and extent of wildfires. For instance, the 2020 wildfires in Australia saw about 80% of the **Greater Blue Mountains Area World Heritage Site**, known for its temperate eucalyptus forest, and 50% of the **Gondwana Rainforests** lost, destroying valuable habitat for a wide range of flora and fauna;[8]
- mass tree mortality in areas like California's Sierra Nevada Mountains, which include **Yosemite National Park** (McMahon et al., 2020);
- changes in seasonal activities of animals, including migration patterns. For instance, Monarch Butterfly populations in the USA and Mexico have drastically changed migratory behaviour in recent years because of climate-change induced alterations to their habitats (Seebacher & Post, 2015). The incidence of sedentary, non-migratory populations in the USA is increasing, with consequences for the ecological integrity of Mexico's **Monarch Butterfly Biosphere Reserve World Heritage Site** (inscribed in 2008).

So how should the natural heritage community respond to these and other pressures? In a briefing note prepared in advance of the COP26 summit in Glasgow in November 2021, IUCN explicitly called for increased efforts regarding the designation and effective management of the natural environment, stating that 'scaling up the proportion of land, inland waters and ocean effectively protected, conserved and restored is necessary to reverse the decline of nature, tackle climate change and attain the UN Sustainable Development Goals' (IUCN & WCPA, 2021, p. 2). In other words, there is an aspiration that by actively protecting natural heritage, some of the worst impacts of climate change might be avoided. Whether one of the outcomes of this call is a renewed effort to inscribe more natural heritage properties on the UNESCO list remains to be seen.

6.4.2 Marine natural heritage

As well as impacting terrestrial natural heritage sites, there is an equally significant challenge associated with climate change for marine World Heritage Sites which are likely to suffer from some or all of the following impacts of climate change (Laffoley et al., 2019):

- Sea level rise (changing coastlines and affecting vegetation cover, morphology and habitats);
- Warming oceans (leading to coral bleaching and species migrating towards the poles or to deeper water for a cooler environment);
- Deoxygenation (leading to species seeking deeper water which is more oxygenated);
- Ocean acidification (affecting the distribution of certain marine species with knock-on effects on local and regional food chains);
- More extreme weather events (increasing problems of flooding in coastal areas with subsequent impacts on habitat as well as on human activity).

UNESCO reports that around two-thirds of marine World Heritage Sites are currently experiencing high risks of degradation[9] and there is concern that in some instances entire ecosystems such as coral reefs will be locally eliminated by warming temperatures (Van Dyke & Lamb, 2020). Where this happens at World Heritage properties, it is likely to have a significant impact on the Outstanding Universal Value that led to inscription in the first place. Natural properties already on the World Heritage List in Danger whose future is likely to be compromised still further by the impacts of climate change include parts of the **Río Plátano Biosphere Reserve** in Honduras; parts of the **Tropical Rain Forest Heritage of Sumatra**; Mexico's **Islands and Protected Areas of the Gulf of California** and the **Everglades National Park** in the United States.

Other coastal and estuarine World Heritage properties that are likely to be significantly impacted by climate change in the medium term, as water temperatures rise and extreme weather events increase in frequency and severity, include the **Djoudj National Bird Sanctuary** in the Senegal River Delta (inscribed 1981) which is home to important populations of White Pelicans, Great Egrets and African Spoonbill; the **Sanganeb Marine National Park and Dungonab Bay-Mukkawar Island Marine National P**ark (Sudan, inscribed 2016) which contains both fragile coral reefs and also important sea grass beds that are home to an important population of dugong, and the **Aldabra Atoll** (Seychelles) and its important population of giant tortoises.

6.5 Engaging communities in tackling the causes and impacts of climate change at heritage properties

There are some interesting community-based initiatives emerging where a suite of low-cost but potentially high impact interventions are being employed to address both the underlying causes of climate change but also the impacts of associated extreme weather events on the heritage of the area. One such example, that is worth examining at length here, can be found at Makli in Pakistan.

Pakistan ratified the World Heritage Convention in 1976, and Makli was its fourth World Heritage property inscribed on the list. The site was proposed for inscription as a World Heritage Property in 1980, but the World Heritage committee deferred the decision, adding it to the World Heritage list the following year in 1981 (inscribed under the site name **Historical Monuments at Makli, Thatta**). This large site of an estimated 500,000 tombs and graves covers an area of about 10 km². It was associated with the city of Thatta, the ancient capital of Sindh from the 14th to 18th century. The site is listed against cultural Criterion (iii), noting: 'The capital of three successive dynasties and later ruled by the Mughal emperors of Delhi, Thatta was constantly embellished from the 14th to the 18th century. The remains of the city and its necropolis provide a unique view of civilization in Sind'.[10]

At the time of inscription concerns were expressed relating to the conservation and management needs of the site, summed up through the ICOMOS evaluation as: 'the inclusion of Thatta on the World Heritage List should occasion a concerted action of protection'. The site's statement of integrity and authenticity acknowledges the conservation needs of the standing structures. The regular state of conservation reports record the range of issues impacting the site and its setting, including the lack of detailed conservation planning, and the long-term erosion of the standing structures, alongside looting.

Record monsoon rains led to flooding in Pakistan in 2010 with flood waters covering at least 37,280 km² (14,390 square miles) between July and September 2010, affecting some 20 million people (Scott, 2011). The cause of the record rains has been connected to the changed behaviour of the Asian Monsoon weather pattern, which was caused by high-pressure north of the Black Sea that trapped hot air over Russia. The impact of the record rains was further exacerbated by deforestation, so the land itself was able to absorb much less moisture. Floodwaters in particular took a long time to retreat from Sind Province. The damage to Makli as a result of the flooding meant it was considered for separate listing on the List of World Heritage in Danger in 2012 (UNESCO, 2012).

Pakistan's leading architect Yasmine Lari co-founded the Heritage Foundation of Pakistan in 1980 and has subsequently worked at Makli and other locations. The conservation work at Makli has been supported by (among others) US Ambassador's Fund, German Government funds, Prince Claus Fund of the Netherlands, Spiritual Chords (South Africa). Motivated by the deep understanding of the site and its local communities – which sometimes resulted in challenging behaviour, such as looting as an economic necessity – the Heritage Foundation of Pakistan has undertaken pioneering work connecting and embedding community development into conservation (and vice versa) through a series of projects:

For instance, the UNESCO/Republic of Korea Funds-in-Trust funded project, 'Revitalization of Ancient Glazed Tiles in Sindh' combined conservation of the standing structures with the revival of kashi (glazed ceramic) skills for local communities, especially women, for income generation. Separately the Chullah stove project has created 'Barefoot Village Entrepreneurs' where marginalised women have been empowered to train others and build innovative low-cost smokeless stoves, through adaptation of the traditional stoves in other communities. The adaptive design of the Chullah stoves uses 50–70% less firewood than traditional stoves, which in turn reduces the amount of time spent gathering fuel, while also reducing deforestation and thus tackling some of the underlying causes of climate change. This is an important connection to wider environmental concerns as deforestation was a known factor in the 2010 floods. Each stove costs US$8, comprising US$2 for training, and US$6 for materials (mudbrick and lime). This is particularly important as four in every five households in rural Pakistan lack access to a clean, safe cooking resource – open-flame stoves are known to cause respiratory and eye problems, and food cooked in floor-mounted stoves can become easily contaminated. Since 2014 more than 40,000 stoves have been built, improving the health of an estimated 300,000 people (UN-Habitat Award, 2018), with ambitions to build 100,000 Chullahs per year.

The creation of the Makli INTBAU Zero-Carbon Training and Eco-centre designed to enable collaborators, researchers, tourists and visiting groups to visit Makli, and it is hoped in time to run conservation and archaeology working holidays. The central structure is a bamboo teaching/seminar space, a library, alongside individual accommodation in huts. The materials are local, natural and sustainable, mudbrick, lime and bamboo all adapted to the site and its low-impact aspirations, again demonstrating how social interventions can be used to support broader moves towards combating climate change.

The state of conservation at Makli World Heritage Site is ongoing, and there is much work still to be done given the complexities of the site, its communities and the impacts of the climate crisis. But by shifting focus from the site and its standing structures to people, and by showing the connection between poverty alleviation and heritage, the work at Makli connects communities with heritage in a meaningful way. The example shown through this productive and prolific series of projects demonstrates the huge potential to use World Heritage as an enabler for locally led sustainable development and the intersection across the different SDGs. The work undertaken by the Heritage Trust for Pakistan at Makli provides inspiration for how World Heritage could be harnessed in a meaningful way.

6.6 Conclusion

One of the challenges in responding to the climate emergency is that the need for 'change' needs to be registered in order for people to respond to it. Yet climate change is long-term, delayed and in contrast individuals and societies are better adapted to considering short-term outcomes (Pahl et al., 2014; Cooke, 2015). Moreover, the example of Chan Chan shows how even with a longer-term perspective on a particular World Heritage property, neither a commitment to action nor a positive outcome can be guaranteed. In contrast to the example of Chan Chan, which shows the problems of conservation and management, there is an emerging aspiration for World Heritage properties (along with biosphere reserves and global geoparks) to be reimagined as climate change observatories, and to be used in climate change communication, where relevant information can be gathered and experimental approaches developed. This is an interesting development from the original concept of Outstanding Universal Value.

Yet from the perspective of early 2022, when this book was being completed, having experienced the near closing-down of 'normal' life as countries entered lockdown as a response to the global coronavirus pandemic, we have seen the rapid speed with which action can be undertaken when the situation demands. And in terms of reversing anthropogenic impacts on the environment, we have seen the almost immediate positive impacts of changing carbon-heavy lifestyles - nature came back to previously busy and now deserted World Heritage properties. For instance, Venice's unique biosphere was 'rediscovered', and air pollution levels in many urban destinations dropped dramatically.[11]

The immediate and dramatic changes to lifestyles that are needed to respond to the climate emergency align to UNESCO's 2019 'Changing Minds not the Climate' initiative[12] that stressed the need to redefine the relationships between people and humans and nature, redefining habits, and refocusing on responsibilities to the planet. This requires implementation of long-term strategies that are grounded in ethics and social justice and thus are appropriate factors to be integrated into World Heritage Site management plans even though, as we explored in Chapter 2, these tend to have a relatively short-term focus.

Notes

1 See https://climate.nasa.gov/resources/global-warming-vs-climate-change/ (accessed 27 November 2021).
2 See https://climate.nasa.gov/resources/global-warming-vs-climate-change/ (accessed 27 November 2021).
3 See https://www.bbc.co.uk/news/science-environment-56901261 (accessed 28 November 2021).
4 See https://www.europanostra.org/climate-heritage-network-launches-race-to-resilience-campaign-at-the-cop26/ (accessed 28 November 2021).
5 See https://whc.unesco.org/en/decisions/7662/ (accessed 5 February 2022).
6 See https://www.theartnewspaper.com/2021/09/07/ancient-chinese-sites-hit-by-flash-floods-this-summer (accessed 28 November 2021).
7 See http://whc.unesco.org/en/list/366 (accessed 4 July 2022).
8 See https://www.theguardian.com/environment/2020/jan/17/its-heart-wrenching-80-of-blue-mountains-and-50-of-gondwana-rainforests-burn-in-bushfires (accessed 28 November 2021).
9 See https://whc.unesco.org/en/review/100/ (accessed 2 December 2021).
10 See https://whc.unesco.org/en/list/143/ (accessed 4 July 2022).
11 See https://www.bbc.co.uk/news/av/world-europe-51943104 (accessed 4 July 2022). https://www.centreforcities.org/publication/covid-pandemic-lockdown-air-quality-cities/
12 See https://en.unesco.org/events/changing-minds-not-climate-science-knowledge-systems-and-ethics-enhanced-ambition-and (accessed 27 November 2021).

References

Cooke, L. 2010. *Conservation Approaches to Earthen Architecture in Archaeological Contexts.* British Archaeological Reports International Series S2147. Oxford: Archaeopress.
Cooke, L. 2015. The heritage of earth buildings: process, substance and climate change. In: D. Harvey & J. Perry (eds). *The Future of Heritage as Climates Change: Loss, Adaptation and Creativity.* Key Issues in Cultural Heritage Series. Abingdon: Routledge, 217–229.

Crutzen, P. 2002. Geology of mankind. *Nature*, 415, 23.

Heathcote, E. 2016. Ghost of Palmyra's arch rises in Trafalgar Square. *Financial Times*, 19 April 2016. https://www.ft.com/content/70a7d9fe-0545-11e6-a70d-4e39ac32c284 (accessed 4 July 2022).

IUCN & WCPA. 2021. *World Commission on Protected Areas (WCPA) Information Note for UNFCCC COP26: Role of Protected and Conserved Areas (PCAs) in Attaining the Paris Agreement Target.* Information Note, November 2021, Gland, Switzerland: IUCN.

Lafoley, D., Baxter, J., Day, J., Wenzel, L., Bueno, P. & Zischka, K. 2019. Marine protected areas. In: C. Shephard, ed. *World Seas: An Environmental Evaluation. Volume III: Ecological Issues and Environmental Impacts.* 2nd ed. London: Academic Press, 549–569.

Le Treut, H., Somerville, U., Cubasch, Y., Ding, C., Mauritzen, A. et al. 2007. Historical overview of climate change. In: *Climate Change 2007: The Physical Science Basis. Contribution of Working Group I to the Fourth Assessment Report of the Intergovernmental Panel on Climate Change.* Cambridge and New York: Cambridge University Press.

McMahon, D., Axelson, J. & Kocher, S. 2020. *Mass Tree Mortality, Fuels, and Fire: A Guide for Sierra Nevada Forest Landowners.* UC ANR Publication 8683. Santa Barbara: University of California.

Pahl, S., Sheppard, S., Boomsma, C. & Groves, C. 2014. Perceptions of time in relation to climate change. *WIREs Clim Change*, 5, 375–388. doi:10.1002/wcc.272.

Philips, H. 2014. Adaptation to climate change at UK world heritage sites: progress and challenges. *The Historic Environment: Policy & Practice* 5 (3), 288–299.

Potts, A. 2021. *European Cultural Heritage Green Paper. Putting Europe's shared heritage at the heart of the European Green Deal.* The Hague and Brussels: Europa Nostra.

Reimann, L., Vafeidis, A. T., Brown, S., Hinkel, J. & Tol, R. S. J. 2018Mediterranean UNESCO World Heritage at risk from coastal flooding and erosion due to sea-level rise. *Nature Communications*, 9, 4161. doi:10.1038/s41467-018-06645-9.

Scott, M. 2011. Heavy rains and dry lands don't mix: reflections on the 2010 Pakistan flood. Earth Observatory, NASA. https://earthobservatory.nasa.gov/features/PakistanFloods (accessed 4 July 2022).

Seebacher, F. & Post, E. 2015. Climate change impacts on animal migration. *Climate Change Responses*, 2 (5). https://climatechangeresponses.biomedcentral.com/articles/10.1186/s40665-015-0013-9 (accessed 4 July 2022).

Turner, L. 2016. Palmyra's Arch of Triumph recreated in London. BBC. 19 April 2016. https://www.bbc.co.uk/news/uk-36070721 (accessed 4 July 2022).

UNESCO. 2006. *Development of Policy Document on Impacts of Climate Change and World Heritage.* https://whc.unesco.org/en/CC-policy-document/36070721 (accessed 4 July 2022).

UNESCO. 2007a. *Case Studies on Climate Change and World Heritage.* https://whc.unesco.org/en/documents/115528. 36070721 (accessed 4 July 2022).

UNESCO. 2007b. *World Heritage Report n°22 – May 2007 Climate Change and World Heritage.* https://whc.unesco.org/en/series/22/36070721 (accessed 4 July 2022).

UNESCO. 2012. Decision: 35 COM 7B.76. https://whc.unesco.org/en/decisions/4484/36070721 (accessed 4 July 2022).

UNESCO. 2014. *Climate Change Adaptation for Natural World Heritage Sites – A Practical Guide.* https://whc.unesco.org/en/series/37/36070721 (accessed 4 July 2022).

UNESCO. 2016. *World Heritage and Tourism in a Changing Climate.* https://whc.unesco.org/en/tourism-climate-change/36070721 (accessed 4 July 2022).

UNESCO. 2021. *World Heritage Review 100: Climate Change.* Paris: UNESCO.

UN-Habitat Award. 2018. Pakistan Chulahs: the smokeless stoves empowering women and changing lives. https://world-habitat.org/world-habitat-awards/winners-and-finalists/pakistan-chulahs/36070721 (accessed 4 July 2022).

Van Dyke, F. & Lamb, R. L. 2020. *Conservation Biology. Foundations, Concepts, Applications.* Cham, Switzerland: Springer Nature Switzerland AG.

World Heritage Centre. 2006. WHC–06/30.COM/7.1 issues related to the state of conservation of World Heritage properties: the impacts of climate change on World Heritage properties. https://whc.unesco.org/en/documents/6523. 36070721 (accessed 4 July 2022).

7

MANAGING THREATS TO MARINE HERITAGE SITES AND PROTECTED AREAS

7.1 Introduction

By the time of the 45th Annual session of the World Heritage Committee in 2021 (the 2020 session being cancelled because of the COVID-19 pandemic), some 50 marine sites had been inscribed on the World Heritage List. While in the early days marine protected areas (MPAs) tended to be designated to protect either threatened species or scenic locations, the contemporary approach to designation and management recognises that the effective protection of marine biodiversity requires protection of a wide range of marine and coastal habitats, not just iconic species or special areas (Laffoley et al., 2019).

Like terrestrial natural and cultural properties, marine sites face a range of threats and pressures that are addressed through management planning. These pressures can broadly be categorised as follows:

- Development pressures associated with competing economic uses, including navigation, tourism and mineral extraction, which threaten habitats;
- Disturbance to specific species associated with tourist access, established community uses (legal and illegal) and other economic activity, including fisheries;
- Pollution, including land-based run-off and river outflows but also marine litter and waste discharged from ocean-going vessels;
- Climate change.

7.2 Development pressures

One of the best-known marine World Heritage Sites is Australia's **Great Barrier Reef** (inscribed 1981) which is a heavily contested area because of the conflicting interests of tourism, conservation and other economic development

DOI: 10.4324/9781003044857-8

interests including shipping and port development. As with any other type of World Heritage Site, there is scope for conflict because of the challenge of reconciling the Outstanding Universal Value for which a site is listed, and the more local values that relate to its position within the local economy and living landscape.

Recent research into the effectiveness of planning for the sustainable future of the Great Barrier Reef revealed that a fragmented management structure and a complex legislative framework reflecting both state and federal policy, combined with the competing values of a wide range of stakeholders, presented considerable challenges for the adoption of responsible and sustainable business practices (Moyle et al., 2018). Approval for the dumping of more than one million tonnes of dredge sludge onto the reef illustrates the challenges of keeping important navigation channels and ports open along the coast with broader environmental protection priorities (SBS News, 2019). And these plans were approved despite UNESCO expressing grave concern and threatening to put the property on the list in danger when previous dredging proposals were mooted to assist in the construction of a new coal terminal at Abbot Point, near Townsville, Queensland (BBC News, 2014).

Other fragile marine ecosystems affected by the pressures of economic growth include the **Sundarban Mangrove Forests** of the Ganges Delta (shared between India and Bangladesh) where power stations and cement factories have been constructed on the fringes of the forests and where navigation channels have been created to facilitate the movement of materials by boat (Hassan et al., 2019). In the Caribbean, prospects of oil exploration a decade or so ago posed a major threat to the **Bacalar Chico Marine Reserve** in Belize which for a while was placed on the List in Danger by UNESCO (Murray, 2021). And proposals to develop coastal tourist resorts on Sudan's Red Sea coast have threatened important populations of Reef Manta Rays including those living in the waters of the **Dungonab Bay – Mukkawar Island Marine National Park** (Kessel et al., 2017).

7.3 Disturbance to species

Given that many marine World Heritage Sites are designated precisely because they support populations of rare or endangered species, it is perhaps inevitable that there will be tourists keen to view them from either shore-based or sea-based facilities. **Shark Bay Marine Park** in Western Australia was inscribed on the World Heritage List in 1991, covers an area of around 7,500 km^2 and is celebrated for three exceptional natural features: its sea-grass beds, which are the largest (4,800 km^2) and richest in the world; its population of dugong ('sea cow') which numbers around 10,000 and its stromatolites (colonies of algae which form hard, dome-shaped deposits and are among the oldest forms of life on earth) (Simpson et al., 2020). The waters are an important staging point for Humpback Whales as they migrate along the coast and the beaches provide important nesting sites for

Loggerhead Turtles. Shark Bay is also home to five species of endangered mammals including two species of Wallaby.

One popular activity at Shark Bay is land-based viewing of dolphins close inshore and researchers have reported up to 200 tourists congregating at one time at the Monkey Mia Dolphin Interaction Zone (Laffoley et al., 2019). Such engagement is closely supervised by park authority staff to minimise disturbance and distress to the dolphins and this fits in more generally with broader management policies of zoning the whole MPA, including the WHS, principally for conservation with widespread restrictions on public access to certain areas (Simpson et al., 2020). A recent concern is the growing number of cruise ships coming to the area with associated expectations of close engagement with the more charismatic species found in the park as well as the associated risks of pollution from (accidental) fuel and waste-water discharges.

BOX 7.1 CASE STUDY 7.1: THE SUNDARBANS, INDIA AND BANGLADESH.

The Sundarban Mangrove Forest in the Ganges Delta comprises both freshwater and marine mangroves and is unique as it is the only mangrove forest in the world with a population of tigers (*Panthera tigris*). Inevitably, these are prone to poaching as community members living around the area seek to profit from the large sums paid for tiger parts because of their role in traditional Chinese medicine (David Shepherd Wildlife Foundation, 2014). Other animals poached in the forests of Sundarban include deer and crocodiles (Hassan et al., 2019). The Indian **Sundarbans National Park** was inscribed on the World Heritage List in 1987 under natural Criteria (ix) and (x) while the Bangladeshi **Sundarbans** were added to the list a decade later in 1997 against the same criteria.

Tourism also has the potential to disturb species and to damage the ecosystem of the Sundarbans. As previously indicated, the mangroves lie within the territories of two nation states – India and Bangladesh – and it is instructive to note the different approaches to managing tourism impacts in this World Heritage property between the two countries. In general, management controls in the Bangladesh Sundarbans are less restrictive than on the Indian side, and monitoring of infringements is far less sophisticated on the Bangladeshi side (Table 7.1). This reflects not least relative resource availability at state and municipal level as well as the significance of tourism to each country's economy. As such, the efforts of each States Party to manage pressures from development generally, and tourism specifically, are unequal.

TABLE 7.1 Comparison of tourist management practices in the Indian and Bangladeshi Sundarbans.

Aspects	Bangladesh Sundarbans	Indian Sundarbans
Accessibility	Tourists can walk on a few trails throughout the forest accompanied by armed guards of the Forest Department	Tourists are not allowed to alight from the boats to walk in the forest – viewing is only possible from onboard tourist boats
Vessel movement	Tourist vessel movement is quite flexible	Tourist boats are not allowed to anchor anywhere except close to the assigned camp of the Forest Department
Vessel fitness	The fitness of the tourists' vessels is not checked at any stage and no measures are taken to reduce noise pollution	Every tourist boat must use a silencer to reduce noise pollution
Pollution control	The legal obligation of waste management is not strict; therefore, disposable plastic garbage is dumped into the rivers and beside the trails of the Sundarbans	Tourists may not take into the area disposable plastic items such as bags, bottles, plastic plates. Floating plastic waste is removed by skimmers
Monitoring and control	The environmental concerns arising from tourism are not monitored in any structured way	Any type of environmental incident associated with tourists or tour operators is immediately reported to the authorities, with penalties including fines or loss of operating licences

Source: (Hassan et al., 2019).[1]

The **Galapagos Islands** are one of the world's most iconic habitats and were inscribed in 1978 as the first property on the UNESCO list because of their ecological and cultural significance. In order to protect marine biodiversity and manage fishing activities around the islands (and to reduce conflict between industrial fishing and artisanal fishing by local people) a zoning plan was introduced for the whole Galapagos Marine Reserve (GMR) in 2000 that identified three discrete zones:

- Zone 1 – the multiple use zone, which includes the deep waters of the GMR, i.e. >300 m deep, where all uses are allowed in addition to navigation and surveillance;
- Zone 2 – the limited use zone, which consists of coastal waters (< 300 m) surrounding the islands, islets and rocks, and includes seamounts;
- Zone 3 – port zones.

The intention was to provide clear guidelines to all interested parties on what activities were appropriate around the islands and by and large it appears to have been successful (Moity, 2018). Commercial, industrial fishing is banned across the whole GMR and only artisanal fishing is permitted within the area, and only for registered fishermen from the local community.

Other marine World Heritage Sites where traditional fishing communities have been involved in the consultations around managing important fisheries include the **Shiretoko Peninsula**, Japan (designated WHS in 2005) and an important salmon, squid, cod and pollock fishery (Makino, 2017), and the **Sian Ka'an Biosphere Reserve** (inscribed 1987) on the east coast of the Mexican state of Quintana Roo (Ayer et al., 2018).

7.4 Pollution of marine areas

Pollution of marine areas comes from a number of sources including land-based run-off and river outflows; waste that is deliberately disposed of into the ocean or that finds its way there having been casually discarded, and waste discharged from ocean-going vessels including bilge water, fuel emissions and solid wastes. Some pollution incidents are point-based (i.e. they occur in a very limited area, next to the point of contamination) while others are much more diffuse. Below we briefly address three key areas of concern:

- Transportation of chemicals, silt and debris downriver and into fragile coastal ecosystems;
- Marine plastics;
- Waste discharged from commercial shipping including ballast water, grey water, fuel oils.

7.4.1 Pollution flowing downriver and out to sea

The obvious forms of land-based pollution from river sources flowing into coastal marine areas would be increases in nutrients, particularly nitrogen and phosphorus from agricultural areas which flow into water courses and which cause eutrophication and 'dead zones'; sewage and wastewater, and plastics – when flooding occurs in urban areas, flooding will worsen the distribution of plastic through water networks. Such pollution is a persistent problem in any situation but is aggravated during periods of high precipitation & flooding (Zoppini et al., 2019). It is likely that in the coming decades the problem will be exacerbated further by climate change and the anticipated intensification of the hydrological cycle, which will increase the frequency and severity of floods around the world.

Australia's **Great Barrier Reef** occasionally suffers from environmental damage caused by large-scale flooding events, which are compromising the Reef's OUV (Moyle et al., 2018). Agricultural activities in the catchment areas of rivers flowing out into the sea along the Reef, mean that when in flood, the rivers bring large amounts of silt that can cover the reef and impact sensitive sea grass colonies as well as corals. At the same time, chemicals from pesticides and fertilisers are also entering watercourses and flowing into the marine environment, disrupting fragile ecosystems to the extent that more than 50% of the Reef's World Heritage attributes have been lost in the last three decades (Tan & Humphries, 2018).

This so-called diffuse pollution requires a more strategic approach to management than does point-based pollution, where the source can often be swiftly identified and appropriate mitigation pressures put in place. Inevitably, it involves a much greater range of stakeholders and is thus more costly, time-consuming and challenging to implement. What is particularly challenging in the case of the Barrier Reef is that the primary industry that is creating the problems – agriculture – doesn't benefit from the WHS inscription at all and thus it is proving difficult to engage farmers and landowners in helping to reduce the amounts of nutrients and pesticides that flow downstream and out to sea, and to try to prevent large amounts of sediments associated with changing land-use practices from entering watercourses.

7.4.2 Marine plastics

Though originating largely from land-based sources, pollution from marine plastics is a widespread problem in all of the world's oceans and not just in World Heritage marine areas. Marine plastics can be subdivided into three basic categories (after Vince & Stoett, 2018):

- macroplastics, including debris such as fishing nets and large pieces of Styrofoam;
- microplastics which are particles under 5 mm in diameter and can be either plastic nurdles (used in various production processes) or the fragments that remain when larger plastic objects enter marine ecosystems and phyto-degrade;
- nanoplastics, which are either manufactured as such or are at the end state of microplastic degradation. These are invisible to the naked eye (1,000 times smaller than an algal cell), and more likely than microplastics to pass through biological membranes and thus can be found inside fish and other marine-dwelling creatures.

Vince & Stoett (2018) report that all categories of plastic litter have been found in even the most remote parts of the world's oceans and along the majority of coastlines (as well as most terrestrial ecosystems). It has been calculated that between 1.15 and 2.41 million tonnes of plastic waste currently enters the ocean every year from rivers, with around three-quarters of emissions occurring between May and October (Lebreton et al., 2017). The authors of that report have estimated that the top 20 polluting rivers, mostly located in Asia, account for 67% of the global total. The Yangtse in China is the worst offender, followed by the Ganges (which flows through the **Sundarban World Heritage Site**), the Xi, Dong and Zhujiang rivers which all flow into China's Pearl River Delta and four rivers on Java, Indonesia. In South America one of the worst rivers for transporting plastic waste is Colombia's Magdalena River which flows into the Gulf of Mexico at Barranquilla.

Tackling such pollution must happen at source, when the materials reach the end of their useful life and thus must be prevented from entering the environment, but rather recycled or otherwise disposed of so that they don't create problems of marine pollution. Recent research with residents of the Galapagos Islands confirms that promoting behavioural change in communities responsible for disposing of plastic waste into the oceans is a crucial step for tackling the problem (Schofield et al., 2020).

7.4.3 Waste discharges at sea

Commercial shipping, cruise ships, naval vessels and motor-yachts can create significant environmental problems for the marine environment because of discharges (deliberate or accidental) of oil, sewage, garbage and ballast water. Atmospheric emissions from burning fuels oils are also a problem but are not addressed here. In 1973, the International Maritime Organization (IMO) adopted the International Convention for the Prevention of Pollution from Ships (MARPOL) to address pollution from ships. It applies to 99% of the world's merchant tonnage (International Maritime Organization, n.d.). We explore the key areas of concern below since all have a potential impact on the health of marine areas whether or not they are of World Heritage Site status.

As far as operational oil pollution is concerned, MARPOL requires all vessels to have an oil discharge and monitoring system that separates oil from bilge water to reduce the levels of discharge of used fuel oils. Annex IV of MARPOL contains regulations regarding what is permissible regarding the discharge of sewage into the sea from ships and the provision of port reception facilities for sewage. It is conventionally understood that the oceans are generally capable of assimilating and dealing with raw sewage through natural bacterial action and so Annex IV of MARPOL prohibits the discharge of sewage into the sea within a specified distance from the nearest land. Annex V prohibits the discharge of all garbage into the sea, except in certain instances of food waste, cargo residues, cleaning agents and additives and animal carcasses.

Since the introduction of steel-hulled vessels in the latter part of the 19th century, water has been used as ballast to stabilize vessels at sea with ballast water being pumped into watertight compartments in the hull to maintain safe operating conditions during the voyage. However, ballast water also contains multitudes of marine species including bacteria, small invertebrates, eggs and larvae of various species which may be transferred across long distances within the hull before being discharged. Once in the new marine habitat, transferred species may survive to establish an invasive, reproductive population in the host environment where they may out-compete native species and multiply into pest proportions (International Maritime Organization, n.d.).

This obviously will create challenges in marine protected areas in particular. Moreover, as the volume of international shipping continues to grow, and as new navigation areas open up in the polar north as sea ice retreats, threats to pristine marine World Heritage Sites like Greenland's **Ilulissat Icefjord** (inscribed 2004) or the seas around Russia's **Wrangel Island Reserve** (inscribed 2004) will increase. The International Convention for the Control and Management of Ships' Ballast Water and Sediments (BWM Convention) was passed in 2004 and requires all marine vessels to implement a ballast water management plan to reduce the risks of this kind of ecological damage.

Generally, therefore, there is appropriate legislation governing operational issues of vessels at sea that, if properly followed, should reduce significantly the threats to the marine environment associated with shipping. However, the IMO notes that compliance is not as full across the world's shipping fleets as it could be and hence more needs to be done to enforce greater adherence to the MARPOL regulations at an international level. Locally, nation-states are able to introduce their own legislation and management regime to reduce risks of pollution from shipping. In Canada, for instance, there are two separate coastal/ marine properties on the coast of British Columbia that are on that country's tentative list for WH status – the **Gwaii Haanas National Park Reserve** and the **Hecate Strait & Queen Charlotte Sound MPA**. Relevant conservation stakeholders have already prepared a toolkit to reduce the risks of pollution in marine protected areas on Canada's Pacific coast that builds on and strengthens MARPOL provisions (WWF-Canada, 2020) and it assumed that if and when WH status is accorded to these sites, that implementation of the toolkit will help reduce risks of pollution.

7.5 Managing marine heritage sites – best practice

From this brief review of some of the issues around the challenges facing marine World Heritage Sites, it appears that management activities must tackle a number of key challenges:

- Involving communities whose livelihoods are dependent totally or partially on a high-quality marine environment at all stages of planning, implementing and reviewing management plans, especially where there may be proposals to restrict access to certain areas, or limits to catch sizes (Makino, 2017; Ayer et al., 2018; Jones, n.d.);
- Ensuring that, as with terrestrial properties in the global south and other peripheral areas, the rights of indigenous peoples are respected. To date this is an under-researched area but as Ban & Frid (2018) suggest, while in the past indigenous management of the oceans was commonplace, such management has declined wherever those communities have suffered from colonisation and marginalisation;
- Tackling the complex situations where economic activities far from the WHS are indirectly creating major problems because of their polluting activities, as is the case with agricultural and other land-use interests in catchment areas that supply rivers flowing into fragile or sensitive coastal areas. In situations like this, national policy makers need to be involved to ensure a coordinated approach to legislation and resource management (Moyle et al., 2018; Tan & Humphries, 2018; Jones, n.d.).

Van Putten et al. (2018) propose an innovative approach to preparing management plans for marine areas that ensure more than just the economic value of the marine resources are taken into account. They propose an approach that builds on five different attributes of the marine environment and to which different individuals and stakeholder groups will bond differently. In effect, their ideas (see Figure 7.1) reflect the idea that, just as the historic environment can be valued in many different ways, so can the marine environment, and that only by understanding how different stakeholder groups 'see the sea' can a truly aspirational and effective management plan be prepared for any marine area. They argue that there are a number of factors to consider that, when combined, help to explain or develop feelings of attachment and a sense of place.

Thus, they argue that is important not just to value these locations because of their ecological or scientific importance, but also because of their significance in traditional folklore and popular culture, their contemporary use for leisure and livelihoods and their aesthetics. This approach, if applied at World Heritage marine sites, would help to establish how local values can support and augment the broader concept of Outstanding Universal Value and presents a further, useful tool for the World Heritage manager.

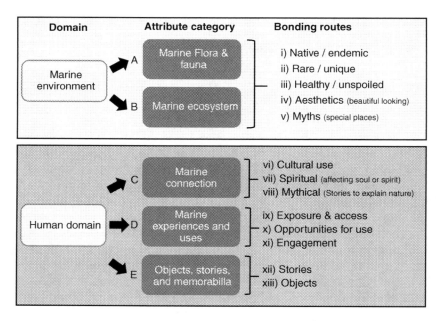

FIGURE 7.1 Conceptual links between domain, five attribute categories, and different processes that are (mostly) linked to well-being and expected to mediate greater Sense of Place in the marine environment.
Source: (Van Putten et al., 2018).

Note

1 Note: slight amendments were made to the vocabulary and grammar of the published version for clarity.

References

Ayer, A., Fulton, S., Caamal-Madrigal, J. & Espinoza-Tenorio, A. 2018. Lessons in building community support for no-take MPAs from the Mexican Caribbean. *OCTO*. doi:10.31230/osf.io/28rqf.

Ban, N. C. & Frid, A. 2018. Indigenous people's rights and marine protected areas. *Marine Policy*, 87 (January), 180–185.

BBC News. 2014. Unesco warns Australia over Great Barrier Reef. https://www.bbc.co.uk/news/world-asia-27233810(accessed 3 May 2021).

David Shepherd Wildlife Foundation. 2014. *Wildlife Matters*, 44, Spring.

Hassan, K., Higham, J., Wooliscroft, B. & Hopkins, D. 2019. Climate change and world heritage: a cross-border analysis of the Sundarbans (Bangladesh–India). *Journal of Policy Research in Tourism, Leisure and Events*, 11 (2), 196–219.

International Maritime Organization. n.d. *Ballast Water Management*. https://www.imo.org/en/OurWork/Environment/Pages/BallastWaterManagement.aspx(accessed 4 May 2021).

Jones, P. J. S. 2021. A governance analysis of Ningaloo and Shark Bay Marine Parks, Western Australia: Putting the 'eco' in tourism to build resilience but threatened in long-term by climate change? *Marine Policy*, 127, May, 103636.

Kessel, S. T., Elamin, N. A., Yurkowski, D. J., Chekchak, T., Walter, R. P. et al. 2017. Conservation of reef manta rays (Manta alfredi) in a UNESCO World Heritage Site: Large-scale island development or sustainable tourism? *PLoS ONE*, 12 (10). doi:10.1371/journal.pone.0185419.

Laffoley, D., Baxter, J., Day, J., Wenzel, L., Bueno, P. &Zischka, K. 2019. Marine protected areas. In: C. Shephard, ed. *World Seas: An Environmental Evaluation. Volume III: Ecological Issues and Environmental Impacts*. 2nd ed. London: Academic Press, 549–569.

Lebreton, L. C. M., van der Zwet, J., Damsteeg, J.-W., Slat, B., Andrady, A. & Reisser, J. 2017. Plastic emissions to the world's oceans. *Nature Communications*, 8 (7 June), 1–10.

Makino, M. 2017. Institutional and economic analysis of Japanese fisheries management and its expansion into marine ecosystem conservation. *Agri-Bioscience Monographs*, 7 (1), 1–24.

Moity, N. 2018. Evaluation of no-take zones in the Galapagos Marine Reserve, Zoning Plan 2000. *Frontiers in Marine Science*, 17 July.

Moyle, B. D., Moyle, C. & Bec, A. 2018. A responsibility-accountability framework for private sector use of a World Heritage Area. *Journal of Environmental Policy and Planning*, 20 (1), 31–44.

Murray, R. 2021. A governance analysis of three MPAs in Belize: conservation objectives compromised by tourism development priorities? *Marine Policy*, 127 (May), 104243.

SBS News. 2019. Dumping sludge in Great Barrier Reef Marine Park given go ahead. https://www.sbs.com.au/news/dumping-sludge-in-great-barrier-reef-marine-park-given-go-ahead (accessed 3 May 2021).

Schofield, J., Wyles, K., Doherty, S., Donnelly, A., Jones, J. & Porter, A. 2020. Object narratives as a methodology for mitigating marine plastic pollution: multidisciplinary investigations in Galápagos. *Antiquity*, 94 (373), 228–244.

Simpson, G. D., Patroni, J., Teo, A. C. K., Chan, J. K. L. & Newsome, D. 2020. Importance-performance analysis to inform visitor management at marine wildlife tourism destinations. *Journal of Tourism Futures*, 6 (2), 165–180.

Tan, P.-L. & Humphries, F. 2018. Adaptive or aspirational? Governance of diffuse water pollution affecting Australia's Great Barrier Reef. *Water International*, 43 (3). doi:10.1080/02508060.2018.1446617.

Van Putten, I. E. et al. 2018. A framework for incorporating sense of place into the management of marine systems. *Ecology and Society*, 23 (4). https://www.ecologyandsociety.org/vol23/iss4/art4/ES-2018-10504.pdf (accessed 5 July 2022).

Vince, J. & Stoett, P. 2018. From problem to crisis to interdiscplinary solutions: plastic marine debris. *Marine Policy*, 96 (October), 200–203.

WWF-Canada. 2020. *Reducing Impacts from Shipping in Marine Protected Areas: A Toolkit for Canada. Reducing impacts from shipping in Scott Islands National Wildlife Area: Pacific Case Study*. Toronto: WWF Canada.

Zoppini, A., Ademollo, A., Bensi, M., Berto, D., Bongiorni, L. et al. 2019. Impact of a river flood on marine water quality and planktonic microbial communities. *Estuarine, Coastal and Shelf Science*, 234 (31 August), 62–72.

8

BENEFITS OF WORLD HERITAGE SITE STATUS

8.1 Introduction

As noted in Chapter 2, many governments are keen to see their cultural and natural heritage represented on the World Heritage list because they perceive there to be real benefits in terms of awareness raising, destination marketing, tourism development and associated positive economic impacts. There is certainly some evidence that this can happen. Buckley's seminal work at Australian World Heritage Sites found that while inscription had limited impact on demand from domestic tourists it did generally yield significant increases in visitation from international tourists (Buckley, 2004). Similarly, Yang et al. (2010) have found that World Heritage designation was a key factor explaining high levels of international tourism interest in certain cultural heritage properties in China, while a major review of tourism flows across 66 countries found that there is a positive relationship between the volume of tourist activity and the number of World Heritage properties in a destination, and that the relationship is stronger for natural heritage sites rather than cultural ones (Su & Lin, 2014).

On the other hand, Ribaudo & Figini (2017) looked at 16 World Heritage Site in Italy and found no clear evidence of a significant increase in tourist demand for such properties post-inscription, while Poria et al. (2013) found, in a survey of domestic and international tourists in Israel, that World Heritage status was sometimes seen as a negative factor as it implied heavy rates of visitation, and hence a crowded and unsatisfactory experience, putting people off the idea of visiting. A more recent study exploring the impact of World Heritage listing on the recreational value of Japan's **Mount Fuji**, (Jones et al., 2017) again found little additional positive benefit post-inscription while Huang et al. (2012), who looked at the case of **Macau**, found just a short-lived benefit. More recently, Adie (2019) has suggested that while the World Heritage Site inscription itself may not drive an

DOI: 10.4324/9781003044857-9

increase in tourist interest in a site, the associated marketing campaigns celebrating inscription may lead to an increase in visitation.

The situation is thus at best ambiguous, yet as Timothy (2021) states, 'Many countries' tourism officials are under the misguided assumption that once a heritage place is inscribed on UNESCO's list, the site will, with certainty, be inundated with more tourists and the destination's economic ills will be cured' (pp. 200–201). Thus, in order to get a more balanced view of the benefits of inscription, one must consider more broadly the types of benefits accruing to destinations and relevant stakeholders, and not just focus on tourism impacts which, as the brief discussion above illustrates, are not always guaranteed.

The framework for the following discussion has been informed by the findings of a review carried out a number of years ago for the UK's main heritage agencies on the costs and benefits of World Heritage status (PricewaterhouseCoopers LLP, 2007). That report identified a number of key benefits delivered by the inscription of a property on the list. From the eight categories of benefit identified in the PWC report and illustrated in Figure 8.1, we focus in this section largely on the following:

- Civic pride and social capital;
- Learning and education;
- Tourism;
- Regeneration.

From our perspective, 'partnership' and 'funding' are aspects of the management process that help to deliver the other outcomes or benefits, while the conservation

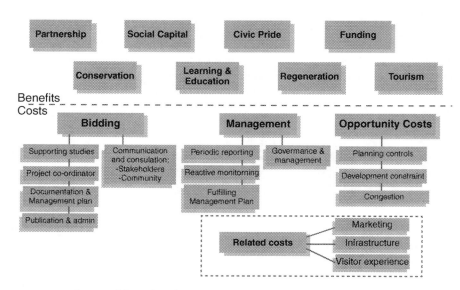

FIGURE 8.1 Costs and benefits of World Heritage Site status.
Source: PricewaterhouseCoopers LLP (2007).

benefits of inscription have already been explored in earlier chapters. In our discussion of learning and education, we focus particularly on volunteering as this
provides a link between that form of constructive engagement on the one hand
and tourism on the other.

8.2 Civic pride and social capital

To commence this discussion of how World Heritage status can help deliver civic
pride and act as a form of social capital, one must first consider what is meant by
the term 'community', since this is the term often used by States Parties to indicate
who some of the prime beneficiaries of a property's inscription will be. People
form and maintain communities to meet common needs (Chavis & Lee, 2015).
While some communities may be rooted in a particular location, communities of
place are not the only ones that exist – people come together for a broad range of
reasons including faith, politics, intellectual or social interests and it is through these
communities that they find a sense of personal and group identity. Moreover, most
people live within multiple communities and, like Russian Matryoshka dolls
(themselves a form of heritage), communities often sit within other communities.
In any given geographic location where people live, as well as the community of
place there may also be different ethnic communities, communities based on
people of different ages and with different needs, and communities based on
common economic interests. As Smith & Waterton state, communities are not a
homogeneous unit but are 'a heterogeneous and changing aggregate of people'
(2009, p. 18). Moreover, they are self-defining, at times having vested interests that
oppose or are opposed by other groups, and can be hard to identify and engage
with without considerable insight into local power structures. And one must also
remember that when dealing with heritage places, engagements with that place will
very rarely be limited to one key community groups and that there may well be
conflicting and competing interests and aspirations (Smith & Waterton, 2009).

All of which makes securing benefits from inscription an even more complex
challenge, because it can be hard to understand which groups are invested in a
property and which are less interested in it, or even not interested at all. The
challenge becomes even greater still when heritage site planners and managers
come in from outside, and when there are indigenous peoples with long-established roots and traditions.

It is particularly important to consider how indigenous peoples are impacted by
World Heritage designation. By indigenous peoples, we mean the descendants of
those who already inhabited an area or region before others came and established
dominance. It is estimated that there are around 370 million indigenous peoples
around the globe (UN Permanent Forum on Indigenous Issues, n.d.). Research
carried out for the Human Rights Council of the United Nations indicated that
the creation of protected areas of any kind, including World Heritage properties,
can often have a negative impact on indigenous peoples because their ancestral
rights over their lands and territories are ignored partially or completely (UN

General Assembly, 2015). Furthermore, the traditional categorisation of World Heritage into discrete categories of either 'natural' or 'cultural' also creates problems for indigenous peoples. Indeed, over one-third of World Heritage Sites designated as 'natural' are home to indigenous peoples with distinct cultures (IIPFWH, n.d.).

An International Indigenous Peoples Forum on World Heritage (IIPFWH) was created in 2017 to provide a voice for all those indigenous peoples affected by the various processes involved in nominating and then managing World Heritage properties. Its stated function is to act 'as a platform dedicated to strategizing and advocating towards the goal of full respect for indigenous rights within World Heritage Conventions and processes'. The principal areas where the Forum is designed to work with the World Heritage Committee and other stakeholders include: promoting the use of indigenous knowledge in understanding conservation and other challenges; ensuring that land, resource and tenure rights are respected and identifying how best to use the capacity of indigenous peoples to act as custodians, owners and decision makers of land to which their community has been attached for centuries but which now is also designated as World Heritage.

What then do communities expect from designation? Noor et al. (2019) found that people living in or near a site inscribed on the World Heritage List were more likely to feel optimistic about receiving potential benefits from tourism activity than those living in a similar environment but lacking that designation. Their research, at the cultural property in **Lenggong Valley** on the Malay Peninsula (inscribed in 2012), also found that residents expected more general community gain as a result of inscription and the resulting government investment in protection, management and related infrastructural works as well as private sector investment in tourism facilities. Similar aspirations have also been found, for instance, with the residents of **Old Rauma** in Finland (Haanpaa et al., 2019); with the ranchers of the **Sierra de San Franscico** World Heritage Site in Baja California (Conway, 2014) and in **Stonetown, Zanzibar** (Okech, 2010). A survey of more than 700 residents of **Old Québec** in Canada found that around 40% felt immense pride in living in a World Heritage city (Evans, 2002).

It is also important to note that attitudes towards tourism held by communities impacted by World Heritage Site status may well change over time and that there is a risk if economic benefits are pursued over and above others (Jimura, 2019). Types of attitudinal change associated with World Heritage Site designation identified by Jimura include:

- Residents may start viewing tourism/ visitors more favourably;
- People may become more interested/ involved in conservation;
- Designation may enhance personal attachment to the place of residence;
- Inscription may also enhance pride in the place of residence.

As a result of all of the above outcomes, World Heritage status can help to strengthen local identity. So how can these perceived and expected benefits be delivered? The role of heritage professionals as catalysts and enablers of community in the commodification and management of heritage sites in general, and World Heritage in particular, has evolved in the last two decades or so, with the emergence of several different ways of involving 'communities of place', (where this is defined as a geographical location where people live, interact, and share a sense of place identity – see, for example, McKnight et al., 2017) and also communities of interest (defined either as a situation where people share a common functional relationship with beliefs, activities or services – see, for example, Fulcher, 1989). These ways in which communities can contribute to the work heritage professionals working at World Heritage properties by sharing their local knowledge include:

- Consultation when preparing management or development plans;
- As part of educational outreach programmes (communities as receivers and sometimes as co-producers of information);
- Community volunteers participating in excavations or other projects, including the preparation and presentation of interpretation materials;
- Community members being employed to support excavations or other projects, including the preparation and presentation of site interpretation.

Based on their experience of working with the community around a dig site in Quseir on Egypt's Red Sea coast, Moser et al. (2002) suggest that the following are essential components for achieving successful community heritage and archaeology projects. We would argue that they are just as important today for ensuring that communities are able to benefit from World Heritage Site inscription, not just through an enhanced sense of pride in their heritage, but materially as well. The seven points made by Moser et al. are:

1.   Communication and collaboration;
2.   Employment and training;
3.   Public presentation, including communities being engaged in interpreting findings and telling their own story;
4.   Interviews and oral history;
5.   Educational resources;
6.   Photographic and video archive;
7.   Community-controlled merchandising.

This approach has increasingly been accepted as good practice by the heritage industry (see for example Smith & Waterton, 2009) and later we examine some examples from World Heritage Sites across the globe where heritage managers have sought to include, rather than exclude, others from their work. This is significant because, as commentators such as Harrison (2010), Meskell (2018) and Adie (2019) have acknowledged, World Heritage in particular is increasingly being used a tool not just for expressing political power but also for stimulating social action and thus without community engagement with the processes of nomination and management, potential benefits will be lost. Because there still exists, in most destinations, what Harrison (2010) refers to as the 'top-down' approach to the 'classification and promotion of particular places by the state as … 'official' heritage' (p. 8), the situation persists where some properties may be inscribed against the wishes and/or without the support of the host community living in the area or a community of interest with a legitimate stake in the heritage property. And when it is the accepted role of States Parties to determine what is and what isn't afforded protection and resourcing, there can be conflict with what Harrison calls the 'bottom-up' relationship 'between people, objects, places and memories which forms the basis for the creation of unofficial forms of heritage (usually) at local level' (Harrison, 2010, p. 8). It is thus essential to involve local communities throughout the planning and delivery phases of any heritage project, and not just the World Heritage Site inscription process, because as noted earlier, communities use their heritage to construct their own identity (see for example Smith & Waterton, 2009). And one must also ensure to recognise and accept different interpretations, definitions and understandings of the past.

In other words, it is important for heritage professionals to understand the lived dimension of World Heritage – the spiritual, immaterial aspects of engagement that some communities have with their homes, as well as embracing more clearly cultural pluralism – 'the multiple meanings that heritage supplies for individuals and peoples with regard to identity and experience, the lives of their ancestors, and their societies' (Graham et al., 2000, p. 221). And these identity issues, the politics of recognition, become even more important when matched against the concept of Outstanding Universal Value because sometimes the value lies with a particular ethnic group, or with people who have a specific political or cultural perspective that isn't necessarily shared universally within that destination. This can particularly be the case at cultural heritage properties and the well-known example of **Uluru– Kata Tjuta National Park** (formerly known as Ayers Rock/ Mount Olga) World Heritage Site, a place sacred to the Pitjantjatjara people of Australia's Northern Territory, demonstrates the need to fully understand these nuances. The site was originally inscribed on the World Heritage list in 1987 under two criteria for natural sites – (ii) and (iii). Only following an extended outcry from a range of sources was this amended so that it was recognised and renominated in 1994 as a cultural landscape and particularly as an 'associative landscape having powerful religious, artistic, and cultural associations of the natural element'.

An example of where communities have been involved in developing interpretation and presentation programmes at World Heritage Sites include work at **Catalhöyük** in Turkey where the principal excavation team has for many years sought to involve the local community in developing multiple perspectives on interpreting the site with largely positive results (Hodder, 2003). Yet there are also instances where accommodating local sensitivities can be a barrier to engagement by some visitors. Graham et al. (2000) reviewed interpretation at the World Heritage Site of **Old Québec**, Canada and reported, with some irony, how increasing emphasis on its French heritage and use of the French language provides a barrier to understanding by the international (mainly US) market who needed interpretation in their own language YET who were going there partly because of its 'Frenchness'. And at the same, the commodification of this Francophone heritage for tourism and the gentrification of the Old City created a sense of alienation and discontent among the long-time residents of the area (Evans, 2002). Thus, reconciling local aspirations with tourist expectations is not always easy.

8.3 Learning and education

8.1.1 UNESCO's own education initiatives for World Heritage

Inevitably, any initiative under the auspices of UNESCO will have an educational aspect as one of its aims, and the World Heritage programme is no exception. Article 27 of the 1972 Convention states that:

1. The States Parties to this Convention shall endeavor by all appropriate means, and in particular by educational and information programmes, to strengthen appreciation and respect by their peoples of the cultural and natural heritage defined in Articles 1 and 2 of the Convention;
2. They shall undertake to keep the public broadly informed of the dangers threatening this heritage and of the activities carried on in pursuance of this Convention.

One can argue that onsite interpretation activities such as guided tours and on-site visitor centres have always been one approach by property managers and other stakeholders to generate awareness of, understanding of, and respect for, World Heritage though as we will demonstrate in Chapter 10, such actions are but one option in a broader toolbox of options.

It is instructive to note that it wasn't until 1994 that a specific education programme was developed by UNESCO for World Heritage (UNESCO, n.d.). The programme is run from the UNESCO World Heritage Centre in Paris and coordinates activities with the UNESCO Associated Schools (ASPnet), UNESCO Field Offices, National Commissions and other partners including ICOMOS, ICCROM, ICOM and IUCN. There are four stated objectives for the programme:

*   To encourage young people to become involved in heritage conservation on a local as well as on a global level;
*   To promote awareness among young people of the importance of the UNESCO World Heritage Convention (1972) and a better understanding of the interdependence of cultures among young people;
*   To develop new and effective educational approaches, methods and materials to introduce/ reinforce World Heritage education in the curricula in the vast majority of the UNESCO Member States;
*   To foster synergies among stakeholders in the promotion of World Heritage Education on a national and international level.

In the last 25 years or so of operation, the programme has accommodated nearly 1,600 young people on more than 40 international and regional youth forums, trained 1,250 teachers and educators, hosted 3,500 volunteers on 359 work camps across 61 countries and produced a 'World Heritage in Young Hands' resource kit in 40 different languages. This latter resource is aimed at pupils in secondary education and adopts an interdisciplinary approach that allows teachers to work across curricula with the objective of raising awareness among young people of the importance of World Heritage (UNESCO, n.d.).

It is interesting to note the geographical spread of the youth forums – of the 44 convened between 1995 and 2019, almost half have been held in Europe, 10 in Asia, 6 in Africa, 3 each in the Americas and Middle East and 2 in Australasia. Spain alone has hosted 5 forums. This doesn't of course represent the spread of World Heritage properties around the world and is instead a reflection of the ability of different national UNESCO commissions and other partners to manage such events and, in recent years, the decision taken to run a youth forum in parallel with the annual meetings of the World Heritage Committee.

A cartoon mascot for the programme – *Patrimonito* ('small heritage' in Spanish) – was created in 1995 and is used in 14 animated films presenting the character's adventures in different World Heritage properties around the world, in an attempt to engage younger children. In particular, the cartoons focus on threats to the specific sites, and possible strategies for reducing these threats. Many of the films are based on original storyboards produced by young people and submitted to annual competitions that ran between 2007 and 2012. It is unclear why activity in this area appears to have ceased while other areas of engagement such as the Youth Forums and the volunteering camps continue to operate.

One more recent initiative is the European Young Heritage Professionals Forum, established in 2019 and which in its first year brought together 28 young heritage professionals from across Europe to discuss issues around the safeguarding of tangible and intangible heritage. The intention is to help develop a network of 'Cultural Heritage Messengers' at the European, national and local levels to support initiatives around the protection and celebration of heritage properties of all kinds, including World Heritage. This programme remains active, running online events as recently as April 2021 (UNESCO, 2021).

To date there appears to have been no formal evaluation of the impact of the World Heritage Education Programme either internationally or nationally.

8.1.2 Volunteering as a tool for increasing engagement with World Heritage

8.1.2.1 Introduction

As indicated above, the World Heritage centre in Paris oversees a number of education initiatives including volunteer camps held in or near World Heritage Sites where young people can gain basic conservation skills in an environment where they also learn about the ethos behind the World Heritage programme and the challenges that sites face in the contemporary world. In doing so, participants are engaging what is an increasingly common activity in civil society around the globe. It is useful, therefore, to explore the idea of heritage volunteering in more detail.

There is of course a long tradition of volunteering at natural and cultural heritage properties in many parts of the world. For instance, in financial year 2018/19 the UK conservation charity The National Trust[1], which is very active at a number of World Heritage Sites, benefited from the unpaid work of some 65,000 volunteers with these people providing more than 4.8 million hours of inputs in more than 500 roles including stewarding visitors, habitat restoration and textile conservation. Trust properties on the World Heritage list that benefit from volunteer inputs include the **English Lake District**, several archaeological sites within the **Frontiers of the Roman Empire** and **Studley Royal Park including the ruins of Fountains Abbey**. Since 1969 the Vindolanda Trust, which manages one of the most significant archaeological sites within the **Frontiers of the Roman Empire World Heritage Site** in Northern England, has had more than 9,700 people volunteer on excavations at this important heritage property. As the Trust itself says on its website 'through that period two generations of Roman archaeologists and specialists have learnt and honed their trade at the site' (Vindolanda Charitable Trust, n.d.). Elsewhere around the world, volunteer divers are used to monitor and cull invasive lionfish populations at the Bacalor Chico Marine Reserve (BCMR), part of the **Belize Barrier Reef Reserve System** World Heritage Site (Anderson et al., 2017). International volunteers, mainly young Australian professionals, have provided development and conservation support to communities on **Mangaliliu and Lelepa Island** (collectively known as 'Lelema'), Vanuatu's first World Heritage Site, in a programme that has been running since the nomination process began in 2004 (Trau, 2015). And in Tanzania, local people living around the **Kilwa Kisiwani** World Heritage Site, a ruined settlement that dates back to the ninth century CE, also volunteer on conservation activities at the property (Lwoga, 2018)

In terms of co-ordinating and promoting volunteering opportunities across global World Heritage, UNESCO has its own programme – the World Heritage Volunteering Initiative (WHVI) – that commenced in 2008 and which in its first ten years of operation saw more than 5,000 young adult volunteers work on 341 separate projects at 138 World Heritage Sites across Latin America, Africa, Europe, the Arab State, and Asia & the Pacific. Together these volunteers contributed 280,000 hours of volunteer work with an estimated economic value of US$7 million (UNESCO, 2020). UNESCO has ambitious aims for this programme, which brings together host community members and international volunteers in its 'Action Camps' (there is a specific requirement that all activities should involve international volunteers, sometimes referred to as voluntourists), arguing that:

> Youth are the future of heritage: by training them in heritage preservation and valorization, by helping them build a local, national and international network of organizations, professionals and individuals, by equipping them with the

intercultural skills needed, by building upon the sentiment of volunteerism, we are building a future of actors who will take the lead in World Heritage protection and conservation. This will help build upon local and international development, and consolidate the role of volunteers in their own societies and internationally.

(UNESCO, 2020, p. 17)

As is demonstrated later, despite these laudable aims for the World Heritage Volunteering Initiative, it has been bedevilled by many of the same challenges faced by more general heritage volunteering schemes around the world. It is therefore useful to explore in a little more detail some of the more general academic literature around volunteering within the context of natural and heritage conservation and management projects, before considering how effective UNESCO's own programme has been.

8.1.2.2 Benefits of volunteering: individual participants and host communities

A comprehensive review of volunteering across multiple sectors of the economy carried out two decades ago (Chinman & Wandersman, 1999) found that most people who volunteer do so for two main reasons: to enjoy personal benefits and to deliver normative, positive outcomes for their community – in other words, to help enhance the overall quality of life in their area. In the UK, the aforementioned National Trust actively uses the emotive appeal of such benefits when seeking to recruit new volunteers, stating on the relevant part of their website: 'Making new friends, working in amazing places and knowing that you're helping a great cause - three fabulous reasons to get volunteering' (National Trust, 2022).

There has been considerable research carried out into volunteering since Chinman and Wandersman's work, and it generally supports these findings. For instance, personal benefits associated with participation in volunteering have been identified as enhanced feelings of belonging to a particular group, and thus improved personal wellbeing; improved mental health (especially for older citizens) (Guiney & Machado, 2018), greater self-confidence (Ali & Rahman, 2019), enhanced awareness of local and global environmental and social problems (Schneller & Coburn, 2018; Pak & Hiramoto, 2020) and improved future employment and salary prospects, particularly for younger people (Pan, 2017; Banki & Schonell, 2018; Wilson et al., 2020). As Wilson et al. note, 'there is evidence that volunteer work in secondary school and college positively affects the status and earnings of one's first job, which in turn has beneficial consequences for wages and salaries later in life' (2020, p. 10). There is, unsurprisingly, considerable debate over the relative balance between altruism and self-interest among volunteers, and particularly volunteer tourists (Wearing & McGehee, 2013; Foller-Carroll & Charlebois, 2016; Bandyopadhyay & Patil, 2017) and this is likely to be reflected among those who volunteer at heritage sites just as it is among those who contribute their time and energies voluntarily in other social situations.

There are also benefits at the community, as well as individual, level. For instance, it has been argued that

> volunteering on heritage sites allows local communities to have a better understanding of their heritage, revealing or identifying heritage values in order to grasp their multiple uses and to finally find a new value. It also draws attention to the needs, desires and rights of the local communities and stakeholders who are most concerned by the sites.
>
> *(UNESCO, 2020, p. 229)*

8.1.2.3 Benefits of volunteering: organisational and instrumental

As well as providing personal benefits to participants, volunteering also provides considerable benefits to the sites themselves. This is particularly the case when property managers have restricted access to funding. The instrumental role of volunteering is noted by UNESCO (2020, p. 229) who argue that: 'Volunteering is the key for engaging communities and increasing participation within a heritage management system. This can be achieved by implementing quality volunteer projects that are community-based'.

Research undertaken by Dearden et al. (2002) found that two-thirds of protected area managers they contacted reported annual budgets falling short of operational requirements and thus as well as spending time trying to secure additional finance, they also spent a lot of time seeking to galvanise more community involvement in aspects of site management by volunteers. This situation has been reported at the **Wadden Sea Protected Area** World Heritage Site, for instance, where volunteer programmes have been created to align with broader site management objectives (rather than necessarily with individual volunteer aspirations) in order to compensate for reduced funding from the state. As the authors of that case study report, 'the need for volunteering at cultural heritage sites is increasing as government funding for such activities is reduced' (Kwiatkowski et al., 2020, p. 305).

The contribution of well-planned and properly supervised volunteer inputs towards ecosystem research and conservation activities in southern Africa is reported by Roques et al. (2018), in the waters off Belize (Anderson et al., 2017) and at the Shirkami-sanchi mountains in Japan (Kato, 2006). Volunteering is not just seen at natural heritage properties of course and there is a long tradition at archaeological sites whether this is by members of the surrounding residential community (Tully, 2007; Appler, 2012; Goh, 2014) or by so-called voluntourists (Benson & Kaminski, 2013; Thomas & Lea, 2014; Möller, 2019).

Goh et al. (2019) argue that in the Malaysian context, developing community archaeology with a strong volunteer inputs represents a new opportunity for managing cultural heritage sites and that it should be fully embraced by site managers who previously had a tendency to ignore local community interests in such locations. This supports the view of Ripp & Rodwell (2018), who argue that good governance of heritage sites needs direct citizen 'participation, involvement, engagement and empowerment' (p. 241).

Again, this provides further evidence of the instrumental role that volunteering can play in both site management but also in broadening public engagement with the heritage, an argument made in the UK context by Lithgow & Timbrell (2014). They were speaking from the perspective of employees of the National Trust, the UK's largest (and wealthiest) conservation charity and one which, as noted earlier, has traditionally enjoyed the voluntary inputs of tens of thousands of individuals across England, Wales and Northern Ireland. Their argument is that volunteering shouldn't be seen as cheap labour, but rather as a tool to augment organisational capacity which in turn will enable the host organisation or site to deliver more outputs, within a shorter timeframe.

The instrumental purpose of volunteering is highlighted by UNESCO in the review of their WHVI suggests that: 'volunteering is an important component of any strategy aimed at poverty reduction, sustainable development and social integration, in particular overcoming social exclusion and discrimination' (UNESCO, 2020, p. 22).

There are of course criticisms of the increasing reliance on volunteer inputs by heritage managers. Alonso Gonzalez et al. (2018) argue that there is a 'new tyranny'[2] of participatory heritage as protected area managers are obliged to follow the discursive and technical requirements of external agencies such as UNESCO, ICOMOS and the EU, all of whom are keen to increase public involvement in protecting and managing heritage assets. In such instances, they argue that managers are obliged to pursue neoliberal forms of governance that alleviate state-created/ imposed financial scarcity under an artificial aura of 'democracy' and that increased public involvement in management activities is a fig-leaf covering structural deficiencies in how heritage conservation is funded (see also Kwiatkowski et al., 2020).

Similarly, the increasing commodification of volunteering opportunities at cultural and natural heritage sites is critiqued by Fredheim (2018) who suggests that such a neo-liberal approaches merely reinforce existing power structures across the sector. There are also criticisms of international volunteering (also referred to as voluntourism) where the predominant flow has mainly young, white volunteers travelling to the Global South (Wearing, 2001). Though originally seen by commentators like Wearing as an alternative, more acceptable form of tourism compared to either mass tourism or backpacking, voluntourism has increasingly been seen as being a contemporary form of colonialism where the benefits to host communities are limited, particularly when compared to the benefits for incoming participants (see for instance Guttentag & Wiley, 2009; Burrai et al., 2014; Burrai & Hannam, 2017; Germann Molz, 2017). In short, there is an argument that importing western specialists with conservation skills, IT skills and associated technology displaces the training and work opportunities for younger, local workers who could be encouraged to develop the traditional skills needed to conserve, in situ, archaeological remains (Meskell, 2018).

8.1.2.4 The World Heritage Volunteers Initiative

It is worthwhile reviewing the recent experience of UNESCO's own programme in the light of the above understanding of the strengths and weaknesses of volunteering at cultural and natural heritage properties. Developed as a tool for engaging younger people with World Heritage, UNESCO launched its World Heritage Volunteers Initiative (WHVI) in 2008 in partnership with the Co-ordinating Committee for International Voluntary Service (CCIVS). Every year since then, until 2020 when the global COVID-19 pandemic caused the temporary cessation of so many initiatives, organisations have submitted bids for funding to support local volunteering projects at World Heritage Site around the world. The WHV Initiative has two key goals: assisting with preservation activities at a property level and more broadly promoting awareness of World Heritage and the work of UNESCO. As indicated earlier, the first ten years saw more than 5,000 volunteers participate in nearly 350 programmes at 138 different World Heritage Sites and properties on State Parties' Tentative Lists.

A review of the programme carried out in 2020 (UNESCO, 2020) found that participants to benefit in two main areas:

- Developing personal skills and life competences such as communication skills, problem solving and increased cultural openness;
- Enhanced heritage knowledge, both in conceptual terms (understanding of World Heritage values) and practically in terms of technical conservation and management skills.

Furthermore, there are benefits to the host organisations in terms of enhanced capacity to deliver against management objectives (albeit time-restricted) and to host communities, in terms of economic benefit. Thus, the WHVI would appear to deliver all of the expected benefits to participants, in terms of personal outcomes.

However, despite the programme's stated goals of involving volunteers from host communities, particularly living in and around World Heritage Site in the global south, the practicalities of funding participation in the programme's Action Camps meant that 'the direction of the exchanges still largely reflect the global economic power imbalance, hindering the essential goals of reciprocity, active participation and solidarity that World Heritage promotes' (UNESCO, 2020, p. 20). In other words, comparatively wealthy young people from the West are disproportionately involved as participants in the programme because they have the means to pay for travel and the participation expenses (the programme's total annual budget is around US$1 million per annum). It appears that the programme's experience re-confirms the criticisms of international voluntourism by commentators such as Guttentag & Wiley, 2009; Burrai & Hannam, 2017; Banki & Schonell (2018) and Fredheim (2018), namely that it is effectively another manifestation of neo-liberal economic activity imposed on the Global South. The reality is that most of the people developing the aforementioned skills return to their home countries and hence any opportunity for a sustained growth in the capacity of people from the local area to contribute towards conservation and management activities at the World Heritage properties hosting these Action Camps is going to be limited.

8.1.2.5 What type of volunteering is appropriate at World Heritage Site?

Notwithstanding the obvious personal benefits to participants in the WHVI camps and the broader positive impacts reported by World Heritage Site managers, the programme highlights the broader concern about the apparent reliance on volunteer inputs by so many heritage sites around the world. In particular, we might ask whether volunteering at heritage sites should be supported, when it is in effect a neoliberal approach to tackling problems of long-standing underfunding in the public sector, which has the overwhelming responsibility for maintaining and managing cultural and natural heritage sites and particularly those of outstanding universal value. As Burrai & Hannam (2017) argue, 'as a result of growth in contemporary capitalism, everyday consumption practices are subject to change to satisfy new consumer's desires for a laudable focus on sustainability, ethics and social justice' (p. 91). As discussed earlier, volunteering at heritage sites has just become another manifestation of contemporary consumption offering what Burrai and Hannam call a 'veneer of respectability', whereby students, young professionals and enthusiastic amatuers provide a range of inputs designed to support management activities at the property. While the personal benefits of volunteering in any context to participants are well recorded, heritage managers seeking to recruit volunteers are not always aware of the 'moral landscape' within which they are operating. These moral landscapes, according to Burrai et al. (2017) are 'co-constructed through myrid assemblage components which are embedded in the connections and orderings between the global North and the global South' (p. 366).

International volunteering at heritage sites is thus yet another component of globalisation, and while on the face of it there is a positive outcome in terms of raising awareness of the universal value of world heritage, there is surely also the negative facet in that it helps mask the underfunding of heritage site management and as such is actually helping to perpetuate the inequalities that exist in many destinations. One can almost hear a Minister of Culture, or Finance, saying 'if tourists from the Global North are prepared to come and volunteer at our heritage properties, why should we invest scarce Treasury resources on those activities when there are other, more pressing needs in our society that need resolution and funding'.

Not withstanding the very valid reasons for questionning the colonial overtones of some volunteering initiatives, it appears that within the World Heritage sector at least, moves are being made to avoid the more negative impacts of international volunteering. In reality, the scarcity of resources for heritage conservation in most parts of the world, whether for natural sites or cultural properties, means that States Parties, individual property managers and other stakeholders will rarely overlook the opportunity to benefit from free labour. So perhaps Lithgow & Timbrell (2014) are right – the heritage sector can't do without volunteering, so we need to accept that and where there are concerns, address them so that host communities and the properties themselves continue to benefit alongside the altruists who give up their time and money to get involved.

8.4 Tourism

As indicated earlier, there is an argument that the brand power of World Heritage Site status is important in terms of generating civic pride and stimulating tourism. Although World Heritage designation is mainly based on preservation criteria, World Heritage Site status has implications for tourism by recognizing the value of preservation and conservation activities, by drawing attention to the site, by raising its profile and, as many destination managers hope, by stimulating demand, particularly for unknown or unexplored sites (Su & Wall, 2014). Indeed, there is an expectation by UNESCO that States Parties will actively mark (not necessarily market, however), properties as having World Heritage Site status. Thus, UNESCO is effectively promoting the concept of World Heritage as a branding exercise (Adie, 2019).

However, there is limited evidence that World Heritage Site status materially increases visitor numbers in most situations. So, while Jimura (2019) argues that 'tourism in many WHSs has developed further after designation' (p. 2) and that 'World Heritage status works as a strong brand in tourism marketing' (p. 2), other researchers contend that at best there is an 'announcement effect' – when there is a very short-term uplift in visitor numbers as inscription is confirmed and publicised (Ribaudo & Figini, 2017). In their work, VanBlarcom & Kayahan (2011) did not find any clear pattern in the trend of tourism demand after World Heritage Site listing and in more than half of the destinations they looked at, growth rates of tourism arrivals and overnight stays were lower in the five years after World Heritage Site listing than growth rates in the five years before the listing. And in some cases, they found that tourism actually declined in the destination despite World Heritage listing. Poria et al. (2013) suggest that World Heritage Site listing is most useful for little-known sites, for which the designation works as a 'quality brand' that might serve as a guarantee for a unique and valuable tourist experience for tourists while du Cros & McKercher (2015) suggest that 'places that are already popular will likely benefit even more, while remote or contested sites may generate few new visitors' (p. 64), adding that tourism at World Heritage Sites is governed more by a property's proximity to main visitor nodes and its fame and image prior to designation.

Ribaudo & Figini (2017) considered the case of 16 Italian World Heritage Sites and the impact of inscription on visitor numbers and found both negative and positive relationships, with further analysis suggesting that these relationships rarely are significant in statistical terms. Perhaps the final word on this topic should go to Adie (2019), who declares that 'the growing body of literature (suggests) that the World Heritage's brand influence may have been greatly overstated' (p. 41).

So, if the jury is out on whether there is a causal relationship between listing and tourism development, why are so many countries concerned to develop tourism at their World Heritage Sites in the first place? International tourism of all kinds, including trips based around visits to cultural heritage and/ or natural areas, can help a country's balance of payments (Timothy, 2021). And domestic tourism ensures that money is retained within the national economy and doesn't leak overseas. Spending by tourists and day excursionists helps support local businesses (and hence jobs) and also generates tax revenue for national and local government. Moreover, when destinations are developed for tourism, the investment in supporting infrastructure and services will generally also benefit the host population. Thus, using the World Heritage brand in markets that respond positively to it seems to be common sense. The case study below of the Blaenavon Industrial Landscape in Wales (inscribed 2000; see Plate 8.1) demonstrates how it can take considerable time and investment for tourism to develop at a World Heritage Site, particularly when the property has not formerly been established as a well-known tourism destination.

PLATE 8.1 Blaenavon Industrial Landscape, Wales – the location for a major effort to use 1209 World Heritage designation as a lever for community and economic regeneration.

Source: Photograph by Grace Sanderson.

BOX 8.1 CASE STUDY 8.1: BLAENAVON INDUSTRIAL LANDSCAPE, UK.

The property was inscribed on the list in 2000 against Criteria (iii) and (iv). The area, at the head of the Avon Llwyd valley in Torfaen, South Wales, represents an exemplar of the impact of more than two centuries of industrial activity on the landscape. The ironworks (established in 1789 and in operation until the 1930s) and the coal mine (operational until 1980) helped drive the preeminent role of South Wales as the world's major producer of iron and coal in the 19th century. Remains of all of the key elements of the industrial concerns can still be seen including coal and ore mines, furnaces, quarries, a tram and railway system as well as worker's homes and the social infrastructure of the community – schools, shops, chapels and the Workmen's Hall.

With the closure of the coal mine in 1980 came the realisation that alternative sources of employment were required and in 1983 it was reopened as a mining museum. However, its location on the fringes of the town of Blaenavon meant that few tourists went in to use the local services and thus a multi-agency partnership was established in 1997 to drive a coordinated approach to heritage-led regeneration (Walker, 2011). One of the first actions of the Blaenavon Partnership was to press for the area's nomination as a World Heritage Site because of its industrial legacy; and inscription was achieved quite promptly in 2000. From the outset, the intention was to use the World Heritage brand as a vehicle for attracting tourism to the area, even though it was acknowledged that the supply-side of the tourism value chain was, at that time, undeveloped (Jones & Munday, 2001) with the first management plan for the property specifically identifying economic decline in the area and public access to the industrial heritage sites as issues to be addressed (Landorf, 2009).

More than £6 million was spent on creating the National Coal Mining Museum for Wales on the colliery site which was re-branded as 'Big Pit', and a further £14 million was spent on other conservation works around the area. Many contracts were 'unbundled' so that small local businesses were able to compete for them, thus reducing leakages of this investment from the local economy. Overall, it was estimated that the investment of more than £20 million over the period 2001–2004 would support more than 100 full-time equivalent (FTE) jobs in the local area per annum and that once tourism associated with industrial heritage was established, around 150 FTE jobs would be created which, as Jones & Munday (2001) suggest, would comprise 'a significant employment impact for a relatively small and deprived locality' (p. 588).

However, despite the anticipated benefits from World Heritage designation, the second Management Plan for the site, prepared for the period 2011–2016, indicated that only 65 FTE jobs had been either safeguarded or created as a direct result of inscription and only ten new businesses had been created. This despite a 100% increase in annual visitor numbers to the town, from 100,000 to 200,000 per annum (Torfaen County Borough Council, 2011).

A few years after inscription the UK's first visitor interpretation centre dedicated to a World Heritage Site opened in the former St Peter's School in the town to present 'a coherent narrative of this tortured, post-industrial landscape' and to position 'the diverse aspects of the scientific advances and entrepreneurial history of the site firmly in the family and community stories of this South Wales powerhouse of the industrial revolution' (Ripp & Rodwell, 2016, p. 95). The focus on interpreting the story of the area in relationship to the lives of the generations who lived and worked there was a conscious attempt to embed the idea behind the nomination within the hearts and minds of the local community though there remained problems – for instance, the investment made in restoring historic shop fronts in the town was exploited by entrepreneurs from outside the area who moved in to open tourist-oriented outlets leaving local shops providing more mundane daily services isolated on the periphery of the main commercial area (Walker, 2011).

As part of a move to better understand the social and economic benefits of World Heritage inscription, consultants for the UK's Department of Culture, Media & Sport explored local residents attitudes towards, and experiences of, the inscription of Blaenavon on the World Heritage list (PricewaterhouseCoopers LLP, 2007). While the majority of residents believed there had been more investment in the area because of the World Heritage designation, two-thirds of respondents to the study would have liked to see more investment in new amenities and services rather than in conservation. Nonetheless, the overwhelming majority of respondents in Blaenavon recognised that designation had also led to an increase in visitor numbers overall and reported that it had increased their sense of local pride in their heritage, with around 25% confirming they had seen an increase in community involvement in supporting conservation and related activities. This ambivalence towards the benefits of inscription in terms of stimulating local economic regeneration was taken on board by the Partnership as it began to work on the second management plan for the World Heritage Site.

One move to overcome this lack of local engagement was the creation of the 'Forgotten Landscape' project, an interpretation initiative aimed particularly at younger adults to encourage them to recognise, learn about and help manage their own heritage landscapes in ways that aimed to stop the regression of the World Heritage Site as a 'theme park' (Knight, 2011). Indeed, a priority of the second Management Plan was to increase levels of community engagement across the World Heritage Site through a range of programmes including the 'Forgotten Landscape' initiative mentioned earlier, as well as through the work of a volunteer ranger service for the World Heritage Site which continues under the name Blaenavon World Heritage Environment Group – BWHEG (Torfaen County Borough Council, 2011). That same plan revealed proposals to reposition the presentation of the World Heritage Site as a 'gateway' to the wider industrial heritage of South Wales which was later formalised in a three-year project under the banner 'The Valleys that Changed the World'.

The third Management Plan, for the period 2018–2023, has sought to build on the successes of the previous two plans and identifies four broad priority areas:

- Enhancing the governance and management of the World Heritage Site, not least by tapping into new sources of funding and support from the Welsh Government;
- Continuing to care for the industrial landscape of Blaenavon;

- Investing in new opportunities for people to explore and enjoy the Blaenavon Industrial Landscape;
- Continuing to invest in encouraging community engagement with, and understanding of, the World Heritage Site.

What is evident is that much of the more recent investment in regeneration activities have been in townscape and infrastructure works that benefit primarily local residents, who have also been the sustained focus of engagement activities which appear designed to sustain their interest in, and support for, the World Heritage Site designation. The aforementioned BWHEG has a core of around 50 local volunteers on its books, of whom around 20 are very active, contributing hundreds of hours a year to a range of activities associated with the conservation and interpretation of the World Heritage Site including monitoring the condition of archaeological structures (carried out in partnership with Cadw – the national heritage organisation for Wales); habitat management on the upland areas including clearing invasive vegetation; recording and reporting wildlife sightings to appropriate conservation bodies; repairing drystone walls and running a programme of free guided walks covering a range of topics associated with the natural, cultural and industrial heritage of Blaenavon. Funding for the group comes partly from the local authority and the group is also represented on the management committee for the World Heritage Site, thus ensuring close alignment between its activities and the broader management objectives for the property thereby reflecting the ideal scenario for volunteer programmes at World Heritage Site as proposed by Kwiatkowski et al. (2020).

One of the issues to consider, therefore, is how actively the World Heritage brand is actually used to support destination marketing. This is important to consider because for many years, UNESCO did not attempt to build World Heritage Site status as a brand, but rather it left it to individual sites to build the World Heritage brand in their own way (Rodger, 2007).

World Heritage Site listed sites can be grouped into four clusters, according to VanBlarcom and Kayahan (2011):

- a celebration designation, for which World Heritage Site listing is seen as a reward for heritage already preserved (many of Europe's great cathedrals that were inscribed in the 1970s and 1980s might fall into this category);
- what they call a 'save our soul' designation, for which World Heritage Site listing is a sign of attention for unique heritage at risk (an example perhaps being the nomination and subsequent inscription of the **Palestine: Land of Olives and Vines – Cultural Landscape of Southern Jerusalem, Battir** site in 2014 which was also immediately placed on the list in danger);
- a branding initiative, for which World Heritage Site inscription is a marketing tool and quality brand to promote the development of tourism and the

territory (certainly the appeal of the World Heritage brand to Chinese tourists would be one reason why the Chinese government has been so keen to see so many properties – cultural and natural – entered on the list);

- a placemaking catalyst, for which World Heritage Site inscription is seen as a multiplier for economic development using heritage to trigger wider socio-economic impacts based on local culture and identity (cynics might argue that this was a strong reason behind the Saudi government pressing for the inclusion of the **Al-Ahsa Oasis, an Evolving Cultural Landscape** on the list in 2018).

In terms of how branding is actually used to promote World Heritage properties, Wuepper & Patry (2017) reviewed the cases of more than 700 locations with World Heritage status and found that rural sites tend to make more use of the World Heritage brand than do urban sites, not least because they seem to benefit more from the association in terms of increasing awareness and throughput. In general, Asian World Heritage Sites were found to be much better branded than those in the Middle East and in richer countries, and in destinations which already have a long-established international tourism sector. Highest levels of visibility of the brand were in Canada, Finland (Plate 8.2) and India with very low levels of visibility across much of Southern and West Africa and the MENA region. They also found that sites using the brand tended to be those with the best conservation state though they made no suggestions as to whether this is a causal relationship. However, common sense suggests that properties with more resources for conservation are likely to promote the World Heritage association in order to demonstrate to visitors and supporters why funding is need for ongoing management activities at the site.

PLATE 8.2 The World Heritage Site logo at The Fortress of Suomenlinna, Finland. Source: Photograph by Simon Woodward.

In terms of how important some World Heritage Sites are in attracting visitors in general, and international tourists in particular, we have collated information on visitor throughput for a range of properties around the world (Table 8.1). What is clear is that the domestic market is generally the most significant in terms of the volume of visitor activity at these properties.

8.5 Regeneration

As indicated at the start of this chapter, a major review carried out for the UK government of the benefits of World Heritage inscription found that many properties use the designation to support broader regeneration initiatives. That is, the

TABLE 8.1 Throughput of domestic and international tourists at selected cultural World Heritage Sites.

Property	Location	Domestic visitors	International tourists	Total	% international tourists	Date and source of data
Agra Fort	Agra, India	371,242	2,810	1,970,000	1%[1]	Government of India, 2022 (data is for 2021)
Borobudur Temples	Java, Indonesia	3,594,684	200,616	3,795,300	5%	Tourism Development International. 2019 (data is for 2017)
Qutb Minar	Delhi, India	2,650,000	304,830	2,954,830	10%	Government of India, 2019 (data is for 2018)
Red Fort	Delhi, India	3,430,000	140,200	3,570,200	4%	Government of India, 2019 (data is for 2018)
Taj Mahal	Agra, India	5,650,000	794,000	6,444,000	12%	Government of India, 2019 (data is for 2018)
Teotihuacan	State of Mexico, Mexico	2,760,000	700,000★	3,460,000	20%	Lopez, 2021 (data is for 2019)

Note: [1]This refers to the period when almost all international tourism to India had ceased because of travel restrictions associated with the global COVID-19 pandemic.

brand value of World Heritage status can be used to justify funding a broad range of planning and management interventions that will help to protect or even enhance the fabric of the property as well as deliver additional benefit to the local community and economy.

Urban regeneration is a process-led approach to tackling infrastructural, environmental, social and economic issues that are affecting the lives of residents in a specific area. One definition is provided by Roberts (2000) who suggests that successful urban regeneration should involve a

> comprehensive and integrated vision and action which leads to the resolution of urban problems and which seeks to bring about a lasting improvement in the economic, physical, social and environmental condition of an area that has been subject to change.
>
> *(p. 17)*

The use of built heritage and culture as a component of urban regeneration initiatives is well established in many parts of the world with sensitive conservation, adaptive re-use of historic buildings combining with new-build works and infrastructural improvements to deliver material changes to the living conditions of local people and often also enhancing the appeal of the location as a tourist destination (Miles & Paddison, 2007). As Orbasli (2008) states, 'tourism is an important means through which architectural heritage contributes to city economics and there has been an increasing realisation that cultural heritage can be a vehicle rather than a hindrance to urban regeneration' (p. 29). This is reflected in the work of Pineros (2017) who promotes the idea of a circle of investment that commences with spending on conservation/ preservation, which then stimulates what he calls the 'tourismification' of the destination and which, because of the profits that are to be made, brings in further funds for conservation as well as for the creation of heritage tourism products and experiences.

For regeneration initiatives to succeed, there are a number of factors to take into consideration. First, it must be seen as a long-term process and while there may be scope for delivering 'quick wins' in the short-term, for regeneration to be successful there will need to be a sustained investment in interventions over a considerable period of time (Roberts & Sykes, 2000). The **Historic Cairo** regeneration programme led by the Aga Khan Trust for Culture (AKTC) in partnership with the Governorate of Cairo and the Supreme Council of Antiquities (SCA), and with the direct participation of the area's residents, for instance, lasted for almost two decades and included investment in building rehabilitation works (especially in the Darb Al Ahmar neighbourhood), the excavation and restoration of stretches of the Ayyubid city wall, open space creation (the Al-Azhar Park), the restoration of various mosques and monuments as well as conservation training, micro-credit initiatives and the delivery of social services and education opportunities (Aga Khan Trust for Culture, 2005).

Second, it is essential that stakeholders from the public and private sectors are involved throughout along with community members themselves. Where the existing residents are marginalised or ignored altogether, there exists the potential for opposition and even unrest. Unfortunately, at times authorities overtly cause the displacement of communities living in areas 'ripe for regeneration' and at other times it happens as a result of the inflationary pressure on property prices (purchase or rent) associated with regeneration and gentrification. Examples of this experience include Brazil's **Historic Centre of Salvador de Bahia** World Heritage Site (Collins, 2008), the **Old Town of Lijiang** in China (Su, 2010), **Blaenavon** in the UK and **Cartagena de Indias in Colombia** (see Box 8.2 Case Study).

BOX 8.2 CASE STUDY 8.2: CARTAGENA DE INDIAS, COLOMBIA.

Cartagena de Indias, inscribed as **Port, Fortresses and Group of Monuments, Cartagena** in 1984 against Criteria (iv) and (vi), is located on the northern coast of Colombia and boasts one of the most complete systems of military fortifications in South America. Because of the city's strategic location, it became one of the most important ports of the Caribbean in the 16th, 17th and 18th centuries and, together with Havana and San Juan, Puerto Rico, an essential link in the trading routes between Central America, South America, the West Indies and Europe.

A network of fortifications surrounds the colonial walled city within which can be found civil, religious and residential monuments located within three neighbourhoods: Centro, the location of the Cathedral of Cartagena, most public buildings and the mansions of the gentry; San Diego (also known as Santo Toribio), where middle class merchants and craftsmen lived; and Getsemaní, the quarter once inhabited by the artisans and slaves whose work fuelled the economic activity of the city.

The renovation of colonial mansions in the heart of the old town of Cartagena commenced in the late 1970s and was led by private individuals who purchased and restored dilapidated colonial mansions for use as vacation/holiday properties. Interest in the destination grew after its inclusion on the World Heritage list in 1984 and by early 1990s the municipality became actively involved in funding renovation works to public buildings. Concern has been expressed that there was undue emphasis on technical aspects of regeneration (i.e. conservation of buildings) rather than on preserving social and intangible heritage and that the inevitable influx of international capital once a tipping point had been reached meant that the demographics of the old town were irreversibly changed (Pineros, 2017). As such, it represents a classic case of the replacement of a resident community of relatively low socio-economic standing, not by a returning gentry but by heritage tourists seeking an 'authentic' colonial experience though one with all mod cons and international branded retail and hospitality opportunities.

Çağlar & Schiller (2018) discuss the case of **Mardin**, a hilltop town in southwest Anatolia which was added to the Turkish state's Tentative List in 2000 and which saw considerable investment in conservation works, new tourism infrastructure and destination branding initiatives during decade or so afterwards. Two attempts at nomination commenced but were subsequently withdrawn (in 2002 and 2015) as the municipality and other stakeholders sought to recreate the old city as it looked at the start of the 20th century, including the restoration of a number of churches associated with Mardin's Syriac Christian community (at times a controversial project in itself because of Turkey's status as a Muslim nation). However, one by-product of this regeneration process, which was designed not least to support the World Heritage nomination, has been the removal of the traditional residents from the old town to alternative accommodation in other parts of the city and associated resentment, not least because the promised benefits of World Heritage inscription have still not been achieved (Çağlar & Schiller, 2018).

And finally, any regeneration initiative based around cultural properties should not only tackle the relatively 'easy' task of building new structures, refurbishing the old and cleaning up the physical environment (including providing new public spaces). It must also embrace the challenge of creating jobs and strengthening the local economy, as was the case in the very successful AKTC initiative in the Darb Al-Ahmar area of historic Cairo (Aga Khan Trust for Culture, 2001).

8.6 Concluding remarks

In this chapter we have sought to explore some of the principal ways how World Heritage Site status can be used to lever economic and community benefits post-inscription. We have noted that there is undoubtedly evidence that local pride in properties inscribed on the list can be enhanced through inscription, and that volunteering activities at sites can stimulate a greater awareness of a property's OUV and of the broader concept of World Heritage. Moreover, the contribution of time and skills can also provide much needed support for ongoing management activities at properties. Using World Heritage status as a tool to support broader community regeneration activities by attracting funding for conservation works, and at the same time using the brand to attract tourists, is an increasingly common phenomenon with examples ranging from Blaenavon in the UK, to Fatamid Cairo in Egypt and Cartagena de Indias in Colombia. Success is not always guaranteed, however, not least because there is conflicting evidence as to whether or not the World Heritage brand is sufficiently well known in many tourism markets and even where it is recognised, whether or not it is the primary factor motivating visits by either domestic or international tourists. Yet there remains a strong movement to share and celebrate properties that have acquired World Heritage Site status with a broad range of audiences, and in Chapter 10 we explore how properties around the world present and interpret their heritage values.

Notes

1 Its full name is The National Trust for Places of Historic Interest or Natural Beauty. There is a separately constituted National Trust for Scotland, meaning the organisation usually known as the National Trust covers only England, Wales and Northern Ireland.
2 Citing Cooke & Kothari (2007).

References

Adie, B. A. 2019. *World Heritage and Tourism*. Abingdon: Routledge.

Aga Khan Trust for Culture. 2001. *Historic Cities Support Programme. The Azhar Park Project in Cairo and the Conservation and Rehabilitation of Darb Al-Ahmar*. Geneva: Aga Khan Trust for Culture.

Aga Khan Trust for Culture. 2005. *Cairo: Urban Regeneration in the Darb Al-Ahmar District. A Framework for Investment*. Historic Cities Support Programme. Geneva: Aga Khan Trust for Culture.

Ali, J. N. & Rahman, A. 2019. Why do people opt for voluntourism in Bangladesh? An exploratory study. *Journal of Tourism Quarterly*, 1 (1–2), 53–65.

Alonso Gonzalez, P., Gonzalez-Alvarez, D. & Roura-Exposito, J. 2018. ParticiPat: exploring the impact of participatory governance in the heritage field. *PoLAR: Political and LEgal Anthropology Review*, 41 (2), 306–318.

Anderson, L. G., Chapman, J. K., Escontrela, D. & Gough, C. L. A. 2017. The role of conservation volunteers in the detection, monitoring and management of invasive alien lionfish. *Management of Biological Invasions*, 8 (4), 589–598.

Appler, D. R. 2012. Municipal archaeology programs and the creation of community amenities. *The Public Historian*, 34 (3), 40–67.

Bandyopadhyay, R. & Patil, V. 2017. 'The white woman's burden' – the racialized, gendered politics of volunteer tourism. *Tourism Geographies*, 19 (4), 644–657.

Banki, S. & Schonell, R. 2018. Voluntourism and the contract corrective. *Third World Quarterly*, 39 (8), 1475–1490.

Benson, A. M. & Kaminski, J. 2013. Volunteering and cultural heritage tourism. Home and away. In: J. Kaminski, A. M. Benson & D. Arnold, eds. *Contemporary Issues in Cultural Heritage Tourism*. Abingdon: Routledge, 303–318.

Buckley, R. 2004. The effects of world heritage listing on tourism to Australian national parks. *Journal of Sustainable Tourism*, 12 (1), 70–84.

Burrai, E., Font, X. & Cochrane, J. 2014. Destination stakeholders' perceptions of volunteer tourism: an equity theory approach. *International Journal of Tourism Research*, 17 (5), 451–459.

Burrai, E. & Hannam, K. 2017. Challenging the responsibility of 'responsible volunteer tourism'. *Journal of Policy Research in Tourism, Leisure and Events*, 10 (1), 90–95.

Çağlar, A. & Schiller, N. G. 2018. *Migrants and City Making. Disposession, Displacement and Urban Regeneration*. Durham, NC: Duke University Press.

Chavis, D. M. & Lee, K. 2015. What is community anyway? *Stanford Social Innovation Review*, 12 May. https://ssir.org/articles/entry/what_is_community_anyway(accessed 17 April 2020).

Chinman, M. & Wandersman, A. 1999. The Benefits and Costs of Volunteering in Community Organizations: Review and Practical Implications. *Nonprofit and Voluntary Sector Quarterly*, 28 (1), 46–64.

Collins, J. 2008. 'But what if I should need to defecate in your neighbourhood, madame?': empire, redemption, and the 'Tradition of the Oppressed' in a Brazilian World Heritage Site. *Cultural Anthropology*, 23 (2), 279–328.

Conway, F. 2014. Local and public heritage at a World Heritage site. *Annals of Tourism Research*, 44, 143–155.

Cooke, B. & Kothari, U. 2007. *Participation: The New Tyranny*. London: Zed Books.

Dearden, P., Bennett, M. & Johnston, J. 2002. Trends in global protected area governance, 1992–2002. *Environmental Management*, 36 (1), 89–100.

du Cros, H. & McKercher, B. 2015. *Cultural Tourism*. 2nd ed. Abingdon: Routledge.

Evans, G. 2002. Living in a World Heritage City: stakeholders in the dialectic of the universal and particular. *International Journal of Heritage Studies*, 8 (2), 117–135.

Foller-Carroll, A. & Charlebois, S. 2016. The attitudes of students and young professionals toward voluntourism: a study abroad perspective. *International Journal of Culture, Tourism and Hospitality Research*, 10 (2), 138–160.

Fredheim, L. H. 2018. Endangerment-driven heritage volunteering: democratisation or 'Changeless Change'. *International Journal of Heritage Studies*, 24 (6), 619–633.

Fulcher, H. 1989. *The Concept of Communities of Interest. A Discussion Paper which Explores the Concept of Community of Interest as it Applies to Local Government Boundaries*, Adelaide: S.A. Department of Local Government.

Germann Molz, J. 2017. Giving back, doing good, feeling global: the affective flows of family voluntourism. *Journal of Contemporary Ethnography*, 46 (3), 334–360.

Goh, H. M. 2014. Cave Archaeology of Lenggong Valley: A Heritage Management Perspective. PhD thesis, Flinders University of South Australia.

Goh, H. M., Saw, C. Y., Shahidan, S., Saidin, M. & Curnoe, D. 2019. Community heritage engagement in Malaysian archaeology: a case from the prehistoric rock art site of Tambun. *Journal of Community Archaeology & Heritage*, 6 (2), 110–121.

Government of India, 2019, *India Tourism Statistics 2018*, Delhi, Government of India, Ministry of Tourism. Market Research Division.

Government of India, 2022, *India Tourism Statistics 2021*, Delhi, Government of India, Ministry of Tourism. Market Research Division.

Graham, B., Ashworth, G. J. & Tunbridge, J. E. 2000. *A Geography of Heritage: Power, Culture and Economy*. London: Arnold Publishers.

Guiney, H. & Machado, L. 2018. Volunteering in the community: potential benefits for cognitive aging. *The Journals of Gerontology: Series B*, 73 (3), 399–408. doi:10.1093/geronb/gbx134.

Guttentag, D. A. & Wiley, J. 2009. The possible negative impacts of volunteer tourism. *International Journal of Tourism Research*, 11 (6), 537–551.

Haanpaa, R., Puolamaki, L. & Karhunen, E. 2019. Local conservation and perceptions of heritage in Old Rauma World Heritage Site. *International Journal of Heritage Studies*, 25 (8), 837–855.

Harrison, R., ed. 2010. *Understanding the Politics of Heritage*. Manchester: Manchester University Press.

Hodder, I. 2003. Social thought and commentary: archaeological reflexivity and the 'local' voice. *Anthropological Quarterly*, 79 (1), 55–69.

Huang, C.-H., Tsaur, J.-R. & Yang, C.-H. 2012. Does world heritage list really induce more tourists? Evidence from Macau. *Tourism Management*, 33, 1450–1547.

IIPFWH. n.d. *Indigenous Peoples Involvement in World Heritage*. https://iipfwh.org/indigenous-involvement-in-world-heritage/ (accessed 28 April 2021).

Jimura, T. 2019. *World Heritage Sites. Tourism, Local Communities and Conservation Activities*. Wallingford: CABI.

Jones, C. & Munday, M. 2001. Blaenavon and United Nations World Heritage Site status: is conservation of industrial heritage a road to local economic development?. *Regional Studies*, 35 (6), 585–590.

Jones, T. E., Yang, Y. & Yamamoto, K. 2017. Assessing the recreational value of world heritage site inscription: A longitudinal travel cost analysis of Mount Fuji climbers. *Tourism Management*, 60, 67–78.

Kato, K. 2006. Community, connection and conservation: intangible cultural values in natural heritage – the case of Shirakami-sanchi World Heritage Area. *International Journal of Heritage Studies*, 12 (5), 458–473.

Knight, E. 2011. The 'forgotten landscapes' conservation, heritage management and lifelong learning in the communty. *Tourism & Management Studies*, 1, 106–113.

Kwiatkowski, G., Hjalager, A.-M., Liburd, J. & Simonsen, P. S. 2020. Volunteering and collaborative governance innovation in the Wadden Sea National Park. *Current Issues in Tourism*, 23 (8), 971–989.

Landorf, C. 2009. Managing for sustainable tourism: a review of six culturalWorld Heritge sites. *Journal of Sustainable Tourism*, 17 (1), 53–70.

Lithgow, K. & Timbrell, H. 2014. How better volunteering can improve conservation: why we need to stop wondering whether volunteering in conservation is a good thing and just get better at doing it well. *Journal of the Institute of Conservation*, 37 (1), 3–14.

Lopez, A. 2021. Number of visitors to the archeological site of Teotihuacán, Mexico from 2009 to 2020. https://www-statista-com/statistics/1052828/teotihuacan-archaeological-site-visitors/ (6 July 2022).

Lwoga, N. B. 2018. Dilemma of local socio-economic perspectives in management of historic ruins in Kilwa Kisiwani World Heritage Site, Tanzania. *International Journal of Heritage Studies*, 24 (10) 1019–1037.

McKnight, M. L., Sanders, S. R., Gibbs, B. G. & Brown, R. B. 2017. Communities of place? New evidence for the role of distance and population size in community attachment. *Rural Sociology*, 82 (2), 291–317.

Meskell, L. 2018. *A Future in Ruins. UNESCO, World Heritage, and the Dream of Peace*. New York: Oxford University Press.

Miles, S. & Paddison, R. 2007. *Culture Led Regeneration*. Abingdon: Routledge.

Möller, K. 2019. Archaeologist for a week: voluntourism in archaeology. In: *Feasible Management of Archaeological Heritage Sites Open to Tourism*. Cham, Switzlerand: Springer, 105–114.

Moser, S., Glazier, D., Phillips, J., Nemr, L., Mousa, M. et al. 2002. Transforming archaeology through practice: strategies for collaborative archaeology and the Community Archaeology Project at Quseir, Egypt. *World Archaeology*, 34 (2), 220–248.

National Trust. 2020. Our spending cut plans in response to coronvirus losses. https://www.nationaltrust.org.uk/news/our-spending-cut-plans-in-response-to-coronavirus-losses (29 April 2021).

National Trust. 2022. Volunteer. https://www.nationaltrust.org.uk/volunteer (6 July 2022).

Noor, S. M., Rasoolimanesh, B. M., Jaafar, M. & Barghi, R. 2019. Inscription of a destination as a World Heritage Site and resident perception. *Asia Pacific Journal of Tourism Reearch*, 24 (1), 14–30.

Okech, R. N. 2010. Socio-cultural impacts of tourism on World Heritage sites: communities' perspective of Lamu (Kenya) and Zanzibar Islands. *Asia Pacific Journal of Tourism Research*, 15 (3), 339–351.

Orbasli, A. 2008. *Architectural Conservation*. Oxford: Blackwell Science Ltd.

Pak, V. & Hiramoto, M. 2020. 'Itching to make an impact': constructing the mobile Singaporean voluntouristm in Instagram travel narratives. *Social Semiotics*, 1–23. doi:10.1080/10350330.2020.1766263.

Pan, T. J. 2017. Personal transformation through volunteer tourism: the evidence of Asian students. *Journal of Hospitality & Tourism Research*, 41 (5), 609–634.

Pineros, S. T. 2017. Tourism gentrification in the cities of Latin America. The socio-economic trajectory of Cartagena de Indias, Colombia. In: M. Gravari-Barbas & S. Guinard, eds. *Tourism and Gentrification in Contemporary Metropolises. International Perspectives.* Abingdon: Routledge, 75–104.

Poria, Y., Reichel, A. & Cohen, R. 2013. Tourist perceptions of World Heritage sites and its designation. *Tourism Management*, 35, 272–274.

PricewaterhouseCoopers LLP, 2007. *The Costs and Benefits of World Heritage Site Status in the UK. Prepared for the Department for Culture, Media and Sport, Cadw and Historic Scotland.* London: PWC.

Reimann, L., Vafeidis, A. L., Brown, S., Hinkel, J. &Tol, R. S. J. 2018. Mediterranean UNESCO World Heritage at risk from coastal flooding and erosion due to sea-level rise. *Nature Communications*, 9, article 4161.

Ribaudo, G. & Figini, P. 2017. The puzzle of tourism demand at destinations hosting UNESCO World Heritage Sites: an analysis of tourism flows for Italy. *Journal of Travel Research*, 56 (4), 521–542.

Ripp, M. & Rodwell, D. 2016. The governance of urban heritage. *The Historic Environment: Policy & Practice*, 7 (1), 81–108.

Ripp, M. & Rodwell, D. 2018. Governance in UNESCO World Heritage sites: reframing the role of management plans as a tool to improve community engagement. In: S. Makavuza, ed. *Aspects of Management Planning for Cultural World Heritage Sites.* Cham, Switzerland: Springer, 241–283.

Roberts, P. 2000. The evolution, definition and purpose of urban regeneration. In: P. Roberts & H. Sykes, eds. *Urban Regeneration. A Handbook.* London: Sage Publications Ltd, 9–36.

Roberts, P. & Sykes, H. 2000. Current challenges and future prospects. In: P. Roberts & H. Sykes, eds. *Urban Regeneration. A Handbook.* London: Sage Publications Ltd, 295–316.

Rodger, J. 2007. *World Heritage Site Branding – The Blaenavon Experience.* Oxford: Archaeopress, 13–16.

Roques, K. G., Jacobsen, S. K. & McCleery, R. A. 2018. Assessing contributions of volunteer tourism to ecosystem research and conservation in southern Africa. *Ecosystem Services*, 30, 382–390.

Schneller, A. J. and Coburn, S. 2018. For-profit environmental voluntourism in Costa Rica: teen volunteer, host community, and environmental outcomes. *Journal of Sustainable Tourism*, 26 (5), 832–851.

Smith, L. & Waterton, E. 2009. *Heritage, Communities and Archaeology.* London: Duckworth.

Su, M. M. & Wall, G. 2014. Community participation in tourism at a world heritage site: Mutianyu Great Wall, Beijing, China. *International Journal of Tourism Research*, 16 (2), 146–156.

Su, X. 2010. Urban conservation in Lijiang, China. Power structure and funding systems. *Cities*, 27, 164–171.

Su, Y. W. & Lin, H.-L. 2014. Analysis of international tourist arrivals worldwide: the role of World Heritage sites. *Tourism Management*, 40, 46–58.

Thomas, S. & Lea, J. 2014. *Public Participation in Archaeology 15.* Woodbridge, Suffolk: Boydell & Brewer Ltd.

Torfaen County Borough Council. 2011. *Blaenavon Industrial Landscape World Heritage Site Management Plan 2011–2016,* Pontypool: Torfaen County Borough Council. Timothy, D. J. 2021. *Cultural Heritage and Tourism. An Introduction.* 2nd ed. Bristol: Channel View Publications.

Tourism Development International. 2019. *Integrated Tourism Master Plan for Borobudur – Yogyakarta – Prambanan. Visitor Management Plan for Borobudur Temple Compounds World Heritage Site.* Dublin: TDI.

Trau, A. M. 2015. Challenges and dilemmas of international development volunteering: a case study from Vanuatu. *Development in Practice*, 25 (1), 29–41.

Tully, G. 2007. Community archaeology: general methods and standards of practice. *Public Archaeology*, 6 (3), 155–187.

UNESCO. 2019. A new network of young cultural heritage professionals emerges from a UNESCO/EU project. https://whc.unesco.org/en/events/1489/ (accessed 4 February 2022).

UNESCO. 2020. *Empowering Youth for Heritage – 10 Years of the World Heritage Volunteers Initiative.* Paris: UNESCO.

UNESCO. 2021. Young Professionals Forum 2021. https://whc.unesco.org/en/whyp f2021/ (6 July 2022).

UNESCO. 2022. World Heritage Volunteers Initiative. http://whc.unesco.org/en/whvo lunteers/ (accessed 8 February 2022).

UNESCO. n.d. World Heritage Education Programme. http://whc.unesco.org/en/whe ducation/ (accessed 4 February 2022).

UN General Assembly. 2015. *Promotion and Protection of the Rights of Indigenous Peoples with Respect to Their Cultural Heritage. Study by the Expert Mechanism on the Rights of Indigenous Peoples. A/HRC/30/53.* New York: United Nations.

UN Permanent Forum on Indigenous Peoples. n.d. United Nations Department of Economic and Social Affairs. https://www.un.org/development/desa/indigenouspeoples/ (accessed 8 February 2022).

VanBlarcom, B. L. and Kayahan, C. 2011. Assessing the economic impact of a UNESCO World Heritage designation. *Journal of Heritage Tourism*, 6 (2), 143–164.

Vindolanda Charitable Trust. n.d. History of the Trust. https://www.vindolanda.com/his tory-of-the-trust (accessed 27 April 2021).

Walker, D. 2011. Towards a beneficial World Heritage: community involvement in the Blaenavon Industrial Landscape. *Museum International*, 631 (1–2), 25–33.

Wearing, S. 2001. *Volunteer Tourism: Experiences that Make a Difference.* New York: CABI Publishing.

Wearing, S. & McGehee, N. 2013. Volunteer tourism: a review. *Tourism Management*, 38, 120–130.

Wilson, J., Mantovan, N. & Sauer, R. M. 2020. The economic benefits for volunteering and social class. *Social Science Research*, 85. doi:10.1016/j.ssresearch.2019.102368.

Wuepper, D. & Patry, M. 2017. The World Heritage list: which sites promote the brand? A big data spatial econometrics approach. *Journal of Cultural Economics*, 41, 1–21.

Yang, C.-H., Lin, H.-L. & Han, C.-C. 2010. Analysis of international tourist arrivals in China: the role of World Heritage Sites. *Tourism Management*, 31, 827–837.

9

MANAGING TOURISM PRESSURES AT WHS

9.1 Introduction

As indicated in Chapter 8, the tourism potential of inscription is often presented as one of the reasons that sites are nominated for inclusion on the World Heritage List. While the impacts of tourism and visitor activity on cultural and natural World Heritage Sites are not specific to only those properties inscribed on the list, where they compromise the Outstanding Universal Value of the property it is conventionally assumed that they require particular attention. It is important to note, however, that of the 52 properties on the List in Danger, only one is currently threatened by potential tourism development: Mexico's **Islands and Protected Areas of the Gulf of California** (inscribed 2005 and added to the List in Danger in 2019). Tourism is currently only mentioned in one other entry, the **Selous Game Reserve** in Tanzania (inscribed 1982 and added to the List in Danger in 2014), where responsibly-managed photographic tourism and hunting are seen as positive factors, generating income for investing in wider conservation projects – in other words, tourism is seen as part of the solution rather than part of the problem!

A summary of the main factors causing properties to be added to the List in Danger is provided in Table 9.1, to show that it is broader issues such as development pressures associated with economic and population growth and a lack of investment in management planning and conservation on the ground that are the key reasons for sites being included in this category.

Inevitably, the scale and nature of impacts associated with anthropogenic activity varies considerably according to levels of visitation, the nature of the property in question and the tools and resources available for managing the site. It is a condition of WHS inscription that in order to mitigate against any threats to a property's OUV, that proper state of conservation reports and management plans are prepared

DOI: 10.4324/9781003044857-10

TABLE 9.1 Reasons for inscription on the List in Danger (52 properties in late 2021).

Issue discussed in UNESCO documentation	Number of sites impacted	% of all properties impacted
Lack of conservation planning	16	31%
Agricultural intrusion, illegal logging	15	29%
Physical processes (including climate change)	14	27%
Development pressures	12	23%
Poaching	11	21%
Military action	7	13%
Vandalism, looting	5	10%
Mining/ mineral extraction	5	10%
Fire	1	2%
Invasive Alien Species	1	2%
Political instability	1	2%
Tourism	1	2%

Source: https://whc.unesco.org/en/danger/ Additional analysis by the authors.

for individual properties. However, in practice this doesn't always happen because of competing demands on management time and resources.

Until the global COVID-19 pandemic of 2020–2022, several WHS sites were experiencing so-called overtourism, where the very weight of visitor numbers across large parts of the year was creating problems for residents living in and around World Heritage Sites. UNWTO considers overtourism to be a situation where the number of visitors in a particular destination creates significant negative outcomes for the quality of life for local residents, and on the experience of tourists in that place. At times both residents and visitors will feel these issues simultaneously (UNWTO, 2018).

Overtourism is evidenced in a number of ways (Milano et al., 2019) including: congestion in tourist hot-spots throughout the year, or at least at peak periods; the replacement of residential accommodation with short-term lets (e.g. Airbnb); the loss of local retail units to businesses catering only for tourists; and the dispersal of tourist activity into areas previously unused to receiving tourists in large numbers and where their presence disturbs normal day-to-day activities (as has been the case at Barcelona's Crypt of the Colònia Güell, for instance). Prior to the pandemic, problems were reported in major European urban destinations such as Amsterdam, Barcelona, Edinburgh, Krakow and Venice – all of whose city centres are on the World Heritage list (apart from Barcelona, where seven Gaudi-designed buildings and structures across the city form the serial inscription '**The Works of Antoni Gaudi**'). But many other World Heritage Sites experience some of these same problems, particularly congestion – witness for instance the long queues to enter the **Church of the Nativity in Bethlehem** (MOTA, 2019) or the lines of tourists climbing up to certain iconic viewpoints in the **Historic Sanctuary of Machu Picchu** in Peru (Larson & Poudyal, 2012).

Thus, understanding how to manage these pressures by pre-empting them where possible, and mitigating against the damage they cause, is a key requirement for all stakeholders involved in managing cultural and natural heritage properties that attract tourists in significant numbers. This will be even more significant as international tourism begins to build back after the COVID-19 pandemic, since there is evidence that many people in the Global North have re-evaluated their travel aspirations in light of the pandemic and the impact it has had on people's perceptions of their own mortality, and are now more determined than ever to visit 'bucket-list' destinations, many of which are likely to be World Heritage Sites (UNWTO, 2021).

In this chapter we first consider some of the main impacts associated with visitor activity at natural and cultural heritage sites, presenting examples of the problems from a wide spread of properties around the world. We also review in some detail some of the issues associated with tourism in historic towns and cities, where the potential for conflict with local residents can become particularly marked. There is obviously some overlap between the types of anthropogenic problems found at cultural and natural heritage sites, particularly where these are associated with improper visitor behaviour (e.g. littering, vandalism, theft of materials) though the onsite approaches used to deal with them may be different. However, the overall strategies available for managing visitation are common to all types of landscape or destination and some of the main conceptual approaches are considered in the second part of this chapter along with an overview of how property managers reconcile all of these issues in visitor management plans.

9.2 Visitor impacts on natural heritage sites

9.2.1 Introduction

Whether tourist activity is restricted to the buffer-zones or extreme margins of natural heritage properties or whether visitor access is possible throughout the whole area, there will inevitably be impacts on the ecosystem, deliberate or accidental. Some of these issues are the same as experienced at cultural heritage properties (e.g. littering, erosion on unsurfaced pathways) but there are other impacts that, if unchecked, can compromise the ecological integrity of the property (Newsome et al., 2005). These impacts become even more significant if they affect the outstanding universal values which support the site's inscription on the WH list. Some of the key issues associated with anthropogenic activity at natural heritage sites discussed below are pollution (particularly of watercourses), damage to vegetation (intentional or unintentional), acting as vectors for the spread of invasive vegetation, and disturbance to wildlife.

It should be noted that different ecosystems, species and landscape types have different levels of resilience to disturbance and this will be a key determinant of how site managers plan for and manage access. Strategies available to managers include concentrating or dispersing activity both spatially and temporally, restricting group size, managing modes of access (e.g. vehicular, ambulatory) and banning certain activities completely (Newsome et al., 2002; Pedersen, 2002) with the primary objective always being to deliver a satisfying visitor experience within the context of sustainable resource usage (Wolf et al., 2019).

9.2.2 Pollution and littering

Pollution associated with tourist activity at natural heritage sites is generally associated with the same practices as those found at cultural properties – careless behaviour by visitors and/or tour operators and/or deliberate discharges into the environment. Here we focus briefly on terrestrial ecosystems - pollution of the marine environment is discussed elsewhere.

Localised problems of fouling associated with urination and defecation in the wild can affect watercourses in many types of environment, possibly leading to eutrophication, as well as affecting the sensory and visual aesthetics of the visitor experience (Hendee et al., 1990). Managing this problem requires educating the visiting public of the implications of their behaviour.

Air pollution from vehicle engines bringing tourists to natural heritage sites can influence the quality of soil and water bodies by polluting precipitation and falling into water and soil environments, with detrimental effects on flora and fauna (Manisalidis et al., 2020). Of particular concern is the release of mercury (Hg) into the atmosphere from vehicle exhausts, from where it contaminates soils and water bodies, is taken up by vegetation and enters the food chain, with predators like the American Bald Eagle (*Haliaeetus leucocephalus*) being susceptible to mercury poisoning if exposed to contaminated prey over a long period of time (though of course this is associated with anthropogenic factors in general and not just tourism activity in an area (Sullivan, 2017)). The American Bald Eagle is found in several North American natural WHS, though protection of its habitat is not the primary purpose of those sites with protected area status and that are inscribed on the WH list.

Pollution from a range of tourism-related sources was identified as a problem more than two decades ago by Goodwin et al., (1998) in and around the main visitation zones in **Komodo National Park,** Indonesia (inscribed 1991). The authors argued that, when combined with overcrowding, this so-called 'point pollution' was diminishing the overall visitor experience. Despite the transfer of management responsibilities for the park from 2005 to 2010 to a joint public–private sector initiative, the Komodo Collaborative Management Initiative (KCMI), which was designed to deliver a more sustainable approach to managing dragon tourism on the island, these issues were not totally resolved because of institutional weaknesses and conflicts over the deployment of resources (Cochrane, 2013). Concerns over pollution associated with developing ecotourism in many parts of Indonesia (four of whose nine WHS are natural properties) remain a concern because of the paucity of resources at local or municipality level to effectively manage waste disposal (Westoby et al., 2021).

Another point to consider is the visual and noise pollution associated with motorised traffic in particular. Research carried out in England's **Lake District** (inscribed 2017) found that this was often perceived to intrude on the quality of the visitor experience, particularly in more open and 'wilder' landscapes (though there is of course an irony in that millions of visitors to that particular World Heritage Site do travel there by car or coach) (Guiver & Stanford, 2014).

In terms of littering, the presence of anthropogenic waste in natural areas can create challenges for wildlife. Small pieces of plastic waste are often mistaken as food, and are ingested with deleterious effects on health. There is evidence that in the marine environment alone, more than 1,400 different species have been affected in this way (Fossi et al., 2018). Birds sometimes use debris for nesting materials and there is evidence that discarded fishing nets can create problems if bird's feet get caught in it (Ryan, 2018). The recent COVID-19 pandemic has led to the widespread littering of Personal Protective Equipment (PPE) items across the globe, and already there are problems reported of ingestion, entanglement and entrapment leading to injury and death of birds, mammals and marine life (Hiemstra et al., 2021).

9.2.3 Damage to vegetation

Trampling by walkers or damage by vehicle tyres can be a problem in any environment. Generally, fertile soils are better able to withstand human use and maintain vegetation whereas thinner and less fertile soils are less able to withstand heavy use. Damage through trampling is often worst at sites of concentrated use (e.g. scenic outlooks and along trails) (Newsome et al., 2002). Compaction of soils through repeated trampling reduces soil pore space and hence the potential for water to infiltrate the soil, creating problems of gullying in periods of heavy rain and the loss of surface soils, exposing root systems and compromising still further the extent and quality of vegetation cover at the local level with knock on effects on dependent fauna. Soil compaction (and the associated environmental impacts on plant communities and associated fauna) is particularly severe where caused by off-road vehicle usage (Newsome et al., 2002). Fire and the subsequent loss of vegetation cover can be associated with deliberate fire-setting or with neglected campfires, cooking stoves, or barbeques and is always a risk, particularly in drier habitats and/ or in times of drought.

Different plant species have different levels of resistance to trampling (Liddle, 1997). In upland areas where there is little ground cover apart from lichens there are particular challenges as these have been found to have low resistance to trampling and tend to grow back very slowly (Bayfield, 1979). As such, in fragile mountain and tundra areas, it is desirable to have very low levels of trekking/ hiking so that vegetation has time to recover (Monz, 2002). When a destination becomes popular for hiking and wild camping, as has happened in the last two decades or two in Iceland for instance (including around the **Vatnajökull National Park** which was inscribed on the list in 2019), levels of vegetation loss and erosion have been found to a function of both altitude and gradient as well as overall levels of use (Olafsdottir & Runnstrom, 2013).

Thus, planning of trails and subsequent management becomes vital to protect the environment from unnecessary or excessive damage. This has implications for managing future tourist access into remote World Heritage sites such as Sweden's **Laponian**

Area (a cultural landscape, inscribed in 1996) or Russia's **Putorana Plateau** (inscribed 2010) though in both instances large reindeer populations may actually create more ecological damage than low-key tourism activity (Eskilinen & Oskanen, 2006).

Similar problems arise in other environments as well, such as the **Stirling Range and Fitzgerald River National Parks** in Western Australia where at certain times of the year large numbers of people arrive to view the wildflower blooms and trample vegetation to get closer to the most scenic parts of the landscape (Mason et al., 2015). On the other side of the Australian continent in the **Wet Tropics of Queensland** WH area (inscribed 1988), mountain bikers have been found to create higher levels of erosion than do hikers (Pickering & Hill, 2007). And similar problems of erosion and habitat damage have been found along the length of the Andes in South America (which contain several WH areas) and even on the cliff tops of the **Jurassic Coast** World Heritage Site in Dorset, England (Barros et al., 2015; May, 2015).

9.2.4 Spreading alien species

Biological invasion, or the deliberate or accidental introduction of invasive alien species (IAS), is a problem that affects a large number of natural World Heritage properties. Recent research suggests that more than half of all natural and mixed WH sites suffer from IAS and that there are more than 300 different species involved (flora and fauna) (Shackleton et al., 2020). Biological invasions often lead to negative impacts on native biodiversity, landscapes and ecosystem services as they lead to the decline or extinction of native species through processes such as predation, disease, competition and hybridisation. Human experience of the affected area can also change, particularly where indigenous communities have their traditional lifestyles impacted (Shackleton et al., 2019).

South Africa's **Cape Floral Kingdom** (inscribed on the list in 2004) has a botanical endemism of around 70% not least because of the so-called Fynbos vegetation, a fine-leaved shrubland that has adapted to the Mediterranean climate experienced in the area and to the periodic fires which allow regrowth to occur. Research has found that botanical IAS are generally present in areas of the Cape Floral Kingdom most susceptible to human disturbance, suggesting that tourists are acting as vectors for alien seed dispersal by inadvertently bringing them into the area on their shoes and/ or clothing (Bouchard et al., 2015).

Preventing this from happening in the first place is a challenging issue since it relies on visitors taking responsibility for checking their clothing before entering a sensitive area which in turn requires awareness campaigns, since it is extremely hard to police. In terms of a management response on the ground, certainly in the Cape Floral Kingdom, active restoration interventions are rarely implemented because resources (finance and labour) are scarce and the focus instead is on removing invasive species, on the assumption that ecosystems can and will self-repair over time (Holmes et al., 2020).

In that particular ecosystem, self-repair has been observed where dense invader stands with short residence times have been cleared and where diverse native plant growth forms survive, either in the vegetation above ground or as seeds within the soil. There is also evidence that lowland fynbos ecosystems are less resilient to invasion, and have a lower capacity for self-repair, than mountain fynbos ecosystems, and this in turn has potential implications for where visitor activity needs to be more closely monitored and managed.

In some instances, IAS have been deliberately introduced for aesthetic reasons (landscape gardening) or for commercial exploitation but have later gone on to create problems. One such species is the Paper Bark Tree (*Melaleuca quinquenervia*) which was native to New Caledonia, Papua New Guinea and coastal Eastern Australia but which was introduced as an ornamental plant to the USA where it is now creating serious problems, particularly in the **Florida Everglades** (inscribed 1979 but on the List in Danger 1993–2007 and 2010 up to the time of writing). This plant has deep tap roots and uses much larger amounts of water relative to its host native plant communities, affecting local hydrological systems (Pejchar & Mooney, 2009).

It isn't just vegetation that can be introduced into a natural environment. For instance, the creation of new routes such as unsurfaced vehicle tracks into rainforest areas allows non-rainforest mammals such as the Canefield Rat (*Rattus sordidus*) and the Grassland Mosaic-tailed Rat (*Melomys burtoni*) to penetrate the area as they make use of the more open habitat created by the presence of the road (Goosem, 2000). That research was carried out in the Kurunda State Forest in Northern Queensland, part of the **Wet Tropics of Queensland** WH area, which also has a problem with feral pigs (Koichi et al., 2013).

At the sub-Antarctic **Macquarie Island** (an Australian possession, inscribed in 1997) both cats and rabbits were introduced into the environment by 19th-century sealing gangs; rabbits for food and cats as pet. Concerns over the impacts these alien species were having on the ecology of the island led to a sustained programme, starting in the 1980s, to completely eradicate feral cats (*Felis catus*) which were predating on the island's important seabird populations. Complete eradication of the cat population was finally achieved in 2001, after which rabbit (*Oryctolagus cuniculus*) numbers increased significantly despite the presence of a biological control action also being put in place (Myxoma virus). The island-wide ecosystem effects were much more widespread grazing by rabbits and in many places, the loss of tall complex grasslands to shorter grazing lawns increasingly being colonised by small herbs and the invasive alien grass *Poa annua* (Annual Meadow Grass, generally found in temperate climates) (Bergstrom et al., 2009). Thus, eliminating one alien species – cats – created a space in the ecosystem for their prey, another IAS, to thrive. Moves are still afoot to eradicate the rabbit population on Macquarie Island.

9.2.5 Disturbance to wildlife

Anthropogenic intrusion into habitats of any kind is generally believed to result in short-term responses such as avoidance or flight by species unaccustomed or not habituated to such invasions. The avoidance of human intruders starts with increased alertness and alarm behaviour, and is generally followed by agitation and finally escape to a safer distance (Newsome et al., 2002). Even so-called 'benign' activities such as observation from a distance are believed to negatively affect wildlife behaviour and biology. In some cases, this might be an increase in boldness (Geffroy et al., 2015) but in other instances, increased timidity, particularly where consumptive use of wildlife resources is involved (Arlinghaus et al., 2016).

Research undertaken in the **Sinharaja Forest Reserve** World Heritage Site in Sri Lanka (inscribed 1988), an 8,800-hectare area of primary tropical rainforest, found that there is considerable impact on the dispersal of birds close to trails used by visitors, and that this disturbance can be felt up to distances of between 75 m and 150 m from the trail itself (Alwis et al., 2016). Flocks of mixed species, one of the attractive features of the forest reserve from an ornithological point of view, were generally more susceptible to disturbance than single species groups.

One concerning implication of this is that the more that birds expend energy on avoiding human contact, the more they eat into their energy reserves that are needed for breeding and possibly migration. And the more that nesting birds are disturbed to the extent that they repeatedly leave their nests, the greater the risk of predation (Newsome et al., 2002). For some bird species, regular use of trails means that corridors either side of the path cease being seen as suitable nesting areas, effectively reducing the available habitat for breeding (Holm & Laursen, 2009). Thus, in destinations where the main tourist season and breeding seasons coincide, there is a risk of fewer possible breeding locations being used, compromising the long-term viability of local populations. In areas where pet dogs are regularly walked, such disturbance to nesting areas can be particularly significant (Banks & Bryant, 2007).

In Australia's **Greater Blue Mountains World Heritage Area** (inscribed 2000), trampling on stream beds associated with the increasingly popular sport of canyoning has been shown to have a short-term impact on local populations of in-stream macroinvertebrate communities, with recovery commencing within a day of trampling and overall community composition returning to its former state within around two weeks (Hardiman & Burgin, 2011).

At the other end of the scale, Dwarf Minke Whales (*Balaenoptera acutorostrata*) are increasingly the subject of whale-watching and 'swim-with' expeditions on the northern parts of the **Great Barrier Reef World Heritage Site**, Australia. As they have become habituated to the presence of boats and swimmers, there is evidence that some individuals are surfacing closer to the tourist vessels than the expected 60 m radius and at times seem happy to aggregate around swimmers (Mangot et al., 2011). This inquisitiveness of the whales can create management challenges including compliance problems for operations that are not licenced to provide a 'swim-with' experience to their guests. Biologists are also concerned about the impacts on the whales' well-being because of close and prolonged association with vessels and swimmers.

Island ecosystems are particularly fragile, particularly more remote properties where species may be endemic (i.e. found nowhere else). On Madagascar, for instance, 50% of the birds and 95% of reptiles and land-snails are endemic (Berry, 2009). There are also important primate populations and at least one of these, the Indri (*Indri Indri*), an endangered species of lemur, has been shown to be more vulnerable to parasites and disease the more anthropogenic disturbance there is to their habitat, whether this is due to tourism or other human intrusion (Junge et al., 2011).

BOX 9.1 CASE STUDY 9.1: MANAGING TOURISM TO THE MOUNTAIN GORILLAS OF EAST AFRICA.

The mountain gorilla (*Gorilla beringei beringei*) is one of the most iconic of all land mammals, certainly from a conservation perspective (Adams & Infield, 2003). There are around 1,000 individuals still left in the wild, with the species listed as endangered by UNESCO. The remaining wild populations of mountain gorillas are found exclusively in Uganda's **Bwindi Impenetrable National Park** (inscribed 1994) and which has around 45% of the remaining wild Mountain gorillas, and in the Virunga Massif which lies within the territory of the Democratic Republic of Congo (DRC), Uganda and Rwanda (Hanes et al., 2018). The **Virunga National Park** in the DRC was Africa's first national park (Parc National des Virunga, 2021), was inscribed on the World Heritage List in 1979 and has been on the list in danger since 1994 (UNESCO, n.d.b). The Ugandan and Rwandan parts of the Virunga Massif enjoy protected area status (Mgahinga Gorilla National Park and Volcanoes National Park respectively) but are not on the World Heritage list at present.

   The tourism potential of the gorilla populations has been exploited for many decades and an ecotourism industry for viewing human-habituated mountain gorillas is present in all three countries (Spenceley et al., 2010; Maekawa et al., 2013; Roga et al., 2017). In Bwindi Impenetrable Forest, for instance, around 15,000 tourists a year come to observe one of the 17 habituated groups, out of 50 or so in the protected area (Weber et al., 2020) paying a fee of between US$600 and US$700 per head. The Volcanoes National Park in northern Rwanda sees between 20,000 and 25,000 visitors per annum visiting 12 habituated groups (Keios, 2015) despite a permit fee of US$1,500 per head, increased from US$750 in 2017 (Volcanoes National Park, 2021). Organised tourist activity in the DRC to view gorillas is slowly rebuilding despite the ongoing political turmoil in the region. Current permit costs are US$400 per head for international tourists and US$200 for Congolese visitors (Virunga National Park, 2020).

   In theory, mountain gorilla tourism should assist with the sustainability of the species by generating much-needed revenue for conservation activities, by increasing international awareness of the precarious position of this species in the wild, and by creating income for communities living around the park fringes so that there is less risk of intrusion into the habitat and of poaching

(Spenceley et al., 2010). Unfortunately, gorilla tourism hasn't always delivered the anticipated level of community benefit either because of ongoing political conflict which has limited the level of tourism that can happen (as has been the case in the DRC) or because residents living on the peripheries of the protected areas have not been sufficiently involved in planning for and delivering eco-tourism activities (Adams & Infield, 2003; Sabuhoro et al., 2021).

A key point to consider in planning and managing tourism based around the gorilla populations of East Africa is the fact that the close genetic relationship between humans and these charismatic primates means there is a major risk for disease transmission from humans to the gorilla, and particularly air-borne pathogens that lead to respiratory disease (Palacios et al., 2011). To manage these risks, interactions with gorilla populations are closely supervised in all three countries. Group sizes are restricted to small numbers, encounters are not permitted without the accompaniment of trained rangers/ guides and there is a minimum distance requirement to be kept between humans and primates. The high costs of trekking permits and the rationing of only a certain number of permits per day – for instance, in Rwanda there are only 96 permits released per day (VisitRwanda, 2021) – acts as a natural brake on demand, as does the relatively high cost of travelling to these destinations from core international markets.

In the DRC it is compulsory for any person (scientists, rangers, tourists) to wear face masks when visiting the gorilla population, though their efficacy has been questioned both in terms of acting as a barrier to spreading disease but also because of their perceived negative impact on the visitor experience, particularly in hot, humid climes (Homsy, 1999). Research carried out with tourists in Bwindi found that more than 50% were prepared to wear a mask if required (Hanes et al., 2018). More recently, the stated level of acceptance has risen to around 75% of visitors (Weber et al., 2020). It is interesting to think that given the widespread adoption of face masks during the global COVID-19 pandemic of 2020–2022 (Pfattheicher et al., 2020) it is quite possible that a much higher acceptance will be found once international tourism re-starts around the world, now that attitudes have shifted towards mask-wearing as people have become more aware of how personal behaviour can impact on the spread of airborne pathogens.

In almost every location there is a minimum distance of 7 m (5 m in Mgahinga Gorilla NP in Uganda) to keep when observing gorillas (Plate 9.1) though this is not always observed, with one study in Bwindi finding an average distance of only 2.7 m, with encounters showing closer proximity often being instigated by the gorillas rather than by tourists, making micro-management of interventions even more challenging (Sandbrook & Semple, 2006). More recently, research observing tour groups in the same protected area found that the 7m distance rule was violated on 96% of trips observed, with 14% of all encounters seeing a distance of less than 3 m between gorillas and tourists (Weber et al., 2020). Given greater awareness of the risks of respiratory illness

PLATE 9.1 Information sign stating minimum required distance, Volcanoes
National Park HQ, Rwanda.
Source: Photograph by Simon Woodward.

because of the COVID-19 pandemic, conservation agencies involved in protecting the remaining populations of this charismatic primate are considering
whether the recommended distance separating tourists from gorillas should be
increased and whether guides and tour operators should be required to ensure
much greater adherence to the guidelines in future (International Gorilla Conservation Programme, 2020).

9.3 Visitor impacts on cultural heritage properties

9.3.1 Opening comments

There are of course many challenges associated with inviting tourists in to visit
heritage sites of any kind, and managers must be aware of these issues from the outset
as well as the strategies available to prevent problems arising where possible, minimise
negative impacts where they can and repair/ recover wherever needed. Pedersen's
widely-read 2002 report for UNESCO, prepared in partnership with UNEP and

TEMA, built on earlier work prepared by Feilden & Jokilehto (1993) for cultural heritage properties. Pederson provides guidance on the basics of planning for and managing visitor activity at heritage sites and destinations of many types and the manual remains a good starting point for considering the basic issues around welcoming people into a cultural World Heritage Site. UNESCO has built on this more recently through its World Heritage and Sustainable Tourism programme which evaluates and presents tools for managing tourism pressures across a wide range of property and destination types (UNESCO, n.d.).

Below we explore some of the main negative impacts associated with tourist behaviour at cultural heritage sites together before identifying suitable management strategies and tools available to heritage site managers. We don't touch upon pollution as this has already been addressed earlier in this chapter.

9.3.2 Accidental damage/wear and tear

Particularly in crowded situations there is always a risk of accidental damage as people move suddenly and bump into damask-covered walls, as rucksacks bash against carved ornamentations or picture frames or as stiletto heels sink into soft timber flooring. Mechanical damage to stone and wood floors in historic places is associated with high volumes of tourist traffic abrading the surface. Where stones and grit are stuck in visitor's shoe treads, the impact can be exacerbated (Lloyd & Lithgow, 2011).

All monuments, sites and buildings can expect to experience general wear and tear as a result of normal daily activities, and it is the role of managers to monitor areas of concern and intervene where appropriate to protect the heritage resource. Particular attention needs to be paid to thresholds and stairs, particularly where fabricated from wood or friable stone (Orbaşli, 2008). Spiral staircases such as those found in castle turrets and cathedral towers are also particularly vulnerable, because visitors are channelled into a narrow space which over time eventually creates wear on treads (Lloyd & Lithgow, 2011).

9.3.3 Change to micro-climate

Enclosed spaces such as tombs, small rooms and caves are sensitive to increased levels of humidity and raised temperatures when large numbers of visitors enter at any one time (Asperen de Boer, 1967; Brown & Rose, 1996; Whitfield et al., 2000). This can encourage the growth of micro-organisms which damage and erode wall paintings which can threaten the heritage values of a site (Lepinay et al., 2018). The most drastic solution is to permanently close off such sites for public access, as this has demonstrably been shown to make the effects of temperature and humidity changes disappear (Li et al., 2017). However, this diminishes the visitor experience and contradicts one of the motivations behind WH inscription, namely to engage people with the legacies of past cultures.

In some cases, such as the Lascaux Caves in France, part of the **Prehistoric Sites and Decorated Caves of the Vézère Valley WHS** (inscribed 1979), public access has been restricted since long before inscription on the list and alternative visitor experiences provided in site museums or replica caves (Alonso et al., 2018). Similarly, the economic contribution of tourism to the area around the **Altamira Caves** in Northern Spain (originally inscribed in 1985 because of the presence of significant palaeolithic cave paintings) has led to the establishment of a site museum, the recreation of one set of paintings in the so-called 'Neocave' and a lottery system that rationed access and which for a while allowed only six tourists to enter the cave each day (Dans & Gonzalez, 2018; Fernandez, 2019).

The long-standing popularity of the **Mogao Caves** near Dunhuang, China (inscribed 1987) also has created challenges for the site's management agency to the extent that replica caves were built inside a visitor centre constructed a few hundred metres away from the 400+ original caves to provide an alternative experience for the 500,000 visitors coming to the site on an annual basis (Demas et al., 2015), as well as providing visitors with an opportunity to take photographs using flash – something forbidden inside the genuine caves. The experiences of visitors to replicas of the **Chauvet-Pont d'Arc Cave** in France's Ardèche Gorge in the South East of France (inscribed 2014) suggests that for many people, seeing a replica is a sufficiently satisfying experience to the extent that there are few concerns about whether or not what they are seeing is 'authentic' (Duval et al., 2020).

In the eastern deserts of Jordan in Wadi Butum, the early eighth-century desert castle of **Quseir Amra** (inscribed 1985) contains some important wall paintings inside what was originally a residence of the Umayyad caliphs. The extensive fresco paintings of the bath building and reception hall are unique for Islamic architecture of the Umayyad period and were a key reason for its inscription. They too have been threatened by increasing numbers of visitors, with research demonstrating that when several groups enter the buildings in rapid succession there is insufficient time for humidity and temperature levels to stabilise, increasing the risks to the frescoes as salts are drawn through the stonework and into the wall paintings (Abebneh, 2015). In response to these challenges, proposals are in place to introduce a management regime that phases access to the property in a more sustainable fashion.

9.3.4 Dust

As Lloyd & Lithgow (2011) suggest,

> Historic wear and tear is often considered attractive or intriguing, imparting a patina of authenticity to the appearance of an historic interior that would be impossible to replicate today. A degree of dust and dirt may suggest antiquity, genteel poverty and romantic neglect.

(p. 55)

In other words, the slightly unkempt appearance of some historic properties becomes important in establishing the 'spirit of place'. Nonetheless, deposits of skin, clothing fibres, hair, mud can create problems on fragile surfaces, particularly fixtures and furnishings in historic houses, and where people regularly touch surfaces, fingerprints leave moisture and chemical deposits that can bond dust to the surface. As this is cleaned off by conservators and housekeepers, the abrasion process can further damage fragile textiles, woodwork, metalwork and stonework. Research carried out by the UK's National Trust found that dust is rarely found in significant quantities more than around 2 metres from visitor routes, thus offering property managers the chance to introduce visitor management interventions that keep people away from the more sensitive parts of a site (Lloyd & Lithgow, 2011).

9.3.5 Littering

A common problem everywhere, and not just at heritage properties, littering creates aesthetic issues in that it detracts from public enjoyment of a place or a view. As indicated earlier when talking about natural heritage properties, certain forms of litter create problems for wildlife in particular. Where resources for gathering litter are scarce and/ or where the infrastructure for disposing of it is limited or non-existent, this creates an additional burden on both property managers and also local municipalities. This is one aspect of visitor damage to WHS that is without doubt best tackled through education and interpretation to prevent its appearance.

9.3.6 Theft of artefacts, building fabric

Theft of artefacts and even building fabric is a risk in many locations though generally not associated with tourists. As indicated earlier, a number of properties have been put on the List in Danger because of the threat of looting and illegal excavations which of course materially damages the archaeological deposit and compromises OUV. And at the visitor centre for the **Mogao Caves** in China, one comes across the interesting case where the historic looting of artifacts from the caves by European and American explorers and adventurers has become a central theme in the interpretation of the property's history (Whitfield et al., 2000; Hopkirk, 2006).

9.3.7 Graffiti, vandalism and other deliberate damage

It seems there has always been a desire among human beings to leave a trace of their presence on walls, plinths, monuments and other structures. As Champion (2017) states, 'virtually all graffiti, with some noted exceptions, is regarded as anti-social, destructive and lacking legitimacy' (p. 6). Graffiti, particularly when created using modern spray paints, as well as being aesthetically distasteful to many observers, can also cause serious damage, especially where surfaces are too fragile to cope with heavy and repeated cleaning. On porous surfaces, such as limestones, sandstones or marble, paint is more easily absorbed, thus creating additional damage (Orbaşli, 2008).

Ironically, in some instances, historic graffiti has become part of the heritage asset itself. At the Sanctuary of Monte Sant'Angelo in Italy, part of the **Longobards in Italy: Places of Power (568–774 AD)** WHS (inscribed 2011), there are Anglo-Saxon runes carved into the walls that were left there by visitors sometime between the seventh and ninth centuries AD and which form part of the rich history of the site (Forbes, 2019). In **Durham Cathedral** (inscribed 1986) there are scratches and scorch marks on the walls dating back to the time of the occupation of the Cathedral by Scottish soldiers, as occupiers in the 1640s and as prisoners in 1650 while next door, in the Deanery, there is a mass of intersecting graffiti between a 15th-century wall painting and earlier 13th-century paintwork on the wall of a former chapel, and that graffiti too is part of the story of this monastic building (Graves & Rollason, 2013). And at **Pompeii** (inscribed 1997), historical graffiti across much of the site, but particularly in the town's brothel (*lupanar*), presents visitors with a vivid insight into social commentary in the period prior to the eruption that destroyed the town (Harper, 2021). Conserving, presenting and interpreting historic graffiti thus becomes yet another important challenge for property managers to consider as they prepare management plans for their sites.

Deliberate damage to historic properties may be 'mindless vandalism' or it may be undertaken for reasons of protest – buildings or monuments that are of spiritual, political or historic value are often targeted because of the additional impact that vandalism has on public sensibilities in a place (Orbaşli, 2008).

9.4 Tourism pressures in historic towns and cities

9.4.1 Introduction

Managing visitors in any historic urban environment will always be complex because of the wide range of economic and social activities present within that space. When that space is also inscribed on the World Heritage List, there is another layer of complexity because of the need to protect the Outstanding Universal Values of the property while at the same time as allowing normal urban life to continue. As Ashworth & Tunbridge suggest, 'few cities, or parts of cities, are exclusively tourist-historic in their functions' (2000, p. 105). In general, managing any urban area is a complex task because of the multiplicity of stakeholders and the competing aims of economic development, tourism, conservation and social life. People dwelling in the suburbs and outlying dormitory areas need swift and easy access to their places of employment and to the commercial and leisure services located in every urban centre, and of course there is also likely to be a permanent resident population living, working and socialising in the city.

The presence of large numbers of people – residents, day trippers or tourists – is an attractive proposition to many commercial enterprises and thus locating within the heart of a historic city brings the potential of higher footfall, more business and potentially higher profits. Yet the maintenance and occupancy of historic buildings, particularly those with a high conservation value or rating, can incur considerable costs because of the requirement to use traditional building techniques and expensive materials (Ashworth & Tunbridge, 2000; Orbaşli, 2000; Orbaşli, 2008). Thus, there is constant pressure on municipal planning authorities and others to provide financial support for conservation and restoration works where they are felt to present an unnecessary burden on tenants and owners of historic buildings whose presence adds to the overall sense of place of a destination, and therefore need to be presented in a particular way.

Indeed, Pendelbury et al. (2009) contend that there is often a conflict between the traditional expectations and approach to conservation in many historic urban areas and the realities of urban dynamism and growth, leading to confusing expectations among visitors expecting a heritage experience. They refer to the case of **Historic Lima** (inscribed 1988, extended in 1991) and its gentrification and sanitisation after receiving WHS status (including the displacement of many street vendors, who were effectively denied the opportunity to benefit from income generation opportunities associated with increased tourism activity) in order to present a 'mythical colonial experience' divorced from the realities of contemporary Peruvian life. Similar negative impacts of gentrification in colonial towns and cities on the World Heritage List that have been actively developed with a view to attracting heritage tourism have been identified in, for instance, **Pelourinho**, Brazil (Nobre, 2002; Leite, 2015; Collins, 2019); **in George Town, Penang**, Malaysia (Beng & Barker, 2016; Foo & Krishnapillai, 2019), in **Colonia del Sacramento** in Uruguay (Conti, 2017; Verdini, 2017) and in **Valletta**, Malta (Markwick, 2018; Dimelli, 2019).

Su (2010) examines the case of the historic town of **Liajing** in Yunnan Province, China which was inscribed on the list in 1997 because of its architecture that blends contributions from several cultures and which retains a high level of authenticity. Su's contention is that in the case of Liajing, conservation is essentially being used as a tool to propel economic development rather than a means of protecting heritage values. The emphasis is on stimulating the growth of tourism in the town, using its WH status as an additional drawcard. Prior to inscription, modern concrete structures were demolished at the behest of the municipal and State authorities in order that the townscape complied with UNESCO expectations of authenticity in a historic settlement (Su, 2010, p. 167) but post-inscription, the emphasis has been more on commercialising public spaces and facilitating economic growth by commodifying the town's historic 'sense of place', with key individuals and power-brokers from the public sector taking the lead and thereby denying smaller businesses the opportunity to benefit from the opportunities of heritage-led tourism development.

An over-emphasis on tourism where heritage sites and urban centres are transformed into venues for tourism and leisure can create problems where the externalities associated with high levels of tourist activity (e.g. congestion, noise, pollution, displacement of traditional activities) reach a level where local residents feel that these sites no longer 'belong' to them but to others, outsiders (Silberman, 2006). This can become even more problematic when traditional residents are displaced either because of gentrification or tourism, or indeed both.

In Seville, for instance, the historic centre became home to a large number of 'lifestyle migrants' in the 1990s and 2000s and over the last decade or so the permanent population of the city has fallen as family apartments have been converted to tourism use (Jover & Diaz-Parra, 2022). Moreover, the rapid growth of Airbnb and similar property letting services has led to an increased concentration of tourism activity in the core of the city, leading to conflicts over access to buildings that formerly housed local families, the loss of local services and even conflicts over access to public spaces. The city's World Heritage Site, **The Cathedral, Alcázar and Archivo de Indias in Seville,** was inscribed in 1987 and the boundaries of the buffer zone, which includes much of the historic core of the city, were refined in 2010 so that it covers an area of some 187 hectares (the Cathedral, Alcázar and archives cover only 12 hectares)[1]. Jover & Diaz-Parra (2022) report that the area around the Cathedral has also traditionally housed the main tourist hotels, but that the emergence of Airbnb accommodation has distributed tourism activity across a much wider area thus also dispersing the externalities associated with tourism more widely as well. Similar issues have been identified in **Barcelona, Dubrovnik, Edinburgh, Florence** and **Rome**, among other European World Heritage cities (see, for instance, Dodds & Butler, 2019; Amore et al., 2020; De Luca et al., 2020; Oskam, 2020).

9.4.2 Traffic management

One problem faced by historic cities, including many of those on the World Heritage list, is that ongoing conservation practices and planning ideologies have led to the retention of the historic urban morphology of narrow, often winding streets, thus imposing challenges on vehicle movement, loading and parking. Yet, as Kamel & Hanks (2009) suggest, the organisation of the visitor journey through an urban WHS is very important in letting tourists develop and experience a sense of place – that intangible feeling associated with the tangible heritage of the destination. So reconciling service provision for businesses within a historic city core and presenting attractive access routes into and around the destination becomes important.

Historic cities, whether or not inscribed on the World Heritage List, generally grew organically around important religious and/ or secular buildings in a time when the principal modes of transport were either pedestrian or carts drawn by domesticated animals (Ashworth & Tunbridge, 2000). In the Middle East, Islamic traditions led to the creation of discrete quarters separating different urban functions from residential areas, with internal barriers further fragmenting the urban form and disrupting access (Bianca, 2000). Inevitably, therefore, most historic cities tend to have narrow streets not suited to high volumes of motorised traffic, particularly larger vehicles such as tourist coaches or delivery lorries. Accessibility issues (and the tourist experience) can be further compromised by conflict between large numbers of visitors walking around the historic city centres in peak periods and the day to day working life of local residents (Orbaşli, 2000). It is therefore instructive to see how different historic cities on the World Heritage list have tackled some of the worst excesses of pedestrian: vehicular conflict.

BOX 9.2 CASE STUDY 9.2: TRAFFIC MANAGEMENT IN TWO UK WORLD HERITAGE CITIES – DURHAM AND EDINBURGH.

The medieval city of **Durham** in Northern England contains one of the UK's most significant cathedrals, which, together with the neighbouring castle and associated buildings, was inscribed on the WH list in 1986. The cathedral is regarded as the finest example of Norman architecture in England and the castle was the home of the Prince Bishops of Durham who enjoyed almost complete autonomy from the King in return for protecting the northern boundaries of England (Pocock, 2013). The castle and cathedral lie on a steep-sided peninsula formed by a bend in the River Wear, a naturally defensive position and one that suited the needs of the time. However, the growth of the city as a focal point for civil administration, trading and learning and, more recently, as a tourism destination meant that the narrow streets of the medieval city leading into the heart of the World Heritage Site were increasingly crowded with motorised traffic, creating congestion and safety problems for pedestrians.

Over the last two decades the relevant authorities have taken a number of steps to relieve the traffic problems in the core of the WHS. Vehicles wishing to access the university, cathedral and castle needed to travel along Saddler Street – a narrow single carriageway – with traffic signals controlling flows of up to 3,600 vehicles per day in a narrow, confined space also occupied by up to 17,000 pedestrians per day (Durham County Council, 2003). Taking advantage of powers available under the UK's Transport Act (2000), a congestion charging initiative was introduced in October 2002, the first of its kind in the UK, whereby motorists were charged £2.00 to drive onto the peninsula at the heart of the World Heritage Site in peak periods (10.00–16.00 from Mondays through to Saturdays).

The scheme had an almost immediate and significant impact on traffic flows, with an 85% decrease in the number of vehicle movements and pedestrian numbers increasing by 10% (Durham County Council, n.d.). At the same time, moves were taken to reduce significantly the long stay parking provision around the city-centre, to encourage commuters to use public transport and park-and-ride provision, thus freeing up city-centre parking spots for short term shoppers and World Heritage Site visitors (Durham County Council, 2016). Catering more for tourists and day visitors, a shuttle bus service was introduced linking the rail station and the main long stay car parks with Palace Green – the heart of the World Heritage Site. More recently, plans have been introduced to enhance the city's cycle route network with one stretch of the National Cycling Network (Route 14) to be re-routed across Prebends Bridge and along South and North Bailey and onto Saddler Street; in other words, instead of bypassing the WHS, cyclists will be taken through the heart of it.

Overall, the impacts of the traffic management initiatives in the heart of the city have led to substantial reductions in vehicle emissions, traffic noise and visual intrusion thus enhancing the experience of the World Heritage Site without materially affecting day to day operations at the Cathedral, the Castle, local traders and the University Departments and Colleges situated on the peninsula.

Further north, Edinburgh's city centre – much larger than Durham – has long suffered from traffic congestion which materially detracts from the experience of the **Old and New Towns of Edinburgh** WHS (inscribed 1995). Following Durham and London's lead, the local authorities sought to introduce a congestion charge but these plans were dropped in 2005 after two years of fierce public opposition. Investment in a tram network linking the airport out to the West with the city centre and Leith did have a marginal impact on traffic levels. Other micro-management initiatives implemented over the last decade or so have included significant uplifts in the costs of resident parking permits (to dissuade city centre residents from owning cars) and charging relatively high prices for on-street visitor parking spaces (to encourage use of public transport by those coming into Edinburgh from outside the city centre for shopping or leisure purposes). The use of hop-on, hop-off buses for tourists to help them explore the core of the city follows well-established practice in many high-volume urban destinations.

However, a more radical approach has now been developed to transform completely traffic movements around the core of the city, including those parts of the Old and New Towns covered by WHS inscription (City of Edinburgh District Council, 2019). Building on guidance from Scottish Planning Policy paragraph 273, which states that all urban mobility projects should prioritise walking, then cycling, then public transport and finally the private car, there is a target to create 'a walkable city centre right at the heart of the World Heritage Site enabled by a pedestrian priority zone and a network of connected, high-quality, car-free streets' (p. 6). Some key streets including parts of the Royal Mile, at the heart of the WHS, will be made entirely traffic free; there will be re-allocation of road spaces including a significant reduction in resident parking provision (thus freeing up space for walking and small open areas), a new pedestrian and cycle-friendly bridge will be created to link the Old and New Towns with an aspiration to reduce private car use by 25% overall. Walking for leisure is difficult in environments dominated by the car, hence the integration of a number of different approaches in the new Edinburgh transport/ mobility strategy.

Other historic urban centres that have tackled traffic management as a tool to improve the quality of life for local people and to enhance the experience of the World Heritage Site include:

- Central **Lisbon**, Portugal, where key streets have been pedestrianised;
- **Amsterdam**, The Netherlands, where the amount of car parking provision has been reduced while at the same time there has been added investment in public transport networks;

- **Vigan**, Philippines, where partial pedestrianisation has been introduced to ease congestion in the heart of the old city (Amistad, 2010);
- **George Town,** Penang (Malaysia), another World Heritage City with increased emphasis on providing safe sidewalks (Zainol et al., 2016) and providing a free local bus service for locals and tourists alike (Zainol, 2016);
- The **Sacred City of Kandy**, Sri Lanka, where use of public transport has declined considerably over the last two decades and where previous attempts at reducing private car use have not been successful, is also planning to increase the restrictions on traffic especially in the heart of the city, close to the Temple of the Tooth Relic (Meetiyagoda, 2018);
- **Dubrovnik**, Croatia where self-guided and guided trails have been created to spread visitors across a wider area and away from the most congested locations (Loades, 2019);
- The area around the **Masjed-e Jame** WHS in Esfahan, Iran where road widening and the provision of open space reduced congestion around the mosque and led to an increase in average traffic speeds, thus reducing pollution and vibration threats to the historic structure as well as improving the urban realm (Seyedashraf et al., 2017).

Of course, it would be remiss at this stage not to mention the controversy caused by the decision of the authorities in Dresden, Germany to construct the Waldschlösschen Bridge over the River Elbe, some 2 km outside the core of the city but still within the buffer zone of the property. This project, designed to alleviate traffic congestion in the area, did so but at the expense of the city losing its status as a World Heritage Site in 2009 (Santos & Zobler, 2012).

This brief review of strategies for managing traffic in historic urban areas (whether or not they are WHS) has revealed a number of possible management tools:

- Physically restricting access on a permanent or temporal basis across all or part of the area;
- Introducing tolls or charges;
- Managing the supply of parking provision for residents and/ or visitors;
- Encouraging modal shifts by increasing provision for walking, cycling and public transport.

Critical success factors for managing traffic in historic areas are, according to Orbaşli & Shaw (2011):

- The careful integration of all types of transport services in a way that meets the needs of local residents first;
- The availability of information about transport options to visitors both prior to, and during, the visit;

- A recognition that all open spaces, car parks and pedestrian zones are part of the urban realm and need to be designed and managed as such;

From a heritage tourism perspective, such measures serve to enhance the overall experience of the historic city. Yet the principal benefits should be felt by local residents who will enjoy a cleaner, safer and aesthetically more pleasing environment. In other words, implementing appropriate traffic management and mobility enhancements in historic places, including WH cities, makes them better for people to live in and better for people to visit.

9.4.3 Walking tours in historic cities

The role of tour guides as intermediaries between tourists and the destination is key to the delivery of a high-quality visitor experience (Cohen, 1985; Salazar, 2005). However, there are often conflicts between large tour groups and other urban centre users, particularly in the cores of historic cities where narrow streets create competition for limited space (Simpson, 1999; Collins, 2008; Orbaşli & Shaw, 2011). These activities are not restricted to day-time; the popularity of ghost tours takes large groups into historic quarters well into the evening in many destinations (Garcia, 2012). Where guides have the opportunity to vary the route according to customer feedback, this can help deflect some of the more disruptive impacts of walking tours (Gentry, 2007).

9.5 Key concepts in visitor management planning

9.5.1 Introduction

It isn't enough for site managers to recognise the specific threats to their properties associated with tourism and visitor activity, and to understand appropriate interventions to mitigate against the impacts of these challenges. There needs to be a structured approach to planning for visitor access across the property that identifies where activity should be focused and how it can be achieved to both protect the site from any unnecessary pressures and deliver a high-quality visitor experience. Thus, the property needs to be managed as a composite resource, and not as separate parts, as this encourages managers to consider the spatial relationships between different parts of the property and the implications for increasing (or decreasing) access to a particular area. This is particularly important at natural heritage sites (Hendee et al., 1990). It is also important to approach site management from a perspective of preventing further degradation or irreversible change. In other words, properties should not be put in a position where their carrying capacities are exceeded.

Two tools that have been in use for many years in natural heritage sites and protected areas are Limits of Acceptable Change (LAC), which considers how best to avoid degradation of sites, and the Recreation Opportunity Spectrum (ROS), which is a form of zoning. Both of these rely on managers having some understanding of the carrying capacity of a site or area.

9.5.2 Carrying capacity

Carrying capacity emerged as a concept in natural resource and environmental management in the 1950s and was originally defined as 'the maximum level of use an area can sustain as set by natural factors of environmental resistance such as food, shelter or water' (Hendee et al., 1990, p216). In effect it allows managers to understand the amount, kind and distribution of use that can occur without leading to unacceptable impacts on the resource in question (Newsome et al., 2002). The idea of carrying capacity is central to best practice in managing heritage sites of any kind, and it is specifically referenced in the ICOMOS International Charter for Cultural Tourism 2021 which states, as Principle 2, that property managers and other stakeholders should 'manage tourism at cultural heritage places through planning instruments and management plans informed by carrying capacity' (p. 4.). The Charter goes on to note that 'carrying capacity indicators and their regular monitoring are the main guidelines for the responsible and sustainable management of tourism at cultural heritage places' (p. 4).

It is very rare that it is possible to identify a static determination of carrying capacity in the natural world, since ecosystems are dynamic and carrying capacity can be increased or decreased through management actions. In landscapes that are used for recreational and leisure purposes (including tourism) there is a further social dimension to be taken into consideration – whether for instance the level of use of a trail or viewpoint at a particular time is seen as too high/crowded and thus impinges on the enjoyment of some or all of the people there. This becomes even more complicated when one considers that different people may be looking for different, potentially conflicting experiences in the same place at the same time – some may want solitude, while others may want companionship. Thus, what is an appropriate level of use for some represents congestion (or loneliness) for others. Introducing the needs and expectations of the host community complicates this point still further. So, there are actually a number of different dimensions of carrying capacity to consider:

- Physical carrying capacity: the ability of a site or destination to accommodate visitors. This will reflect the condition, fragility and conservation status of the property and the scale and range of visitor services available;
- Ecological carrying capacity: the ability of the ecosystem to accommodate anthropogenic interventions while maintaining sustainability, functionality and also heritage values;
- Social and cultural carrying capacity: the degree to which the host community is prepared to accept visitors within a context that delivers the required quality of tourist experience;

- Infrastructural carrying capacity: the ability of the supporting services (e.g. water and power supply, waste disposal, transportation) to accommodate various human uses;
- Perceptual carrying capacity: a reflection of how crowded (or not) a particular environment feels to people there at the time and the impact that this has on their overall experience of the place;
- Economic carrying capacity: the level to which tourism can sustain economic activity at an appropriate spatial scale.

Calculating the physical carrying capacity of historic properties or ancient monuments is, in theory at least, slightly easier than estimating the carrying capacity of a natural area because there is a fixed amount of floor space available for circulation. Where it becomes more complicated again, however, is when one considers the experience that visitors are seeking – again, some may be perfectly happy sharing an archaeological site with hundreds of other people at the same time while others may feel that sharing a site with large numbers of others prevents them from spending time in certain parts of that place, or that their enjoyment is diminished because their views of certain features are obscured by the presence of others. There is also a very practical issue to consider and that is that as the number of people on one site at one time increases, so do the prospects of accidental damage to fragile features. And in enclosed spaces, larger numbers of visitors increase humidity levels and the risks of damage to wall paintings.

Research at **Jerash** in Jordan (on that country's tentative list since 2004) calculated a figure of around 10 m^2 per head as a comfortable measure for an open archaeological site, though the authors noted that this was very rarely exceeded except at key pinch points and viewing locations (Makhadmeh et al., 2020). As suggested above, it is perhaps more useful to consider the perceptual aspects of carrying capacity. Research carried out at **Petra** in Jordan (inscribed 1985) explored the difference between visitor density (an objective measure) and crowding (subjective), and investigated how different types of cultural tourist perceive crowding (Al Azaizeh et al., 2016). The authors found that carrying capacity indicators based on visitor density across a large heritage site such as Petra ignores the very significant spatial variations in activity that can be found in such extensive locations. And such indicators also ignore the number of encounters that visitors have with others, particularly when being guided in groups. They suggest that cultural tourists seeking a 'deep' experience want to see fewer people at one time and want to be in smaller tour groups compared to those wanting a 'shallow', more entertainment-based experience. Tourist's perceptions of crowding at Petra are also affected by the physical space. For instance, encountering a relatively small number of people while walking through the *Siq*, the narrow gully leading into the site, can lead to perceptions of crowding while the same number of people standing in the open area in front of *Al-Khazneh* (The Treasury) is seen as being acceptable.

One final point to consider about carrying capacity is that there are also cultural variations in what constitutes 'crowding'. Research carried out for the **Meidan**

Emam, Esfahan, Iran (inscribed on the list in 1979) identified cultural variations in what was considered an acceptable level of crowding at this early 17th-century mosque, and stressed that a site's social (or perceptual) carrying capacity is generally quite different than any theoretical physical capacity calculated on the basis of a permissible number of square metres per visitor at any one time and that a key differential reflects individual expectations and prior knowledge (Aminian & Khodayar, 2016). And the same seems to be true of natural heritage sites: a survey of some 2,000 visitors to Waitomo Caves in New Zealand (not a WHS but an important natural visitor attraction on the North Island) found that Japanese, Korean and other Asian visitors were less concerned about crowding than those from NZ, the UK and other Europeans (Doorne, 2000). This led to individual tour operators targeting the Asian tourism market since they could increase revenue without risking customer complaints about a poor-quality experience.

9.5.3 Limits of Acceptable Change (LAC)

Despite these complicating factors around perception and tourist expectations, understanding the basic concept of carrying capacity is vital for any heritage site manager since it requires an insight into those elements of the property that are particularly susceptible to damage as a result of human activity. That then allows consideration of whether or not to use the concept of Limits of Acceptable Change (LAC) in the preparation of a management plan for the property. LAC emerged out of research carried out by the US Forest Service in the 1970s (Frissell Jr & Stankey, 1972, cited in Hendee et al., 1990), and recognizes the inevitability that any anthropogenic use of a natural resource will bring change, and that the role of the land/ resource manager is to determine how much change can be permitted without materially compromising the resource, how change should be measured (i.e. what indicators to use) and what interventions are appropriate once these indicators demonstrate change has reached a critical level.

The value of LAC as an approach is that it is not determined by the absolute number of people in an area at one time, or using a resource over a given period. Rather, it considers the cumulative impact that these users have on the resource base. Moreover, it recognizes that different parts of a larger natural area (or indeed a built heritage site) may be managed to provide different types of visitor experience (originally referred to as 'opportunity classes' but now generally referred to as zones) and therefore the acceptable conditions and the triggers for intervention may also vary across a site.

The four main components of the LAC process are:

- The specification of acceptable and achievable resource and social conditions, defined by a series of measurable parameters;
- An analysis of the relationship between existing conditions and those judged acceptable;

- Identification of management actions judged to best achieve these desired conditions;
- A programme of monitoring and evaluating management effectiveness.

Source: (Hendee et al., 1990)

Essentially, LAC is a process that requires inputs from a broad range of stakeholders, each of whom will have their own perspectives on what is an appropriate level of change and how and when interventions should be made to avoid irreversible decline in the quality of the resource. It is time-consuming and costly to prepare a management plan based on the LAC process and in the case of World Heritage Sites, may be further complicated by the primacy of the relevant characteristics that give the site its Outstanding Universal Value since these may not accord with the interests of some stakeholders. As a reminder, almost one-third of the properties currently on the List in Danger are threatened by agricultural intrusion, an indication that these properties (all bar one of which are natural heritage areas, the exception being the **Chan Chan Archaeological Zone** in Peru) are not currently meeting the basic needs of the surrounding communities in terms of them avoiding hunger or even starvation.

There are 9 steps in the LAC planning system, as indicated in Figure 9.1.

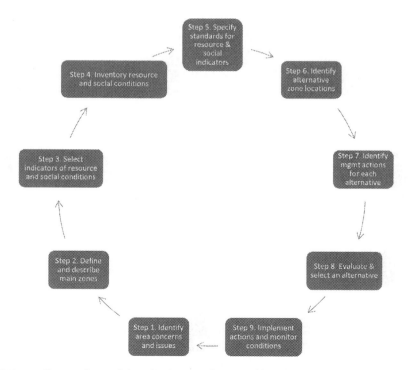

FIGURE 9.1 Process for applying the Limits of Acceptable Change planning framework. Source: Derived from (Hendee et al., 1990).

Although LAC has been well used in planning for access to wilderness areas across the US and in Australia (Newsome et al., 2002), there is limited evidence of its sustained use as a planning tool at World Heritage Sites, though it has been used at the Jenolan Caves in Australia's **Greater Blue Mountains Area WHS** (McArthur, 2000, cited in Newsome et al., 2002). Consultants preparing a visitor management strategy for **Hadrian's Wall World Heritage Site** in the mid-1990s also proposed its employment in the second Management Plan being prepared for that property (ASH Consulting Group & Transport for Leisure, 1996) though this was never followed up by English Heritage and the other property managers along the line of the Wall.

However, the LAC process has been in use for nearly two decades on the Hadrian's Wall Path National Trail, that runs through that same World Heritage Site for some 84 miles (135km) (McGlade, 2014). Nonetheless, the main principles of the LAC framework – understanding issues and concerns, identifying appropriate interventions and monitoring the impact of those interventions – can be found in almost every management plan prepared for both cultural and natural heritage sites[2].

9.5.4 The Recreation Opportunity Spectrum (ROS)

The Recreation Opportunity Spectrum (ROS) also came out of work carried out by the US Forest Service and is based around the principles of how easy (or difficult) it is to access a particular place and the implications that this has for the provision of visitor services, for levels of interaction between groups of visitors and for the amount of management intervention and investment required (Newsome et al., 2002). Again, ROS is essentially a process that combines knowledge of the demand (existing and latent) for different types of recreation or leisure experience with an understanding of the capacity of the host environment to provide for different opportunities without compromising either the ecological integrity of the area or the quality of the visitor experience. Its main application is in planning for visitor access into and around protected areas, and again has been used principally in the USA, Australia and New Zealand where it is used to advise zoning those destinations (Newsome et al., 2002).

As such, it is similar to the conventional approach used by planners when zoning for different land-uses in urban areas (Kalman, 2014) and the principles are equally transferable to management planning for large archaeological sites in particular. For instance, the Masterplan for the **Group of Monuments at Hampi WHS** in India (inscribed 1986), as well as identifying the core zone and buffer zone for the property, distinguishes quite specifically between a number of different location types for tourist activity onsite, including: Interchange Nodes, where visitors leave their vehicles and change into different mode of transport; Stoppage Nodes, where visitors can stop to view monuments, and Destination Points where visitors go for a specific activity such as pilgrimage or recreation (HWHAMA, 2007). And at the Borobudur WHS in Indonesia, a similar strategy was adopted to try to relieve pressure on the most fragile and congested parts of the **Borobudur Temple Compound** on the one hand, and across the broader Borobudur – Yogyakarta – Prambanan area on the other (TDI, 2019).

9.5.5 Concluding comment

To conclude, there are a number of useful ideas that have come originally from management planning in wilderness and forest environments but which, over time, have been adapted for use in a much broader range of heritage properties including cultural landscapes, archaeological sites and historic urban areas. The concept of carrying capacity (however that is defined in practice) and the two complementary ideas of Limits of Acceptable Change and the Recreation Opportunity Spectrum provide guidance to World Heritage property managers and other stakeholders on how to reconcile visitor access to sites in their guardianship with their obligations to protect the often fragile resource base which they are dealing with. Wherever possible, these ideas are used to inform the preparation of management plans for World Heritage Sites which, as we have already seen earlier, is one of the principal obligations of every State Party with properties on the list.

The strategies available to manage tourism pressures such as those described in this chapter are not unique to the World Heritage community and can be found on every continent at every type of cultural or natural heritage property. Briefly, the main approaches one can find are to:

- Influence visitor behaviour during the time on site so that negative impacts (deliberate or accidental) are reduced;
- Disperse activity on a spatial or temporal basis (or both) to avoid problems of congestion and the associated pressures;
- Divert activity away from fragile or sensitive areas towards parts of a property better able to accommodate visitors. This may involve preventing access completely to some locations;
- 'Hardening' the landscape or resource base in certain areas, to enhance its capacity to absorb visitor activity.

Some of these approaches can be enforced in legislation while others may require physical investment, but in all cases they generally need to be supported by education and interpretation activities targeting a broad range of audiences – tour operators, transport providers, tourists themselves as well as local residents – so that the rationale for such management interventions is clear and transparent to all concerned. If not, then investment in management planning is often not as effective as it could be.

9.6 Summing up

This chapter has explored some of the negative effects of tourism at World Heritage properties that are a by-product of introducing higher levels of use at a site than would be expected were there to be no tourism. Some issues are minor, localised and can be solved through prompt intervention by relevant stakeholders while others are much more fundamental and harder to resolve. It should also be noted that many problems addressed here may be caused equally by local resident behaviour. And finally, they are not specific to World Heritage though in some instances if not addressed they may compromise a property's OUV and risk its long-term presence on the list.

Similarly, strategies for tackling these problems are not specific to World Heritage and the sector has learned considerably from management approaches developed around the world in different contexts, from the wildernesses of the USA managed by the US Forest Service, to the work of the UK's National Trust as it oversees the conservation of hundreds of historic properties, and to the experience of the Disney Corporation in managing long queues in its theme parks. One role of World Heritage managers should always be to learn from experience elsewhere, and to apply that knowledge to their understanding of the particular challenges at their own site.

Notes

1 See https://whc.unesco.org/en/list/383/ (accessed 6 July 2020).
2 See chapter 5 of Kalman (2014) for a detailed discussion of managing change at built heritage properties.

References

Abebneh, A. 2015. Qusair Amra (Jordan) World Heritage Site: A Review of Current Status of Presentation and Protection Approaches. *Mediterranean Archaeology and Archaeometry*, 15 (2), 27–44.

Adams, W. M. & Infield, M. 2003. Who is on the gorilla's payroll? Claims on tourist revenue from a Ugandan National Park. *World Development*, 31 (1), 177–190.

Al Azaizeh, M. M., Hallo, J. C., Backman, S. J., Norman, W. C. & Vogel, M. A. 2016. Value orientations and heritage tourism management at Petra Archaeological Park, Jordan: a comparative study of McKercher's five types of heritage tourists. *Tourism Management*, 57, 149–158.

Alonso, L., Creuzé-des-Châtelliers, C., Trabac, T., Dubost, A., Moënne-Loccoz, Y. & Pommier, T. 2018. Rock substrate rather than black stain alterations drives microbial community structure in the passage of Lascaux Cave. *Microbiome*, 6 (1), 1–15.

Alwis, N. S., Perera, P. & Dayawansa, N. P. 2016. Response of tropical avifauna to visitor recreational disturbances: a case study from the Sinharaja World Heritage Forest, Sri Lanka. *Avian Research*, 7 (15), 1–13.

Aminian, N. & Khodayar, S. 2016. Tourism carrying capacity assessment for historical sites – Isfahan Emam Mosque. *Travel and Tourism Research Association: Advancing Tourism Research Globally*, 12. https://scholarworks.umass.edu/ttra/2011/Student/12 (14 July 2022).

Amistad, F. 2010. Assessment of the Pedestrianization Policy in Vigan City: UNESCO World Heritage City. *Journal of Urban Planning and Development*, 136 (1), 11–22.

Amore, A., Falk, M. & Adie, B. A. 2020. One visitor too many: Assessing the degree of overtourism in established European urban destinations. *International Journal of Tourism Cities*, 6 (1), 117–137.

Arlinghaus, R., Alos, J., Klefoth, T., Laskowski, K., Monk, C. T., Nakayama, S. & Schrö- der, A. 2016. Consumptive tourism causes timidity, rather than boldness, syndromes: a response to Geffroy et al. *Trends in Ecology and Evolution*, 31 (2), 92–94.

ASH Consulting Group and Transport for Leisure. 1996. *Visitor Management Plan for Hadrian's Wall World Heritage Site*. Edinburgh: ASH.

Ashworth, G. J. & Tunbridge, J. E. 2000. *The Tourist-Historic City. Retrospect and Prospect of Managing the Heritage City.* Oxford: Elsevier Science Ltd.

Asperen de Boer, J. V. 1967. Humidity in walls in relation to the preservation of works of art. *Studies in Conservation,* 12 (sup1), 109–117.

Banks, P. B. & Bryant, J. V. 2007. Four-legged friend or foe? Dog walking displaces native birds from natural areas. *Biology Letters,* 3 (6), 611–613.

Barros, A., Monz, C. & Pickering, C. 2015. Is tourism damaging ecosystems in the Andes? Current knowledge and an agenda for future research. *Ambio,* 44 (2), 82–98.

Bayfield, N. G. 1979. Recovery of four montane heath communities on Cairngorm, Scotland, from disturbance by trampling. *Biological Conservation,* 15 (3), 165–179.

Beng, L. Y. & Barker, T. 2016. *Hipsters, Festivals and Evictions: Gentrification and the Rise of the Neuvo-Creative Class in George Town Penang.* Bangkok: School of Communication Arts, Bangkok University.

Bergstrom, D. M., Lucieer, A., Kiefer, K., Wasley, J., Belbin, L., Pedersen, T. K. & Chown, S. L. 2009. Indirect effects of invasive species removal devastate World Heritage Island. *Journal of Applied Ecology,* January, 73–81.

Berry, R. J. 2009. *The Natural History of Islands.* London: Collins.

Bianca, S. 2000. *Urban Form in the Arab World.* London: Thames and Hudson.

Bouchard, E. H., Little, L. E., Miller, C. M., Rundell, S. M., Vlodaver, E. M. & Maciejewski, K. 2015. Undeclared baggage: do tourists act as vectors for seed dispersal in fynbos protected areas? *Koedoe,* 57 (1), 1–9.

Brown, J. P. & Rose, W. B. 1996. Humidity and moisture in historic buildings: the origins of building and object conservation. *APT Bulletin: The Journal of Preservation Technology,* 27 (3), 12–23.

Champion, M. 2017. The priest, the prostitute, and the slander on the walls: shifting perceptions towards historic graffiti. *Perigrinations: Journal of Medieval Art and Architecture,* 6 (1), 5–37.

City of Edinburgh District Council, 2019. *Edinburgh City Centre Transformation.* Edinburgh: City of Edinburgh District Council.

Cochrane, J. 2013. Exit the dragon? Collapse of co-management at Komodo National Park, Indonesia. *Tourism Recreation Research,* 38 (2), 127–143.

Cohen, E. 1985. The Tourist Guide: the origins, structure and dynamics of a role . *Annals of Tourism Research,* 12 (1), 5–29.

Collins, J. 2008. 'But what if I should need to defecate in your neighbourhood, madame?': empire, redemption, and the 'Tradition of the Oppressed' in a Brazilian World Heritage Site. *Cultural Anthropology,* 23(2), 279–328.

Collins, J. F. 2019. Vital properties and Afro-Brazilian lives: on promiscuities of gentrification and personhood in Salvador, Bahia's Pelourinho Historical Center. *International Journal of Heritage Studies,* 25 (9), 870–881.

Conti, A. 2017. The impacts of tourism on Latin American World Heritage Towns. In: L. Bordeau, M. Gravari-Barbas & M. Robinson, eds. *World Heritage Sites and Tourism: Global and Local Relations.* Abingdon: Routledge, 175–188.

Dans, E. P. & Gonzalez, P. A. 2018. The Altamira controversy: assessing the economic impact of a world heritage site for planning and tourism management. *Journal of Cultural Heritage,* 30, 180–189.

De Luca, G., Shrivani Dastgerdi, A., Francini, C. & Liberatore, G. 2020. Sustainable cultural heritage planning and management of overtourism in art cities: lessons from Atlas World Heritage. *Sustainability,* 12 (9), 3929.

Demas, M., Agnew, N. & Fan, J. 2015. *Strategies for Sustainable Tourism at the Mogao Grottoes of Dunhuang, China.* New York: Springer.

Dimelli, D. 2019. Modern conservation principles and their application in Mediterranean Historic Centers – the case of Valletta. *Heritage*, 2, 787–796.

Dodds, R. & Butler, R. 2019. The phenomena of overtourism: a review. *International Journal of Tourism Cities*, 5 (4), 519–528.

Doorne, S. 2000. Caves, cultures and crowds: carrying capacity meets consumer sovereignty. *Journal of Sustainable Tourism*, 8 (2), 116–130.

Durham County Council, 2003. *Saddler Street Road User Charge Scheme. Monitoring Report.* Durham: Durham County Council.

Durham County Council, 2016. *Durham City Sustainable Transport Strategy 2016–2033*, Durham: Durham County Council.

Durham County Council, n.d. *Transport Innovation in an Historic City. A Demand Management Proposal for Durham City by Durham County Council*, Durham: Durham County Council.

Duval, M., Smith, B., Gauchon, C., Mayer, L. & Malgat, C. 2020. 'I have visited the Chauvet Cave': the heritage experience of a rock art replica. *International Journal of Heritage Studies*, 26 (2), 142–162.

Eskilinen, A. & Oskanen, J. 2006. Changes in the abundance, composition and species richness of mountain vegetation in relation to summer grazing by reindeer. *Journal of Vegetation Science*, 17, 245–254.

Feilden, B. M. & Jokilehto, J. 1993. *Management Guidelines for World Cultural Heritage Sites.* Rome: ICCROM.

Fernandez, A. M. 2019. Altamira: integrity and authenticity as a political tool. In: S. Doempke, ed. *World Heritage Watch Report 2019.* Berlin: World Heritage Watch, 142–144.

Foo, R. & Krishnapillai, G. 2019. Preserving the intangible living heritage in the George Town World Heritage Site, Malaysia. *Journal of Heritage Tourism*, 14 (4), 358–370.

Forbes, H. F. 2019. Writing on the wall: Anglo-Saxons at Monte Sant'Angelo sul Gargano (Puglia) and the spiritual and social significance of graffiti. *Journal of Late Antiquity*, 12 (1), 169–210.

Fossi, M. C., Panti, C., Baini, M. & Lavers, J. L. 2018. A review of plastic-associated pressures: cetaceans of the Mediterranean Sea and Eastern Australian Shearwaters as case studies. *Frontiers in Marine Science*, 5, 173–182.

Frissell Jr, Sidney S. & Stankey, George H. 1972. Wilderness environmental quality: search for social and ecological harmony. In: *Proceedings of the 1972 National Convention; 1972 October 1–5, Hot Springs, AR.* Washington, DC: Society of American Foresters, 170–183.

Garcia, B. R. 2012. Management issues in dark tourism attractions: the case of ghost tours in Edinburgh and Toledo. *Journal of Unconventional Parks, Tourism & Recreation Research*, 4 (1), 14–19.

Geffroy, B., Samia, D. S. M., Bessa, E. & Blumstein, D. T. 2015. How nature-based tourism might increase prey vulnerability to predators. *Trends in Ecology & Evolution*, 30 (12), 755–765.

Gentry, G. W. 2007. Walking with the dead: the place of ghost walk tourism in Savannah, Georgia. *Southeastern Geographer*, 47 (2), 222–238.

Goodwin, H., Kent, I., Parker, K. & Walpole, M. 1998. *Tourism, Conservation and Sustainable Development: Case Studies from Asia and Africa.* Wildlife and Development Series No. 10. London: IIED.

Goosem, M. 2000. Effects of tropical rainforest roads on small mammals: edge effects in community composition. *Wildlife Reearch*, 27, 151–163.

Graves, C. P. & Rollason, L. 2013. The monastery of Durham and the wider world: medieval graffiti in the prior's chapel. *Northern History*, 50 (2), 186–215.

Guiver, J. & Stanford, D. 2014. Why destination visitor travel planning falls between the cracks. *Journal of Destination Marketing & Management*, 3 (3), 140–151.

Hanes, A. C., Kalema-Zikusoka, G., Svensson, M. S. & Hill, C. M. 2018. Assessment of health risks posed by tourists visiting mountain gorillas in Bwindi Impenetrable National Park, Uganda. *Primate Conservation*, 32, 1–10.

Hardiman, N. & Burgin, S. 2011. Effects of trampling on in-stream macroinvertebrate communities from canyoning in the Greater Blue Mountains World Heritage Area. *Wetlands Ecology and Management*, 19, 61–71.

Harper, E. 2021. *Graffiti in The Wolf Den*. https://aspectsofhistory.com/the-wolf-den/ (21 May 2021).

Hendee, J. C., Stankey, G. H. & Lucas, R. C. 1990. *Wilderness Management*. 2nd ed. Golden, CO: North America Press.

Hiemstra, A. F., Rambonnet, L., Gravendeel, B. & Schilthuizen, M. 2021. The effects of COVID-19 litter on animal life. *Animal Biology*, 71 (2), 215–231.

Holm, T. & Laursen, K. 2009. Experimental disturbance by walkers affect behaviour and territorial density of Black-Tailed Godwit Limosa Limosa. *Ibis*, 151, 77–87.

Holmes, P. M., Esler, K. J., van Wilgen, B. W. & Richardson, D. M. 2020. Ecological restoration of ecosystems degraded by invasive alien plants in South African Fynbos: Is spontaneous succession a viable strategy?. *Transactions of the Royal Society of South Africa*, 75 (2), 111–119.

Homsy, J. 1999. *Ape Tourism and Human Diseases: How Close Should We Get? A Critical Review of the Rules and Regulations Governing Park Management & Tourism for the Wild Mountain Gorilla, Gorilla gorilla beringei*. Kigali: International Gorilla Conservation Programme.

Hopkirk, P. 2006. *Foreign Devils on the Silk Road: The Search for the Lost Treasures of Central Asia*. London: John Murray.

HWHAMA. 2007. *Masterplan 2021 for Hampi Local Planning Area*. Hospet, India: Hampi World Heritage Area Management Authority.

International Gorilla Conservation Programme. 2020. Mountain gorilla tourism in the wake of Covid19: how close should we get?https://igcp.org/updates/mountain-gorilla-tourism -in-the-wake-of-covid-19-how-close-should-we-get/ (9 May 2021).

Jover, J. & Diaz-Parra, I. 2022. Who is the city for? Overtourism, lifestyle migration and social sustainability. *Tourism Geographies*, 24 (1), 9–32.

Junge, R. E., Barrett, M. A. & Yoder, A. D. 2011. Effects of anthropogenic disturbance on indri (Indri indri) health in Madagascar. *American Journal of Primatology*, 73 (7), 632–642.

Kalman, H. 2014. *Heritage Planning. Principles and Process*. New York: Routledge.

Kamel, E. & Hanks, L. 2009. *Towards Self-Interpreting World Heritage Sites: A Proposal of Design-Guiding Principles for the Landscape of Interpretive Sites*. Hanoi: Forum UNESCO.

Keios, 2015. *Revised Sustainable Tourism Masterplan Volume 1: Strategic Plan. Report to the Republic of Rwanda Ministry of Trade & Industry*. Rome: Keios Development Consulting.

Koichi, K., Cottrell, A., Sangha, K. K. & Gordon, I. 2013. What determines the acceptability of wildlife control methods? A case of feral pig management in the wet tropics World Heritage area, Australia. *Human Dimensions of Wildlife*, 18 (2), 97–108.

Larson, L. R. & Poudyal, N. C., 2012. Developing sustainable tourism through adaptive resource management: a case study of Machu Picchu, Peru. *Journal of Sustainable Tourism*, 20 (7), 917–938.

Leite, R. P. 2015. Cities and Gentrification in Contemporary Brazil. *Current Urban Studies*, 3, 175–186.

Lepinay, C., Mihajlovski, A., Touron, S., Seyer, D., Bousta, F. & Di Martino, P. 2018. Bacterial diversity associated with saline efflorescences damaging the walls of a French decorated prehistoric cave registered as a World Cultural Heritage Site. *International Biodeterioration & Biodegradation*, 130, 55–64.

Li, H., Wang, W., Zhan, H., Qiu, F., Guo, Q., Sun, S. & Zhang, G. 2017. The effects of atmospheric moisture on the mural paintings of the Mogao Grottoes. *Studies in Conservation*, 62 (4), 229–239.

Liddle, M. J. 1997. *Recreation Ecology: The Ecological Impact of Outdoor Recreation and Ecotourism*. London: Chapman Hall.

Lloyd, H. & Lithgow, K. 2011. Agents of deterioration. In: H. Lloyd, ed. *The National Trust Manual of Housekeeping. Care and Conservation of Collections in Historic Houses*. Swindon: National Trust, 55–67.

Loades, C. M. 2019. Heritage and Scale – Challenges to wellbeing and place management in Dubrovnik's World Heritage Site. *Journal of Urban Culture Research*, 19, 5–32.

Maekawa, M., Lanjouw, A., Rutagarama, E. & Sharp, D. 2013. Mountain gorilla tourism generating wealth and peace in post-conflict Rwanda. *Natural Resources Forum*, 37 (2), 127–137.

Makhadmeh, A., Al-Badarneh, M., Rawashdeh, A. & Al-Shorman, A. 2020. Evaluating the carrying capacity at the archaeological site of Jerash (Gerasa) using mathematical GIS modeling. *Egyptian Journal of Remote Sensing and Space Science*, 23 (2), 159–165.

Mangot, A. H., Birtles, R. A. & Marsh, H. 2011. Attraction of dwarf minke whales Balaenoptera acutorostrata to vessels and swimmers in the Great Barrier Reef World Heritage Area - the management challenge of an inquisitive whale. *Journal of Ecotourism*, 10 (1), 64–76.

Manisalidis, I., Stavroploulou, E., Stavropoulous, A. & Bezirtzoglou, E. 2020. Environmental and health impacts of air pollution: a review. *Frontiers in Public Health*, 8 (14), 1–13.

Markwick, M. 2018. Creative clusters in the regeneration of Valletta and the cultural politics of Strait Street. *Urban Research and Practice*, 11 (2), 87–110.

Mason, S., Newsome, D., Moore, S. & Admiraal, R. 2015. Recreational trampling negatively impacts vegetation structure of an Australian biodiversity hotspot. *Biodiversity and Conservation*, 24 (11), 2685–270.

May, V. 2015. Coastal cliff conservation and management: the Dorset and East Devon Coast World Heritage Site. *Journal of Coast Conservation*, 19, 821–829.

McArthur, S. 2000. Visitor Management in Action. An Analysis of the Development and Implementation of visitor Management Models at Jenolan Caves and Kangaroo Island. PhD thesis, University of Canberra, ACT, Australia.

McGlade, D. 2014. Hadrian's Wall Path National Trail and the World Heritage Site. A Case study in heritage access management. In: P. Stone & D. Brough, eds. *Managing, Using, and Interpreting Hadrian's Wall as World Heritage*, 47–61.

Meetiyagoda, L. 2018. Pedestrian safety in Kandy Heritage City, Sri Lanka: lessons from World Heritage cities. *Sustainable Cities and Society*, 38 (April), 301–308.

Milano, C., Novelli, M. & Cheer, J. M. (2019) Overtourism and degrowth: a social movements perspective. *Journal of Sustainable Tourism*, 27 (12), 1857–1875.

Monz, C. 2002. The response of arctic tundra plant communities to human trampling disturbance. *Journal of Environmental Management*, 64, 207–217.

MOTA. 2019. *Birthplace of Jesus. Church of the Nativity and Pilgrimage Route. Conservation Management Plan for the World Heritage Site*. Ramallah, Palestine: MOTA.

Newsome, D., Dowling, R. & Moore, S. 2005. *Wildlife Tourism*. Clevedon: Channel View Publications.

Newsome, D., Moore, S. A. & Dowling, R. K. 2002. *Natural Area Tourism. Ecology, Impacts and Management*. Clevedon: Channel View.

Nobre, E. A. C. 2002. Urban regeneration experiences in Brazil: Historical preservation, tourism development and gentrification in Salvador da Bahia. *Urban Design International*, 7, 109–124.

Olafsdottir, R. & Runnstrom, M. C. 2013. Assessing hiking trails condition in two popular tourist destinations in the Icelandic highlands. *Journal of Outdoor Recreation and Tourism*, 3–4 (December), 57–67.

Orbaşli, A. 2000. *Tourists in Historic Towns. Urban Conservation and Heritage Management.* London: E & FN Spon.

Orbaşli, A. 2008. *Architectural Conservation.* Oxford: Blackwell Science Ltd.

Orbaşli, A. & Shaw, S. 2011. Transport and visitors in historic cities. In: L. M. Lumsdon & S. J. Page, eds. *Tourism and Transport. Issues and Agenda for the New Millennium.* Abingdon: Routledge, 93–104.

Oskam, J. A. 2020. Eiffel Tower and Big Ben, or 'off the beaten track'? Centripetal demand in Airbnb. *Hospitality and Society*, 10 (2), 127–155.

Palacios, G., Lowenstine, L.J., Cranfield, M. R., Gilardi, K. V., Spelman, L., Lukasik-Braum, M., Kinani, J. F., Mudakikwa, A., Nyirakaragire, E., Bussetti, A. V. & Savji, N. 2011. Human metapneumovirus in wild mountain gorillas, Rwanda. *Emerging Infectious Diseases*, 17 (4), 711–713.

Pedersen, A. 2002. *Managing Tourism at World Heritage Sites. A Practical Manual for World Heritage Site Managers*, Paris: UNESCO World Heritage Centre.

Pejchar, L. & Mooney, H. A. 2009. Invasive species, ecosystem services and human well-being. *Trends in Ecology and Evolution*, 24 (9), 497–504.

Pendelbury, J., Short, M. & While, A. 2009. Urban World Heritage Sites and the problem of authenticity. *Cities*, 26, 349–358.

Pfattheicher, S., Nockur, L., Böhm, R., Sassenrath, C. & Petersen, M. B. 2020. The emotional path to action: empathy promotes physical distancing and wearing of face masks during the COVID-19 pandemic. *Psychological Science*, 31 (11), 1363–1373.

Pickering, C. M. & Hill, W. 2007. Impacts of recreation and tourism on plant biodiversity and vegetation in protected areas in Australia. *Journal of Environmental Management*, 85, 791–800.

Pocock, D. 2013. *The Story of Durham.* Stroud: The History Press.

Roga, N. B., Ferguson, W. & Bagoora, F. 2017. Transboundary conservation areas in African mountains: Opportunities and challenges for addressing global change. *Earth Sciences*, 6 (6), 117–126.

Ryan, P. G. 2018. Entanglement of birds in plastics and other synthetic materials. *Marine Pollution Bulletin*, 135, 159–164.

Sabuhoro, E., Wright, B., Munanura, I. E., Nyakabwa, I. N. & Nibigira, C., 2021. The potential of ecotourism opportunities to generate support for mountain gorilla conservation among local communities neighboring Volcanoes National Park in Rwanda. *Journal of Ecotourism*, 20 (1), 1–17.

Salazar, N. B. 2005. Tourism and glocalisation 'local' tour guiding. *Annals of Tourism Research*, 32 (3), 628–646.

Sandbrook, C. & Semple, S. 2006. The rules and the reality of mountain gorilla Gorilla beringei beringei tracking: how close do tourists get? *Oryx*, 40 (4), 428–433.

Santos, C. A. & Zobler, K. A. 2012. The bridge on the River Elbe: World Heritage in a modern city. *Annals of Tourism Research*, 39, 484–486.

Seyedashraf, B., Ravankhah, M., Weidner, S. & Schmidt, M. 2017. Applying Heritage Impact Assessment to urban development: World Heritage property of Masjed-e Jame of Isfahan in Iran. *Sustainable Cities and Society*, 31, 213–224.

Shackleton, R. T., Shackleton, C. M. & Kull, C. A. 2019. The role of invasive alien species in shaping local livelihoods and human well-being: a review. *Journal of Environmental Management*, 229, 145–157.

Shackleton, R. T. et al. 2020. Biological invasions in World Heritage Sites: current status and a proposed monitoring and reporting framework. *Biodiversity and Conservation*, 29, 3327–3347.

Silberman, N. 2006. The ICOMOS–Ename Charter Initiative: rethinking the role of heritage interpretation in the 21st century. *The George Wright Forum*, 23 (1), 28–32.

Simpson, F. 1999. Tourist impact in the historic centre of Prague: resident and visitor perceptions of the historic built environment. *Geographical Journal*, 165 (2), 173–183.

Spenceley, A., Habyalimana, S., Tusabe, R. & Mariza, D. 2010. Benefits to the poor from gorilla tourism in Rwanda. *Development Southern Africa*, 27 (5), 647–662.

Su, X. 2010. Urban Conservation in Lijiang, China. Power Structure and Funding Systems. *Cities*, 27, 164–171.

Sullivan, T. J. 2017. *Air Pollution and Its Impacts on U.S. National Parks*. Boca Raton, FL: CRC Press.

TDI, 2019. *Integrated Tourism Master Plan for Borobudur – Yogyakarta – Prambanan*, Dublin: Tourism Development International.

UNESCO. n.d. Sustainable tourism. UNESCO World Heritage and Sustainable Tourism Programme. https://whc.unesco.org/en/tourism/ (8 July 2022).

UNESCO. n.d.b Virunga National Park. https://whc.unesco.org/en/list/63 (accessed 4 February 2022).

UNWTO. 2018. *'Overtourism'? Understanding and Managing Urban Tourism Growth beyond Perceptions*. Madrid: UNWTO.

UNWTO. 2021. *UNWTO Inclusive Recovery Guide Sociocultural Impacts of COVID-19 Issue 2: Cultural Tourism*. Madrid: UNWTO.

Verdini, G. 2017. Planetary urbanisation and the built heritge from a non-Western perspective: the question of 'how' we should protect the past. *Built Heritage*, 1 (3), 73–82.

Virunga National Park. 2020. Congo gorilla trekking permits. https://www.virungaparkcongo.com/information/congo-gorilla-trekking-permits/ (accessed 7 July 2022).

VisitRwanda. 2022. Gorilla tracking. https://www.visitrwanda.com/interests/gorilla-tracking/ (accessed 7 July 2022).

Volcanoes National Park. 2021. Gorilla trekking permits in Rwanda 2021. https://www.volcanoesparkrwanda.org/information/gorilla-trekking-permits-rwanda-2021/ (accessed 7 July 2022).

Weber, A., Kalema-Zikusoka, G. & Stevens, N. J. 2020. Lack of rule-adherence during Mountain gorilla tourism encounters in Bwindi Impenetrable National Park, Rwanda, places gorillas at risk from human disease. *Frontiers in Public Health*, 8 (1), 1–13.

Westoby, R., Gardiner, S., Carter, R. W. & Scott, N. 2021. Sustainable livelihoods from tourism in the '10 New Balis' in Indonesia. *Asia Pacific Journal of Tourism Research*, 26 (6), 702–716.

Whitfield, R., Whitfield, S. & Agnew, N. 2000. *Cave Temples of Mogao. Art and History on the Silk Road*. Los Angeles: The Getty Conservation Institute and the J. Paul Getty Museum.

Wolf, I. D., Croft, D. B. & Green, R. J. 2019. nature conservation and nature-based tourism: a paradox?. *Environments*, 6 (9), 104.

Zainol, R. 2016. Auditing a Central Area Transit (Cat) bus service in a Malaysia's world heritage site: a case study of Georgetown, Penang. *Malaysian Journal of Society and Space*, 12 (5), 61–73.

Zainol, R., Wang, C., Ali, A. S., Ahmad, F., Aripin, A. W. M. & Salleh, H. 2016. Pedestrianization and walkability in a fast developing UNESCO World Heritage City. *Open House International*, 41 (1), 112–119.

10

PRESENTING AND INTERPRETING WORLD HERITAGE

10.1 Introduction

There is increasing understanding among all heritage stakeholders that it is important for a broad range of reasons – economic, social, political – that both natural and cultural World Heritage Sites are made accessible to as broad a range of visitors as possible. One reason for this is that the more the public understands why properties are protected, the more likely they are to support and perhaps even help to fund conservation measures (see for example Kalman, 2014; Matthews, 2020), And one way of delivering this understanding is through interpretation. As has been suggested by Jameson Jr (2008), 'the public interpretation of archaeological and cultural sites has come to be recognised as an essential component in the conservation and protection of cultural resources and sites and in fostering public stewardship around the world' (Jameson Jr, 2008, p. 427).

Former Director of the UNESCO World Heritage Centre, Francesco Bandarin, said in 2002 that

> the very reasons why a property is chosen for inscription on the World Heritage List are also the reasons why millions of tourists flock to those sites year after year. In fact, the belief that World Heritage sites belong to everyone and should be preserved for future generations is the very principle on which the World Heritage Convention is based.
>
> *(cited in Pedersen, 2002, p. 3)*

Thus, understanding what different types of tourists expect from their visit, particularly as regards understanding why a particular site is 'important', and knowing how to deliver this without compromising the integrity and authenticity of the heritage assets in question, is another essential aspect of site management. The

DOI: 10.4324/9781003044857-11

tourism potential of World Heritage has been explored previously in this book, with the key conclusion being that there are multiple different stakeholders with interests in World Heritage, all of whom require different levels of physical and intellectual access so that their expectations and aspirations for engaging with that heritage can be met.

Some of the key challenges of providing physical access to certain types of World Heritage Site have also been outlined in previous chapters and later we will look at the implications of providing access to and managing visitor pressures at both natural and cultural heritage locations. But first it is important to consider how different types of World Heritage Site are presented to the public and made intellectually accessible, and to explore in more detail some of the main strategies that have been adopted across the globe to facilitate and encourage access to World Heritage Site and to raise awareness of the significance of different properties on the list.

Having previously looked at how visitors are able to get close to the physical realities of heritage locations, it is also important to understand the role of inter-pretation as a tool for promoting public understanding of World Heritage as a con-cept on the one hand, and as a tool for facilitating engagement with the OUVs of individual sites on the other. This is significant because, as Shackley pointed out some two decades ago, 'Most World Heritage Sites, particularly those in developing countries or where tourism and visitor management policies are poorly developed, have a very basic level of on-site interpretation (or even none at all)' (2000, p. 7). Yet understanding why a site has been afforded WH designation, and what it actu-ally means to different communities of interest, is essential for all stakeholders across the heritage planning, tourism and economic development sectors of local and national government, as well as being a key component of the tourist experience at such locations.

This chapter considers a number of important themes. We consider the presentation and interpretation of heritage sites as covered by the 2008 Ename Charter and review some of the practical ways in which the interpretation of World Heritage values and indeed other aspects of a property's history is delivered. We focus on the role of interpretation as a tool for allowing site managers and others to explain specific aspects of a site's Outstanding Universal Value as well as other stories associated with both its history and its con-temporary context, by considering the different ways in which interpretation is used by heritage site managers, building on the work of David Uzzell and Roy Ballantyne in particular (Uzzell, 1989; Uzzell & Ballantyne, 1998). We look in some detail at the benefits and drawbacks of reconstructions at heritage sites, the role of tour guides as intermediaries between tourists and the heritage sites they are visiting, costumed interpretation and finally the growing role of Augmented Reality (AR) and Virtual Reality (VR) as key assets within the heritage site manager's toolbox. We start however with a brief consideration of the Ename Charter and its implications for presenting and interpreting World Heritage.

10.2 The Ename Charter

In 2008 the ICOMOS Charter for the Interpretation and Presentation of Cultural Heritage Sites (also known as the Ename Charter) was ratified at the organisation's General Assembly in Quebec 'to define the basic principles of Interpretation and Presentation as essential components of heritage conservation efforts and as a means of enhancing public appreciation and understanding of cultural heritage sites' (Ename Center, 2020). The Charter defines interpretation in quite broad terms, including all activities that seek to raise public awareness and enhance public understanding of cultural heritage sites including lectures, informal and formal education initiatives, community-based learning activities and research. It also presents a quite nuanced view of presentation, which it sees as being 'the successfully planned communication of interpretive content through the arrangement of interpretive information through a variety of technical means, including informational panels, museum displays, formalized walking tours, lectures and multi-media applications' (Jameson Jr, 2008, p. 435).

Thus it is a relevant consideration for heritage and tourism planners dealing with situations where visitors are already within a World Heritage property – unsuprisingly it says nothing about how physical access to a particular location should be managed, since there are so many site-specific factors to take into consideration that generalities would be meaningless.

Seven principles are stated within the Charter designed to guide public communication, education and learning at cultural heritage sites, detailed in Table 10.1.

TABLE 10.1 Ename Charter Principles.

Principle 1: Access and Understanding – Facilitate understanding and appreciation of cultural heritage sites and foster public awareness and engagement in the need for their protection and conservation.

Principle 2: Information Sources – Communicate the meaning of cultural heritage sites to a range of audiences through careful, documented recognition of significance, through accepted scientific and scholarly methods as well as from living cultural traditions.

Principle 3: Context and Setting – Safeguard the tangible and intangible values of cultural heritage sites in their natural and cultural settings and social contexts.

Principle 4: Authenticity – Respect the authenticity of cultural heritage sites, by communicating the significance of their historic fabric and cultural values and protecting them from the adverse impact of intrusive interpretive infrastructure, visitor pressure, inaccurate or inappropriate interpretation.

Principle 5: Sustainability – Contribute to the sustainable conservation of cultural heritage sites, through promoting public understanding of, and participation in, ongoing conservation efforts, ensuring long-term maintenance of the interpretive infrastructure and regular review of its interpretive contents.

Principal 6: Inclusiveness – Encourage inclusiveness in the interpretation of cultural heritage sites, by facilitating the involvement of stakeholders and associated communities in the development and implementation of interpretive programmes.

Principal 7: Research, Evaluation and Training – Develop technical and professional guidelines for heritage interpretation and presentation, including technologies, research, and training. Such guidelines must be appropriate and sustainable in their social contexts.

Source: ICOMOS, 2008.

As noted by Silberman (2009, p. 7) the Charter's principal contribution to advancing the interpretation and presentation of public heritage is that it argued that these activities should not just be seen as the 'communication of factual scientific, artistic, or historical data about archaeological sites, cultural landscapes, and historic buildings – but as a complex public exercise of historical reflection among many stakeholders, characterized by a concern for open access, sustainability, and inclusiveness'. In other words, it encouraged all those involved in this aspect of facilitating public engagement with heritage to consider the views and expectations of a much broader range of interest groups than was often the case previously. And notwithstanding the fact that the Charter was prepared for cultural heritage properties, there has long been general acceptance that these principles apply to natural heritage sites as well.

There is often great interest in such charters when they are published, though their currency can be somewhat time limited. For example, a survey of the 380 members of the UK's Association for Heritage Interpretation (AHI) carried out to inform the preparation this book found that fewer than 50% of its members had heard of the Ename charter, and of those, fewer than half used it to inform their practice. In other words, not much more than a decade after it had been prepared, the Charter was, for many people working in the field, effectively irrelevant. One respondent, a professional interpreter with more than 20 years' experience, felt that it was 'too simplistic' and that it 'provided a nice idea to aim for rather than an effective, operational tool'. Where it did have some impact, however, was at an organisational level, with representatives of one leading public sector heritage organisation saying that it had informed their corporate interpretation principles and access policies, and was regularly provided to their contractors in order to guide the initial planning and installation of interpretation at the heritage sites in their guardianship.

Similarly, a review of the most recent Management Plans for all of the UK's World Heritage Site at the time of writing found that only one specifically mentioned the charter – that was the plan for the **Slate Landscape of Northwest Wales**, inscribed in 2021 and which specifically states that:

> interpretation of The Slate Landscape of Northwest Wales is guided by the ICOMOS Ename Charter (2008) for interpretation and presentation, and is based on its first, fifth and sixth principles: access and understanding; planning for sustainability, and concern for inclusivity.
>
> *(Gwynedd Council, 2020, p. 165)*

These observations tend to support Silberman's (2009) contention that the principal value of the Charter is as a conceptual guide for planning interpretation and presentation of heritage sites, rather than as a template for delivering specific interventions on the ground.

10.3 Presenting and interpreting World Heritage

10.3.1 The conventional view of heritage interpretation

American conservationist Freeman Tilden (1883–1980), acknowledged by many as the founder of modern heritage interpretation, defined interpretation as 'an educational activity which aims to reveal meaning and relationships through the use of original objects, by first-hand experience, and by illustrative media, rather than simply to communicate factual information' (Tilden, 2007, p. 8). Within the heritage and tourism sectors, interpretation is generally acknowledged as being a valuable tool used by site managers to promote greater public awareness and understanding of heritage (see for example Bryant, 2006 or Hodges, 2020). Stewart et al. (1998) suggest that 'interpretation, either explicitly or implicitly, aims to stimulate, facilitate and extend people's understanding of place so that empathy towards heritage, conservation, culture and landscape can be developed' (p. 257). Some heritage professionals go even further, and argue that 'interpretation enriches our lives through engaging emotions, enhancing experiences and deepening understanding of places, people, events and objects from the past and present' (Association for Heritage Interpretation, 2020).

In other words, interpretation is an instrumental part of the manager's toolbox, conveying through a broad range of media the significance of a building, place, object or cultural practice to host communities, visitors and other interested parties and adding value to the visitor experience. It is particularly important in the context of World Heritage Sites where there is an expectation by UNESCO that the Outstanding Universal Value of such locations are clearly understood by the broadest range of stakeholders possible while at the same time, site managers are keen to ensure that people are aware of the reasons why funds are always required to protect and maintain heritage sites.

10.3.2 Critiques of Tilden

There are, however, dissenting voices. The validity of the instrumental use of interpretation as a management tool has been questioned by, for instance, Staiff (2014) who suggests that it is not appropriate to employ interpretation to change attitudes and behaviour.

Staiff also critiques Tilden's philosophical approach to interpretation, feeling that Tilden tended to assume ignorance on the part of visitors to heritage sites and that the conventional approach to interpretation delivery developed by Tilden, and implemented to this day by professional interpreters, perpetuates a hierarchical relationship between the expert and the non-expert, between those assumed to be have knowledge of a site and those assumed to lack such knowledge. In other words, Staiff is suggesting that within the field of interpretation there remains an element of the so-called Authorise Heritage Discourse as championed by Laurajane Smith (2006). Similar concern is expressed by Jameson Jr (2008) who stresses that it is important to recognise the need for multivocality whereby several, possibly competing, perspectives on a site's heritage are considered and presented to the public. In other words, one must move beyond just presenting one central, 'authorised' perspective on a site's importance. He highlights both the importance of values-based management as a tool for uncovering multiple views on heritage (even where these views may differ between groups), but also stresses the need to recognise the views of groups who have traditionally been marginalised in discussions about heritage, suggesting that 'philosophical movements in Australasia towards inclusiveness of indigenous perspectives ... set an example for other countries' (Jameson Jr, 2008, p. 428).

As is demonstrated in our case study of Hadrian's Wall in northern England (part of the **Frontiers of the Roman Empire,** or Roman Limes, World Heritage Site), including a diversity of interpretive messages and themes relevant to different stakeholders tends to provide a broader and more nuanced tourism experience as well as enabling a more coherent and appropriate approach to site management that reflects and protects the property's Outstanding Universal Value. Moreover, as indicated earlier in Section 10.2, this is actually an expectation for all cultural World Heritage Sites as laid out in the 2008 Ename Charter. Nonetheless, many interpretation practitioners working at World Heritage Sites continue to follow Tilden's core ideology of using a broad range of media to convey prescribed or authorised messages to one or more audiences.

10.3.3 'Hot' interpretation

Another critique of traditional approaches to heritage interpretation is that they have tended to focus on non-controversial, safe topics and position historical fact over emotion (Uzzell & Ballantyne, 1998). A counter-point to this which recognises the emotional significance of places, of events, to some visitors, is so-called 'hot-interpretation', defined by Uzzell & Ballantyne as 'interpretation that appreciates the need for and injects an affective component into its subject matter' (1998, p. 153). The authors argue that providing interpretive content that stimulates an affective response in those engaging with it is particularly important when talking about more challenging subjects such as environmental concerns (including climate change and species depletion); power, class and caste issues (almost always an under-represented story at built heritage sites) and of course armed conflict and its impact on society. Thus 'hot interpretation' is entirely appropriate at many World Heritage Sites, either because their designation has been used to mark or celebrate some of these difficult issues, or because the property itself is challenged by the impacts of climate change, conflict or international politics.

Such issues were brought to the forefront in summer 2020 by the 'Black Lives Matter' movement and the challenges it raised about the way that the legacy of slavery and the oppression of Africans and African-Americans continue to be memorialised through statues of prominent individuals who benefited financially from that abhorrent trade. This contemporary movement reflected protests a few years earlier associated with the 'Rhodes Must Fall' campaign which began at the

University of Cape Town, South Africa in 2015 and which saw mass protests initially directed against a statue on campus that commemorated Cecil Rhodes, the 19th-century politician, but which later extended to cover the decolonisation of the curriculum. Those protests spread not just to other South African universities but also to the University of Oxford in the UK, where students called for a statue of Rhodes to be removed from Oriel College and to Harvard Law School in the USA, directed at its association with the slave-owning history of the Royall family who were early benefactors of the University's Law School. A number of internal commissions and collaborative working groups currently exist in major historic universities globally, focusing on how universities profited from the slave trade either in endowments or in the use of slave labour. Interestingly, one of these is a World Heritage Site – The **University of Virginia** (UVa) in Charlottesville – which has itself committed to 'exploring and commemorating its relationship with slavery, as well as the lives of the enslaved people who were an integral part of early life at Jefferson's University' (University of Virginia, 2018). As Woodward & Carnegie (2020) show, this represents what is a recent change in emphasis of interpreting the heritage of the UVa campus, a World Heritage Site since 1987, where the convention was always to ignore the history of slavery associated with the campus and the discrimination against students of colour that extended well after the Civil War.

This is not to say that the history of slavery, and the difficult questions it raises for many people today, has not been explored at World Heritage locations. In 1994, UNESCO launched the Slave Route Project in Benin, with the aim of 'breaking the silence' surrounding the slave trade and slavery. A suite of initiatives and programmes covering historical, memorial, creative, educational and heritage themes have been implemented in many African, Caribbean and South American countries to raise awareness of that terrible period of history and the impact it had on so many lives. The legacy of slavery is presented at several important WH properties including **National History Park – Citadel, Sans Souci, Ramiers** (Haiti, inscribed 1982); the **Aapravasi Ghat and the Le Morne Cultural Landscape** (Mauritius, inscribed 2006 and 2008 respectively) the **Blue and John Crow Mountains** in Jamaica (inscribed 2015) and at **Kunta Kinteh Island and Related Sites** in the Gambia (see case study in Chapter 11).

So from a heritage interpretation view, it is important to note the words of Wallis (2019) who argues that 'there is no single way to view the past and to apply historical lessons to the present' (p1) and that it is important, when discussing the complex legacies of conflict and imperialism, that we are all willing and able to engage with our personal discomfort while at the same time acknowledging that the past was not a simple binary of good versus evil or right versus wrong. Crucially, heritage property managers and interpreters need to acknowledge and engage with controversy in order to tackle established cultural understandings and political positions, and to energise social change for the better while understanding that, as Richter (2005), suggests 'the most important political issue surrounding heritage tourism is whether even an extensive exposure to it leads to a better informed or perhaps more tolerant individual' (p. 269). In effect, it is important to offer what Copeland (2006) refers to as a constructivist approach to interpretation rather than a more positivist one, whereby visitors are allowed or even encouraged to bring their own ideas, preconceptions and theories to the discussion, thus becoming more active players in the interpretation of a site or property and acting as agents of their own experience.

10.3.4 Uses of interpretation

Different authors provide differing opinions of what interpretation is actually for, or what it can be used for. For instance, Uzzell (1989) suggests that interpretation can be put to four uses:

- Interpretation as 'soft' visitor management (raising awareness, increasing understanding);
- Interpretation as 'hard' visitor management (guiding or directing visitors around a site)
- Interpretation as propaganda (promoting the values of a particular site or activity);
- Interpretation as a value-added element of the tourism industry (where interpretation is used to create a heritage product – possibly an event, temporary or permanent attraction).

Park (2014) reports the views of Light & Prentice (1994) who see interpretation as a valuable aspect of product development at heritage sites because of its limited impact on the perceived authenticity of such sites, by which they mean it is an investment in product development that does not necessarily require making physical changes to the heritage assets themselves. As such, it is an important tool for informing different audiences about what they are looking at, and why it is significance. He proposes three slightly different functions of interpretation than does Uzzell, namely that interpretation should be used for:

- Constructing and enhancing the visitor experience;
- Encouraging conservation/ preservation through education;
- Ensuring the sustainability of tourism.

Like Uzzell, Park states that it is more than just about conveying knowledge and factual information, though he is less committed to the role of interpretation in hard visitor management. Jameson Jr (2008), following Kohl (2003), argues that a key role of interpretation should be moving beyond site-specific resource protection to a 'larger system of information and beliefs that affect how civilization treats natural and cultural entities' (p. 437), thus supporting Park's second objective for interpretation as a tool of heritage managers.

This view is further developed by Benton (2009) who argues that interpretation should generally perform two main functions: first, it should convey resource management topics and second, and what is in his view its seminal goal, it should connect visitors to natural and cultural heritage. To do this, Benton argues there are four key aspects to good interpretation: connecting visitors to resources, conveying agency mission and influencing behaviour, encouraging environmental literacy, and generally promoting tourism outcomes. For the purposes of the next part of this chapter, however, Uzzel's four functions of interpretation will provide the framework around which to explore the use of interpretation at World Heritage Sites.

10.3.5 Interpretation as a tool of soft visitor management

Tilden's proposal that only if people understand and appreciate the values embodied in heritage assets will they be prepared to engage with and support their conservation and protection was first made in the 1950s but remains relevant today. Interpretation of sensitive landscapes, their special values and their rationale for designation as protected areas, has long been seen as a tool for promoting sustainable tourism both through overt and covert means (Moscardo, 1998). Achieving site management objectives through interpretation is particularly important at fragile cultural and natural heritage properties, as visitors need to be aware why they are being asked to behave in a certain way (Bryant, 2006). Bryant also contends that interpretation should go further than just explaining why certain landscapes have been or are being protected, and that property managers should be more proactive by raising public awareness of contemporary social, political and economic issues around sustainable development, environmental protection, cultural diversity, access and inclusion. This of course fits right into the UNESCO agenda for World Heritage Sites, as well as the organisation's broader aspirations for global economic development laid out in the Sustainable Development Goals (see Chapter 11).

10.3.6 Hard visitor management

In terms of delivering hard visitor management through interpretation, the careful placing of interpretive panels and the use of guided trails or routes is used to direct visitors to locations where site managers wish visitors to spend time and away from more fragile locations (Pedersen, 2002). Guided walks are a well-established interpretive tool that, avoid the need for investment in costly supporting infrastructure, can create employment opportunities in rural areas and which, because of their flexibility, can direct visitors towards particular locations thus maximising desired management outcomes (Crawford & Black, 2012).

How visitors to protected areas such as natural World Heritage Sites react to different scales of interpretation provision was addressed by Hughes & Morrison-Saunders (2005), who investigated whether visitors at sites that are intensively interpreted gain a better understanding of the site than those at sites where interpretation is relatively modest in scale. They found that the intensity of interpretation did not appear to affect visitors' perceptions or influence attitudes towards a site. Rather, it is the nature of the site itself, the demographic profile of the visitor and their pre-existing level of background understanding that were more important. They also found that repeat visitors are less responsive to new interpretive messages than one-off or first-time visitors which, they suggested, can present challenges to site managers who wish to put across a strong conservation message, particularly where the conservation imperative is relatively recent.

10.3.7 Interpretation as propaganda

The propaganda angle is a reflection of Laurajane Smith's (2006) concept of the Authorised Heritage Discourse (AHD), whereby those in authority determine what is and what is not protected, conserved and presented for public consumption. There can be tension when there are multiple opinions of what is valued at a site, with different stakeholders valuing the location in different ways and wishing to see their own understanding of 'heritage' given primacy. This reflects the concern noted earlier by Staiff (2014) who suggests that community interests in heritage are often subsumed or even ignored by approaches to interpretation that celebrate the national interest. This point is taken even further forward by Shackel & Palus (2006) who argue that there is often a political agenda to remembering, celebrating and interpreting industrial landscapes in particular, and that the role and conditions of the workforce tend to be ignored in favour of technical achievement and architectural design. Given that there are many industrial heritage sites on the UNESCO list, telling the stories of those workers who toiled in uncomfortable workplaces such as tin mines, coal mines, textile factories and saltpetre works is important because it sustains the memory of their contribution to economic development and social life at the time those facilities were active (see for instance Hale, 2001; Walker, 2011).

10.3.8 Adding value through interpretation

The final of Uzzell's four functions for interpretation is to add value to the visitor product and, to paraphrase Mazel (2017, p. 422), to enhance the personal experience of engaging with heritage sites and places. In other words, there may be occasions when there is a need to augment what already exists in order to attract and satisfy visitors and create an experience or indeed to provide intellectual access to the property away from the site, most usually these days through ICT. This is particularly the case where interpretive provision is seen essentially as part of a destination's tourism product. Examples might include the provision of stand-alone visitor centres that offer an immersive and stand-alone experience, or holding costumed re-enactments that are events in their own right.

When thinking about the challenges of using interpretation to add value to the visitor experience, West & Ndlovu (2010) make the interesting point that interpretation of the landscape is particularly challenging in contexts where there is little or no continuity of community understanding, in other words where there are generational gaps between those who 'created' a cultural landscape and those coming later to explore it from a leisure perspective. This is particularly the case in the West, they argue. How does one add value when there is a generational or a cultural disconnect between those who created the observed industrial heritage landscape and those who are consuming it? That, obviously, is where interpretation that talks about the human condition, past and present, in these locations, becomes even more important.

Another interesting point raised by Richter (2005) relates to the implications for the heritage experience associated with the growing trend towards downsizing the public sector and introducing neoliberal ideologies in many economies, a phenomenon that has seen resources for national, regional and local heritage organisations cut back. She questions whether this has had a knock-on effect on the increasing levels of entrepreneurship and entertainment evidenced at many heritage sites, as site managers try to compete with theme parks and other leisure attractions. Indeed, many sites have seen the emergence of so-called 'edutainment', defined by Okan (2003) as an IT-based approach to learning that relies on visual materials, on narrative or game-like formats, and on more informal, less didactic styles of address that engage the participant's emotions; by Moss (2009) as 'recreational learning and knowledge transfer in non-traditional informal settings' (p. 248), and by Park (2014) merely as a hybrid of entertainment and education.

For some critics, such as Okan (2003) edutainment represents a 'dumbing-down' of learning though others, including Park (2014) argue that it shouldn't be seen as a threat to more 'authentic' experiences but rather as an enhanced approach to delivering interpretation that appeals to certain specific markets who have often been under-represented at heritage sites in the past. There is certainly evidence of what Hertzman et al. (2008) refer to as Edutainment Heritage Tourist Attractions (EHTAs) delivering valuable learning experiences, arguing that 'many visitors consider the historical representations they encounter at EHTAs to be important, legitimate and reliable sources of historical information' (2008, p. 170).

10.4 Delivering effective interpretation

The key to successful interpretation is in responding sensitively to the needs of the audience, to the 'sense of place' in which the interpretation will be used, and finally to the significance of the site (Uzzell, 1989; Masters & Carter, 1999; Tilden, 2007; Benton, 2009). This is particularly important at World Heritage Sites where there may be multiple understandings of why the site is significant – both the factors represented in the statement of Outstanding Universal Value but also other meanings that are more locally understood. Good interpretation enhances a visit and in no way detracts from the experience. Most importantly, good interpretation stimulates a genuine response from its users, whereby they are more inclined to value the site or resource once they know more about it (the principal aim of inscription, many would argue). Excellent interpretation succeeds in inspiring visitors to actually change their behaviour, for example by taking more care of the resource in some way – treading carefully so as not to damage plants or disturb wildlife, by making a donation towards the preservation of a building, or by volunteering to guide visitors or to pick up litter. In other words, it helps with the delivery of effective 'hard' interpretation as well as adding value to the experience, although it is important to remember that interpretation must be appropriate to the target audience and their own cultural and social norms.

Some two decades ago, Masters & Carter (1999) prepared guidelines on how to evaluate interpretation to advise a nationwide project looking at developing a coordinated approach to cultural and natural heritage interpretation across Scotland and despite its age, their work remains valid. Of particular importance, they argue, is that heritage site interpretation should be based around a clearly defined idea or message on the basis that people tend to remember thematic ideas much better than they remember facts and figures. Their recommended approach to the delivery of high quality, effective interpretation, and requires site managers and other relevant stakeholders to address the following questions:

- Is the interpretive item clearly and specifically related to features, objects, or events in the immediate surroundings?
- How much does it encourage visitors to look at, touch, listen to, smell, taste or otherwise explore the things around them?
- How much does it relate to the audience?
- Does the interpretation communicate either a single or limited number of linked idea(s) or message(s) about its subject?

A decade after these were first published, similar sentiments were expressed in the Ename Charter prepared by ICOMOS to guide the preparation and installation of interpretation at World Heritage Sites and other cultural heritage properties (see Section 10.2), and indeed they remain valid today as a guide to evaluating the success of any interpretive provision at heritage properties, cultural or natural.

10.5 Interpretive tools

10.5.1 Introduction

There are many different tools available to interpretive planners, site managers and other practitioners. Figure 10.1 categorises some of the main tools according to their flexibility at the time of use/ interface with the visitor on the one hand, and the capital and revenue costs associated with installation, delivery and ongoing maintenance on the other. There is not time here to explore the costs and benefits of all of these tools, and hence we focus on three that we propose are of particular relevant and interest to World Heritage Site managers and their partners in the tourism industry. These are:

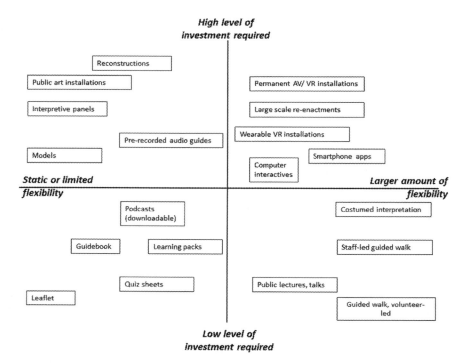

FIGURE 10.1 Categorisation of interpretation tools according to flexibility and cost of delivery and maintenance.

- Reconstructions – a fact of life at archaeological sites for centuries (Bold et al., 2018);
- Guided tours – again, a traditional feature of cultural and heritage tourism since the days of the Grand Tour (Machin, 2016);
- Augmented Reality and Virtual Reality – an emergent trend in both placed-based and remote interpretation (Guttentag, 2010).

10.5.1 Reconstructions as an interpretive tool

One of the main challenges at archaeological sites in particular is that all that many visitors see are the foundations and a few courses of stonework of long abandoned or destroyed sites. The removal for re-use of building materials by later occupiers of the same place can leave a site devoid of meaning for many, unless there is appropriate interpretation. The reconstruction or recreation of structures on the site, or nearby, is one tool which, while expensive, can help bring to life past settlements and structures. Within the context of World Heritage, reconstruction can be very contentious because it is a reinterpretation of the past; even when based on firm evidence it is not the original, 'authentic' structure (Orbaşli, 2008). The Burra Charter is quite clear that reconstruction is appropriate only where a place is incomplete through damage or alteration, and where sufficient evidence exists to reproduce an earlier state of the structure in question. It is also important that any reconstructions are identifiable as new work, either to the naked eye or through additional interpretation. In other words, the casual observer should not be put in a position where they think they are viewing an authentic historic place (Kalman, 2014).

This issue of whether or not the visitor or tourist completely understands that they are looking at reconstructions that might or might not be exact replications of what existed earlier has a long tradition. For instance, Jameson Jr (2008) expresses concern at the legacy of the approach to historic interpretation championed at Colonial Williamsburg in Virginia, USA since the 1930s, where reconstructions of historic buildings based partly on the examination of surviving archaeological and architectural evidence and partly on speculation have proved to be immensely popular with visitors, yet still concern some professionals precisely because conjecture remains a key tool in the presentation and interpretation of the past. He contrasts the work of the Rockefeller Foundation (and later the Colonial Williamsburg Foundation) with that of the US National Park Service, which distinguishes very clearly between reconstruction and restoration, arguing that the latter is most appropriate wherever possible (and which of course reflects the sentiment behind the Burra Charter). Nonetheless, he agrees that reconstructions are particularly valuable in stimulating public imagination of past cultures and civilisations and that they are of considerable benefit to the tourism sector in many destinations.

There are some interesting issues to consider here in terms of what one can see at some World Heritage Sites. For instance, much of the central section of Hadrian's Wall in the North of England, part of the **Frontiers of the Roman Empire World Heritage Site**, does not date back to the first to fourth centuries of Roman occupation, but was effectively rebuilt, using original materials, under the instruction of the 19th-century antiquarian and local landowner John Clayton (Allason-Jones, 2014). On the other hand, in the 1970s, original masonry from the Walltown area was used in the reconstruction of a stretch of curtain wall and a turret at the very popular archaeological site and visitor attraction at Vindolanda (Symonds, 2021). Without additional interpretation, the visitor may not understand exactly what it is they are looking at, and whether or not it is the 'authentic' original.

A similar situation can be found in the **historic centre of Warsaw** (inscribed 1980), almost all of which was reconstructed from plans, drawings and photographs after its destruction by the German Wehrmacht between 1939 and 1944. It took more than two decades of investment to meticulously reconstruct the original built form of the historic area – city walls, street patterns and buildings. The 26-hectare site was eventually listed as a World Heritage Site in 1980 in recognition of its position as 'an outstanding example of a near-total reconstruction of a span of history covering the 13th to the 20th century' (UNESCO, 2021). Again, the average visitor may not recognise the place they are visiting as a mid-to-late-20th-century recreation of a medieval landscape without additional interpretation, and may not recognise that to Polish nationals in particular, it is actually the spirit behind the fact of the reconstruction that gives the place its value as much as the aesthetic virtues of the urban landform in question.

Esquerra (2007) considers the merits of reconstructions as a means of increasing public knowledge and understanding of archaeological sites, looking in particular at the Spanish experience (though not necessarily at World Heritage Sites). She found that where such sites were a legacy of experimental archaeology (i.e. researchers had sought to replicate historic building forms using the original construction materials and building techniques) there was often an academic benefit yet only limited visitor appeal, except to 'better-educated' [sic] visitors. However, she also notes that many reconstructed heritage sites, where they are built away from the original archaeological remains, are effectively dependent on making themselves attractive to visitors through a range of additional interpretive provision in order to appeal to their main market, which is visitors looking for entertainment.

Her research with visitors to a number of ruined archaeological sites and reconstructed heritage attractions in Catalonia found that 'the romantic archaeological site confers an element of prestige on its visitors which the reconstructed monument lacks' and that 'the cultural veneer conferred by the preserved archaeological site is not always available at a reconstruction' (Esquerra, 2007, p. 45). Nonetheless, there was more evidence of personal learning among people visiting reconstructions than visiting unrestored ruins.

Reconstruction of ruined sites and buildings is expensive, time-consuming and fraught with challenges over authenticity and originality. Perhaps then we should leave the last word to Richter, who suggests that 'some tourist sites are more interesting as ruins than they would be if everything were rebuilt' (2005, p. 265).

10.5.2 The tour guide

Whether delivered by a trained interpreter on the staff of a heritage site, or by an enthusiastic amateur with a passion for the heritage in question, guided tours of cultural or natural properties are a standard way of conveying key messages about both past and present, and indeed about the future prospects for the site in question. Tour guides play a vital role in many destinations, acting as mediators between the place that is being visited, and the visitors themselves – in the words of Cohen (1985), the guide is a 'professional pathfinder' (p. 7). As noted by Dahles (2002), guides are expected to have not only a specific insight into the topic or place they are talking about but also a high level of communication skills. Only when both are in place are guides able to be effective in their role as mediator building bridges between host and guests, between visitors and the place being visited. Where tour guides are drawn exclusively from the host community, as is the case at the **Kunta Kinteh Island and Associated Sites** World Heritage Site in the Gambia (see case study in Chapter 11) then the rationale behind World Heritage Site status as well as the more personal associations with the site can be shared with visitors in greater detail.

It is important, as Salazar (2005) notes, that guides are mindful of the different expectations of different audiences or visitor groups, and are able to tailor both the way they communicate and also the facts that they communicate to these different groups. This can be particularly complex at some World Heritage Sites where there may be many different nationalities represented in a tour party, with differing levels of language ability, differing levels of familiarity with the history and heritage of the location and indeed different levels of interest in learning more! Yet, as Salazar (2005, p. 640) determines, it is 'the human contact, the close encounters with people … the feeling one has of actively participating in the lived life' that tourists remember about tours. But this relies on the tour guides themselves having the ability to convey messages about Outstanding Universal Value and a property's heritage succinctly, accurately and consistently. Sadly, this isn't always the case. Research undertaken on guided tours at the **Historic Centre of Macao World Heritage Site** found that many guides tended to conflate the inscription of the whole area with the heritage status of individual buildings, presenting a confused message to many visitors and thus providing a less than satisfactory experience (Io & Hallo, 2011).

Alazaizeh et al. (2019) consider the mediating role of tour guides on the visitor experience and satisfaction at one of the Middle East's most iconic World Heritage Sites – the **Petra Archaeological Park** in Jordan (inscribed 1985). As well as confirming the important role that tour guides can play in encouraging more sustainable behaviour on the part of site visitors, their research also demonstrated that tour guide 'performance' can add significantly to the overall quality of the visitor experience, and hence enhance overall visitor satisfaction. In short, they found that the more that visitors appreciated the performance by the tour guide, the better the overall experience, the higher their satisfaction with the trip and the greater the likelihood that they would act in a sustainable or responsible fashion. In other words, their research confirmed the old adage often used in heritage interpretation, that 'with greater understanding comes appreciation, and with appreciation comes better protection'. They suggest that 'the role and behaviour of the tour guides is therefore highly significant since visitors come from diverse backgrounds in terms of their culture, education, religion, etc. and they have various expectations towards the site they visit' (Alazaizeh et al., 2019, p. 1719).

There is evidence that tour guides are sometimes not just able to adapt their messages to suit the interests of a particular group, but indeed that they may be required to do so. Some early research into tour guiding in Indonesia by Dahles (2002) for instance, found a high level of state intervention on the messages transmitted by tour guides to tourists while Su & Teo (2009) recognised the challenges that guides faced in balancing contested and at times contradictory opinions in the World Heritage city of **Lijiang**, China (inscribed 1997). A similar situation has been identified in **historic Macao** by Ong et al. (2014) where it is suggested that the involvement of UNESCO in training new cadres of guides post-inscription has led to a situation where local tour guides are encouraged 'to seek ways to become cultural experts and to become local cultural champions or ambassador-activists'

(2014, p. 231). In other words, they are expected not just to interpret the history of the destination and its peoples, but broader themes championed by UNESCO and expressed through World Heritage Site inscription.

Just as heritage is effectively a political process (Smith, 2006), so is tour-guiding. Decisions are made about what stories to tell, to whom, and what to leave out. And as we now explore, the democratisation of information available through the internet, and particularly the growing significance of AR and VR, provide one route for some interested parties to bypass the services offered by guides and to seek out alternative ways of understanding a heritage place.

10.6 Augmented reality and virtual reality: an introduction

The widespread availability of portable, low-cost mobile ICT devices over the last two decades has been instrumental in stimulating the emergence of new approaches to interpreting cultural and natural heritage sites using either Augmented Reality (AR) or Virtual Reality (VR). However, the use of reality technologies in archaeology has been commonplace for the last two decades, with researchers modelling the reconstruction of individual buildings, urban and rural environments and specific finds and objects in 3D.

It took time, however, for the potential of AR and VR to interpret heritage properties to lay visitors to take root. For instance, Zollner et al. (2009) talked about how museum interpretation could benefit from augmented reality layers being added onto site photographs so that visitors were better able to understand the original locations from where finds were excavated. They talk particularly about the effectiveness of 3D reconstructions of historical sites presented through head-mounted displays (HMDs). This is an obvious benefit to site interpretation since there is no actual physical reconstruction of a ruined site, just a hypothesised virtual one which, as long as it is clearly marked as such, avoids the risks of presenting an inauthentic perspective of what a building or complex looked like in the past.

And it should be noted that some World Heritage Site have been using AR to provide visitors with an understanding of what a property looked like in the past for some time now – for instance, Vlahakis et al. (2002) reviewed work carried out two decades ago to prepare digital reconstructions of **The Archaeological Site of Olympia**, Greece (inscribed 1989). At that time, users viewed the digital reconstructions using a palm-held device rented for the duration of their visit – this was before the widespread adoption of smartphones and when there was still an obligation for site managers to provide the hardware and software that facilitated VR provision.

Elsewhere in the Middle East, the potential of AR has also been explored at the **Erbil Citadel** in Iraq (inscribed 2014). Research by Mohammed-Amin et al. (2012) at the ancient site of Arbela led them to propose that implementing mobile AR systems at historic and archaeological sites has the potential to enrich visitor experiences by enabling instantaneous, onsite access to historic information in different languages and formats, a task which would be much more costly using conventional technology. Such tools also have the opportunity to deliver more personalised self-guided experiences (though this of course then denies local people the chance to work as tour guides to visitors unfamiliar with the property).

Below we explore the various ways in which some of these new technologies are being adopted by World Heritage Site managers and other interested parties to interpret heritage places, and the stories associated with them, to different audiences. Prior to getting into that detail, however, it is important to be clear about the difference between AR and VR, and how they relate to the more modern concept of Mixed Reality (MR).

Augmented reality, as the terminology suggests, is an enhanced version of a real image that is created by overlaying digital information onto an image being viewed through a device such as a smartphone camera or a Head Mounted Display (HMD) screen. HMD screens may be partially see-through and computer-generated graphics are optically superimposed onto the either the smartphone camera or HMD, so that the user sees both the graphic and the real-world view. Depending on the level of sophistication of the technology, the viewer may have some element of control over the content that is viewed and the part of the site or building being examined.

In contrast to VR, where the user is immersed in the world of the computer, AR incorporates the computer into the reality of the user so that the user can interact with the real world in a natural way, with the computer providing both information and assistance. In effect, the AR function of whatever tool is being used provides additional information to the user which augments the reality of the situation or location they are in at that precise moment, providing additional information such as what the landscape might have looked like in the past (Stanco et al., 2012). The importance of Augmented Reality for interpreting heritage properties and landscapes is that it makes possible the combination of virtual elements with the real world, without necessarily making these virtual aspects the focus of activity. With Virtual Reality on the other hand, the experience is predicated on the fact that one enters an entire virtual world to the exclusion of 'Real Reality'.

Virtual reality refers to an artificial, computer-generated simulation of an environment which a viewer experiences through sensory stimuli such as sights or sounds, or even touch and smell, and where the viewer's own actions partially determine what can happen in the environment. This interaction can appear seemingly real to the person engaging with the VR interface who will use a HMD, generally either a helmet or pair of googles with a screen inside and earphones attached (visual and aural stimulus), or gloves fitted with sensors (tactile stimulus). Another way of putting it is to say that VR simulates real scenarios whereas AR focuses on enhancing physically based reality through computer-generated sensory outputs (Gavish et al., 2015).

The term 'Mixed Reality' (MR) is more recent and defines a more complex panorama (not to be confused with the AR one), placing itself at the centre of the 'Virtuality Continuum' first conceived of by Milgram & Kishino (1994) – see Figure 10.2.

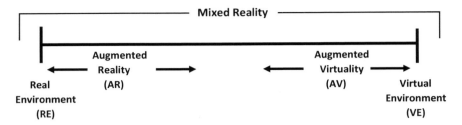

FIGURE 10.2 Simplified representation of a 'virtuality continuum'.
Source: Milgram & Kishino (1994).

In MR, virtual objects are inserted into a real context in an immersive and interactive way where the user still has real-world perception and where the real and virtual contents interact with each other in real time (Venditti, 2020). Vendetti mentions two possible MR scenarios: one where the viewer starts with the real world into which digital objects such as holograms are inserted to give the appearance they are present; and a second which starts in an anchored, virtual world which screens out some of the landscape or building features which are present in reality.

10.7 Applications of AR and VR in presenting and interpreting World Heritage

10.7.1 Introduction

AR has been a feature of archaeological and architectural research for some time. For instance, Palma et al. (2019) report on the effectiveness of AR when scanning and recording complex carved architectural features such as baroque entrance halls in Turin, including some in buildings that form part of the **Residences of the Royal House of Savoy** World Heritage Site (inscribed 1997). However, as noted earlier, it is only relatively recently that the visitor-focused utility of these tools has been developed. This is largely due to the rapid development of mobile technology including GPS receivers, smartphones and tablets, and the widespread adoption of this technology – one estimate is that in 2020, more than 6 billion people on earth had a smartphone (Statista, 2021).

This has then paved the way for a multitude of mobile augmented reality (MAR) applications (apps) across the cultural heritage and natural heritage sectors. Examples include museum, monument and site guides which visually augment physical exhibits with background or interpretive information. In some instances, these apps are able to use the device's GPS receiver and inertial sensors to superimpose virtual objects on the physical environment framed by the camera's display. This then allows the mobile device to display AR views of a building or landscape, to receive additional location-based information, or to play audio and 3D-enhanced narrations. Positive outcomes are not always guaranteed. For instance, (Bernardini et al., 2012) found that augmented reality helped visitors understand past ways of life a little better but that many still found it hard to place the current ruins they were looking at as intact buildings within an historic landscape.

While much of the emphasis to date has been on the built and archaeological environments rather than the natural world, there are some examples of its use in the landscape. For instance, researchers in Germany have used AR to enhance interpretation in nature reserves and other protected areas to show users what rare and endangered species look like in their natural habitat, in an attempt to raise awareness of the need for conservation and protection (Weil et al., 2019).

10.7.2 Offsite use of AR and VR

Zollner et al. (2009) consider the potential for interpreting remote cultural heritage sites through AR by superimposing interactive annotations like 3D reconstructions, historic and contemporary images and film clips onto large floor- or wall-mounted photographs of the particular heritage site – in their case, the *Forum Romanum* – part of the **Historic Centre of Rome** World Heritage Site (inscribed 1980). Their particular installation, based in a museum in the Netherlands, used video see-through tablets as the interface between the visitor and the digital experience, but they argue it could also work with head-mounted displays (HMDs) – either optical see-through displays which project images onto a semi-transparent layer in front of the viewer's eyes or a video seen through HMD which films the environment and which shows it on a micro-display built into the headset. The experience provided allowed the viewer to perceive 3D reconstructions of the original built state of some of the now partially ruined structures across the Forum, as well as understand the deterioration of the property over time through a sequence of geo-located historical photographs. This particular use is helpful since it isn't site-based and thus can be used to protect fragile properties from over-visitation.

10.7.3 Onsite use of AR and VR

AR can also be used to enhance the visitor experience onsite. For instance, researchers working in the southwestern district of ancient Syracuse, named Neapolis (inscribed 2005 as part of the **Syracuse and the Rocky Necropolis of Pantalica** site) recre-ated using Augmented Reality part of a ruined Greek temple – the altar of Hieron II – and then used a mobile phone app to make it accessible to tourists. Similar work has been done at Peel Gap on Hadrian's Wall in the North of England, where AR has been used to help interpret the historic landscape to visitors, showing them how it changed over the four centuries of Roman occupation (Eve, 2012).

One benefit of this approach is that once the cost of preparing the AR tool is covered, it can be rolled out at very limited additional cost to site managers since the tourists themselves already own (or lease) the hardware needed to make it work – the mobile phone or tablet. In this way, AR applications that can be downloaded represent a major step forward to the traditional recorded audio guides since there is much more flexibility for the visitor in terms of how they use the provision to enhance their experience of the site. Indeed, the ability of property managers, conservators and other professionals to meet the ever-increasing demand for AR and VR applications that can be downloaded as cell-phone applications will remain a pressing need for some time to come – as Moro et al. (2019) suggest, most AR and VR technology used in tourism will remain based around mobile devices rather than wearable technology such as smart glasses primarily for cost reasons as well as technical barriers.

Such technology is best applied when it can add value to the overall visitor experience and encourage a greater appreciation for how a property may have looked in the past. Falconer et al. (2020) have reviewed a VR simulation of Avebury Stone Circle & Henge Complex (inscribed 1986 as part of the **Stonehenge, Avebury and Associated Sites** nomination) and found that

> the more believable the simulation appeared, the greater the sense of place experienced by the participants. We also found that personal characteristics had very little influence upon visitor reactions to the simulation, suggesting that such simulations might have wide appeal for heritage and museum visitors, regardless of age, gender or familiarity with technology.
>
> *(p. 1)*

One of their intentions was to create a sense of place that viewers could emotionally respond to – so sound was as important as visual imagery, and for many respondents it was sound – particularly voice and animal sounds – that made the difference. This issue of eliciting an emotional response to interpretation is important since it reflects one of the primary objectives of the professional heritage interpreter (see for instance the AHI's views on interpretation presented in Section 10.4.1). In Falconer et al.'s research, the four most frequently cited emotions were interest, curiosity, excitement and absorption. All respondents reported emotional responses to VA, with the majority reporting positive emotions. Some did report feeling nervous and/or over-whelmed, which is important to recognise when deploying VR at heritage sites. Only 4% of respondents felt it wasn't a believable landscape they had experienced, suggesting that when done well, VR can be a powerful tool for interpretation.

That same research project also investigated whether VR appealed more to younger than older visitors (following the argument sometimes made that it is necessary to adopt the latest ICT based technologies to attract a younger audience to heritage sites). What they found is that although older visitors may need more encouragement to use VR experiences but once engaged, their experience seems to differ little from that of younger visitors.

10.7.4 Routes and tours

AR and VR doesn't just offer site-specific interpretation – there is also the opportunity to use it along specific routes or across a whole urban destination so that the visitor/ user can navigate their way through a whole landscape whose heritage is unfurled and revealed to them along the way. The use of mobile phone apps to guide visitors along themed cultural routes and to function as an interface for more detailed interpretation has been reviewed by while Kourouthanassis et al. (2015) consider the use of MAR as a tool available via smartphones (CorfuAR) for enhancing navigation around **historic Corfu** (inscribed 2007). Their findings are most instructive, namely that the more functional a tool is, the greater the pleasure the user derives from it and hence the more likely they are to adopt it and use it to guide themselves round a destination and engage with its heritage/ experience the sense of place. Personalisation remains an important function, whereby users can select, for example, which period of history they wish to engage with, or which particular heritage theme (e.g. religion; power; the role of women etc).

Tussyadiah et al. (2018) conducted two studies to analyse how the sense of presence during virtual walkthrough of a tourism destination influenced users' attitudes toward a future visit. Though only one of their case study examples is a World Heritage Site, the findings are nonetheless instructive. They had 202 participants in Hong Kong who were shown a VR street view of Tokyo, Japan, viewed with Google Cardboard, or VR video of Porto, Portugal, viewed with Samsung Gear VR; and 724 people in the United Kingdom who were able to view a 360-degree VR video of the **English Lake District** (inscribed 2017), using Samsung Gear VR. They concluded that the feeling of being in the virtual environment increases enjoyment of VR experiences; that the heightened feeling of 'being there' results in stronger liking and preference for the destination, and that positive attitude change leads to a higher level of visitation intention. Thus, even when made available at a distance from the destination itself, VR can be valuable not only as a tool for immersing a user in a new environment (current, historical or even a future world) but as a marketing instrument, promoting the idea of travel to that destination.

10.7.5 Games

One final aspect of ICT-based interpretation to consider is gamification. The argument expressed by authors such as Hammady et al. (2016) is that gamification of VR environments might make visits to heritage sites more appealing to younger visitors. They provide examples of scenarios that could be used around different ancient Egyptian Gods in the new Grand Egyptian Museum in Giza which, though not itself a World Heritage Site, once officially opened will provide a supporting visitor experience to the nearby Pyramids and Sphinx, part of the **Memphis and its Necropolis – the Pyramid Fields from Giza to Dahshur World Heritage Site** inscribed in 1979.

There is evidence that this can work from research carried out by Ardito et al., (2007) in Italy. They developed a basic mobile augmented reality game that could be accessed on a basic smartphone and promoted it to school children visiting Egnathia in Apulia, Italy – ruins of a city that goes back 2,500 years. They found that gameplay is able to trigger a desire among most young users to learn more about ancient history, by making the visit itself more engaging and exciting, and thus the learning more effective. A further benefit they noted was that, because the system was run on students' own cell phones, investment requirements were lower than would have been the case were it the site managers' responsibility to provide software AND hardware.

10.8 Concluding remarks

It is vital, for sustained public support for the World Heritage Site programme, that people from across the globe are able to access such sites and understand: why they have been protected; what they mean to different stakeholders and how their own behaviour and attitudes are important to perpetuating an understanding of Out-standing Universal Value in particular, and of community/ national heritage in gen-eral. The challenges around first of all making such sites accessible physically are many and varied but rarely pose unsurmountable challenges to site managers. The vast panoply of interpretive tools available to site managers and their partners can play a major role in enhancing both the quality of the visit experience, but also the personal understanding of why such properties are important. The emergence of AR and VR tools in interpretation add particular value because they can provide alter-native experiences that do not threaten the integrity of the actual properties they relate to, and at the same time support more traditional approaches to interpretation that have been practiced for centuries, such as reconstruction and guided tours.

BOX 10.1: CASE STUDY 10.1: PRESENTING AND INTERPRETING HADRIAN'S WALL.

Stretching for around 80 Roman miles (120 km) across the north of England, **Hadrian's Wall** (inscribed 1987) has been referred to as 'the largest, most spectacular and one of the most enigmatic historical monuments in Britain' (Moffat, 2009, p. 1). Along the Wall was a sequence of milecastles, turrets, defensive earthworks either side of the structure itself and 15 garrison forts which were generally spaced between 11–13 km apart (Hodgson, 2017), which when taken together represented what (Collins, 2020, p. 19) refers to as 'the monumental focus of the Roman frontier'.

The Wall was abandoned around the start of the fifth century AD (Fleming, 2011; Breeze, 2014; Symonds, 2021) and the fortifications provided a useful resource for later builders – many farmhouses and ecclesiastical structures in the area contain stones robbed from it. From the middle of the 18th century onwards, local antiquarians developed an interest in the Wall and its associated remains, writing up accounts of their forays along the monument and giving talks to contemporaries about their experiences (Higgins, 2013). During the 19th century John Clayton, a Newcastle lawyer and businessman, started buying up large tracts of land in Northumberland that included Roman archaeological deposits and his fascination with the Wall led to him reconstructing stretches of it to the extent that parts of the central section of the monument are often referred to as 'Clayton's Wall' (Moffat, 2009).

Late 19th- and early 20th-century quarrying threats to the stretch of the Wall, along with growing visitor interest in the archaeological remains from the 1920s onwards led to enhanced protection for the structure (Moffat, 2009), with upstanding sections of the Wall, fort ruins, associated earthworks and other related sites either taken into the guardianship of the then Ministry of Works, being purchased by the National Trust or at least being accorded protection under the 1931 Ancient Monuments Act (Symonds, 2021).

From the 1940s onwards there seems to have been a policy at properties along the Wall in the guardianship of the Ministry of Works to consolidate only Roman materials and to remove traces of later structures, despite there being ample evidence at many sites of post-Roman occupation (Symonds, 2021). It is suggested that this may have been because 'as the Roman Wall became specifically associated with Hadrian, so too visitors expected to encounter *his* Wall' (p. 153; emphasis original). Yet of course the construction of the first suite of fortifications had not even been completed by the time of Hadrian's death in AD 138, thus in reality visitors were seeing layers of archaeology associated with almost three centuries of Roman occupation.

The popularity with visitors of various sites along the Wall, and particularly within the central section, led to increased investment by various stakeholders in site museums, visitor centres, onsite interpretation panels and other infrastructure. By the 1970s, the four main paid-entry sites along the Wall (Chesters, Housesteads, Vindolanda and Corbridge Roman Town) were attracting more than 450,000 visitors per annum between them and numbers continued to rise slowly in the following decades to more than 1 million by 2011 (Stone, 2014; Tuttiett, 2014).

Throughout that period there was an increased realisation of the need to differentiate between the main paid entry sites and museums along the Wall by focusing on different themes – thus civilian life was a topic covered at Vindolanda and Corbridge while the Roman Army Museum at Greenhead interpreted military life, as did Chesters Roman Fort. Religion was a key theme at the Senhouse Roman Museum at Maryport on the Cumbrian coast while the broader history of Roman occupation of the region was a core theme at Newcastle's Museum of Antiquities (replaced in 2008 by the Great North Museum) (Allason-Jones, 2014).

More effort was also made to holding special events, particularly in the shoulder months, to attract visitors across the whole of the World Heritage Site. For instance, on the evening of 13 March 2010, a chain of more than 500 flaming torches was lit along the whole 120 km of the Wall to mark the 1600th anniversary of the collapse of Roman rule in Britain. The event involved more than 1,000 volunteers, attracted around 50,000 visitors on the day and generated around £3 million for the regional economy (BBC News, 2010).

In their review of interpretation at Hadrian's Wall, Adkins & Mills (2014) report that successive visitor (and non-visitor) surveys carried out in the 1990s and 2000s had revealed that visitors to individual sites along the Wall rarely understood the relationship of the place they were in at the time to the larger (longer) monument and that 'the standard of interpretation at sites was poor and lacked a *wow* factor' (p. 101; emphasis original).

There was little understanding of the scale of the monument and of the relationship between the different sites along it (at the time, there were 13 major visitor attractions associated with Hadrian's Wall as well as many other smaller locations where visitors could engage with the monument). Nor was there sufficient differentiation in visitors' minds about the experience on offer at different locations. A key reason for this was the fact that properties and visitor attractions along the monument were in the ownership and/ or managed by many different organisations including English Heritage, the National Trust, local authorities and charitable trusts (including the Vindolanda Trust which operates at two locations).

From around 2004 attempts were made to alert visitors to the scale and complexity of the World Heritage Site and its tourist offer through a branding campaign that referred to 'Hadrian's Wall Country', with themed orientation panels being installed at various sites along the whole length of the World Heritage Site locating the place within the broader context of the monument, associated remains and local services (Plate 10.1). The intention was to inform the visitor about what else could be seen in the surrounding area, hopefully leading to an extended period of stay and hence greater local economic benefit.

PLATE 10.1 Orientation panel for Hadrian's Wall Country.
Source: Photograph by Simon Woodward.

The re-designation in 2005 of Hadrian's Wall as part of the larger, transnational **'Frontiers of the Roman Empire'** World Heritage Site provided an opportunity to revisit the interpretation of the monument as a whole by presenting it within the context of a wider narrative that considered the Roman occupation of Britain and the growth and decline of the Empire in that period (Adkins & Mills, 2011). After an extensive programme of site audits, interviews and focus groups with visitors and non-visitors and consultations with relevant stakeholders, a number of core themes were identified for the framework covering three main areas:

- People of the Empire;
- The Roman Army;
- Exploration, Discovery and Values.

This framework then allowed owners and managers of different properties and visitor attractions along the whole length of Hadrian's Wall to design and deliver interpretation that built on each site's particular heritage within this broader discussion of the role of the frontier from the first to the fifth centuries AD. By moving the focus of interpretation away from the archaeology of each site to broader topics and by utilising a wider range of interpretive media, a more varied visitor experience would be possible thus hopefully leading to an increase in audiences across the whole of the property and an uplift in the associated economic benefits.

Launched in 2011, the framework was quickly used to advise major investment projects at a number of attractions along the Wall including Roman Vindolanda, the Roman Army Museum, Tullie House Museum in Carlisle and Housesteads Roman Fort. Aspects of the framework were also used to inform some of the interpretation in The National Landscape Discovery Centre (also known as The Sill) at Bardon Mill, a mile or so south of some of the most dramatic sections of the central sector of the monument (Plate 10.2).

Unfortunately, the demise of the Regional Development Agency network in England in 2012 and cuts to the budgets of UK public-sector agencies and local authorities meant that funding for major new interpretation projects became more difficult to secure, and thus some of the anticipated re-presentations were put on hold across the property.

Nonetheless, there has been a largely successful reimagining of Hadrian's Wall in visitors' minds from a traditional (19th- and 20th-century) viewpoint of it being a broken chain of archaeological military ruins to a more nuanced perspective that appreciates the original function of the Wall as a frontier operating within a complex socio-economic and landscape context. Moreover, greater emphasis on a narrative that relates themes of historic frontier and occupation to today's global issues, and that also explores the contemporary cultural landscape of the Wall, allows the regional destination marketing organisations as well as individual site operators to attract as broad an audience as possible to the World Heritage Site. In recent years this has included marking

PLATE 10.2 The Sill, Northumberland – a major interpretation facility providing insights into the geology, natural history and cultural heritage of this part of Northern Britain, including Hadrian's Wall, part of the Frontiers of the Roman Empire WHS.
Source: Photograph by Simon Woodward.

PLATE 10.3 Marking the line of Hadrian's Wall in Central Newcastle through sensitive urban design.
Source: Photograph by Simon Woodward.

the line of the wall through central Newcastle via some creative urban design (Plate 10.3) and, during 2022, a major programme of public lectures, exhibitions and special events across the whole extent of the World Heritage Site to mark its 1900th birthday (see https://1900.hadrianswallcountry.co.uk/).

References

Adkins, G. & Mills, N. 2011. *Frontiers of the Roman Empire World Heritage Site – Hadrian's Wall Interpretation Framework*. Perth: Hadrian's Wall Heritage Ltd.

Adkins, G. & Mills, N., 2014. Managing interpretation. In: P. G. Stone & D. Brough, eds. *Managing, Using and Interpreting Hadrian's Wall as World Heritage*. New York: Springer, 101–113.

Alazaizeh, M. M., Jamaliah, M. M., Mgonja, J. T. & Ababneh, A. 2019. Tour guide performance and sustainable visitor behaviour at cultural heritage sites. *Journal of Sustainable Tourism*, 27 (11), 1708–1724.

Allason-Jones, L. 2014. Hadrian's Wall as World Heritage: the museums. In: P. G. Stone & D. Brough, eds. *Managing, Using, and Interpreting Hadrian's Wall as World Heritage*. New York: Springer, 89–100.

Ardito, C. et al. 2007. *Re-Experiencing History in Archaeological Parks by Playing a Mobile Augmented Reality Game*. Berlin and Heidelberg: Springer, 357–366.

Association for Heritage Interpretation. 2020. AHI Ethos. https://ahi.org.uk/ (accessed 29 June 2020).

Atkins. 2007. *The Palace of Westminster and Westminster Abbey including St Margaret's Church. World Heritage Site Management Plan*. London: Westminster World Heritage Site Management Plan Steering Group.

Avci, E. 2019. Enhancing the cultural tourism experience through augmented reality. In: C. Cobanoglu, M. Cavisoglu & A. Corbaci, eds. *Advances in Global Business and Economics*. Volume 2. Sarasota, FL: ANAHEI Publishing, LLC, 215–230.

Baker, E. L. 1998. Travel advisory: recovering the calm at Westminster Abbey. https://www.nytimes.com/1998/02/15/travel/travel-advisory-recovering-the-calm-at-westminster-abbey.html (accessed 16 April 2021).

BBC News. 2010. Lit-up Hadrian's Wall 'brought £3m boost to economy'. https://www.bbc.co.uk/news/uk-england-11010555 (accessed 12 February 2011).

Benton, G. 2009. From principle to practice: four conceptions of interpretation. *Journal of Interpretation Research*, 14, 7–31.

Bernardini, A., Delogu, C., Pallotti, E. & Constantini, L. 2012. *Living the Past: Augmented Reality and Archaeology*. New York: IEEE, 354–357.

Blockley, M. 1999. Preservation, restoration and presentation of the industrial heritage. A case study of the Ironbridge Gorge. In: G. Chitty & D. Baker, eds. *Managing Historic Sites and Buildings. Reconciling Presentation and Preservation*. Abingdon: Routledge, 141–156.

Bold, J., Larkham, P. & Pickard, R. 2018. *Authentic Reconstruction. Authenticity, Architecture and the Built Heritage*. London: Bloomsbury.

Bramley, L. 2019. Access for all at UK World Heritage Sites. MSc thesis, Leeds Beckett University.

Bramwell, B. 2012. Interventions and policy instruments for sustainable tourism. In: W. F. Theobald, ed. *Global Tourism*. Abingdon: Routledge, 406–425.

Breeze, D. J. 2014. The archaeology, history and significance of Hadrian's Wall. In: P. G. Stone & D. Brough, eds. *Managing, Using, and Interpreting Hadrian's Wall as World Heritage*. New York: Springer, 9–13.

Bryant, M., 2006. Tilden's children: interpretation in Britain's National Parks. In: A. Hems & M. Blockley, eds. *Interpreting Heritage*. Abingdon: Routledge, 173–188.

Causevic, S. 2020. Hagia Sophia: turning this Turkish treasure into a mosque is at odds with its Unesco status. https://theconversation.com/hagia-sophia-turning-this-turkish-treasur e-into-a-mosque-is-at-odds-with-its-unesco-status-143372 (accessed 16 April 2021).

Caval, S. 2021. Social landscapes as multicultural spaces: stecci in Bosnia and Herzoegovina. *Antiquity*, 95 (380), 1–9.

Cohen, E. 1985. The tourist guide: the origins, structure and dynamics of a role. *Annals of Tourism Research*, 12, 5–29.

Cohen, E. & Cohen, S. 2012. Authentication – hot and cool. *Annals of Tourism Research*, 39 (3), 1295–1314.

Collins, R. 2020. *Living on the Edge of Empire. The Objects and People of Hadrian's Wall*. Barnsley: Pen & Sword Books Ltd.

Copeland, T. 2006. Constructing pasts: interpreting the historic environment. In: A. Hems & M. Blockley, eds. *Heritage Interpretation*. Abingdon: Routledge, 83–96.

Crawford, K. R. & Black, R. 2012. Visitor understanding of the geodiversity and the geo-conservation value of the Giant's Causeway World Heritage Site, Northern Ireland. *Geoheritage*, 4 (1–2), 115–126.

Czifra, S. et al. 2019. *Smart Solutions for Guided Cultural Routes along the Iron Age Archaeological Sites of the Danube Basin*. Sofia: Institute of Mathematics and Informatics.

Dahles, H. 2002. The politics of tour guiding. Image management in Indonesia. *Annals of Tourism Research*, 29 (3), 783–800.

du Cros, H. & McKercher, B. 2015. *Cultural Tourism*. 2nd ed. Abingdon: Routledge.

Ename Center. 2020. Who we are. http://www.enamecenter.org/EEC2013/index-E.html (accessed 8 April 2020).

English Heritage. n.d. Live! See the skies above Stonehenge. https://www.english-heritage.org. uk/visit/places/stonehenge/history-and-stories/stonehenge360/ (accessed 1 April 2020).

Esquerra, C. M. 2007. Presenting archaeological heritage to the public: ruins versus recon-structions. *EuroREA Journal of Reconstruction and Experiment in Archaeology*, 4, 41–46.

Etxeberria, A. I., Asensio, M., Vincent, N. & Cuenca, J. M. 2012. Mobile devices: a tool for tourism and learning at archaeological sites. *International Journal of Web Based Communities*, 8 (1), 57–72.

Eve, S. 2012. Augmenting phenomenology: using augmented reality to aid archaeological phenomenology in the landscape. *Journal of Archaeological Method and Theory*, 19 (4), 582–600.

Falconer, L. et al. 2020. Virtual Avebury: Exploring Sense of Place in a Virtual Archaeology Simulation. *Virtual Archaeology Review*, 11 (23), 1–13.

Fleming, R. 2011. *Britain after Rome. The Fall and Rise, 400–1070*. London: Penguin Books Ltd.

Fortescue, S. 2020. *No visitors, no income: The impact of Covid-19 on the Galapagos – and how we can help*. https://www.boatinternational.com/destinations/impact-of-covid-galapagos-isla nds-yachting (accessed 20 April 2021).

Fyall, A., Leask, A. & Barber, S. B. 2020. Marketing archaeological heritage for tourism. In: D. J. Timothy & L. G. Tahan, eds. *Archaeology and Tourism. Touring the Past*. Bristol: Channel View Publications, 69–86.

Galatis, P. et al. 2016. *Mobile Augmented Reality Guides in Cultural Heritage*. Proceedings of the 8th EAI International Conference on Mobile Computing, Applications and Services (MOBICASE), January. 11–19.

Gavish, N. et al. 2015. Evaluating virtual reality and augmented reality training for industrial maintenance and assembly tasks. *Interactive Learning Environments*, 23 (6), 778–798.

Graziano, T. & Privitera, D. 2020. Cultural heritage, tourist attractiveness and augmented reality: insights from Italy. *Journal of Heritage Tourism*, 15 (6), 666–679.

Guttentag, D. A. 2010. Virtual reality: applications and implications for tourism. *Tourism Management*, 31 (5), 637–651.

Gwynedd Council. 2020. *The Slate Landscape of Northwest Wales. Nomination as a World Heritage Site. Property Management Plan, 2020–2030*. Caernarfon: Gwynedd Council.

Hale, A. 2001. Representing the Cornish. Contesting heritage interpretation in Cornwall. *Tourist Studies*, 1 (2), 185–196.

Hammady, R., Ma, M. & Temple, N. 2016. *Augmented Reality and Gamification in Heritage Museums*. Cham, Switzerland: Springer, 181–187.

Han, D. et al. 2019. Virtual and augmented reality technologies to enhance the visitor experience in cultural tourism. In: T. Jung & M. C. tom Diek, eds. *Augmented Reality and Virtual Reality for Business*. Cham, Switzerland: Springer, 113–128.

Harrison, R., ed. 2010. *Understanding the Politics of Peritage*. Manchester: Manchester University Press.

Hertzman, E., Anderson, D. & Rowley, S. 2008. Edutainment heritage tourism attractions: a portrait of visitors' experiences at Storyeum. *Museum Management and Curatorship*, 23 (2), 1555–1175.

Higgins, C. 2013. *Under Another Sky. Journeys in Roman Britain*. London: Jonathan Cape.

Hodges, S. 2020. Interpreting the past: telling the archaeological story to visitors. In: D. J. Timothy & L. G. Tahan, eds. *Archaeology and Tourism. Touring the Past*. Bristol: Channel View Publications, 167–185.

Hodgson, N. 2017. *Hadrian's Wall. Archaeology and History at the Limit of Rome's Empire*. Marlborough: Robert Hale.

Hughes, M. & Morrison-Saunders, M. 2005. Influence of on-site interpretation intensity on visitors to natural areas. *Journal of Ecotourism*, 4 (3), 161–177.

Hwang, S.-N., Lee, C. & Chen, H.-J., 2005. The relationship among tourists' involvement, place attachment and interpretation in Taiwan's National Parks. *Tourism Management*, 26, 143–156.

ICOMOS. 2008. *The ICOMOS Charter for the Interpretation and Presentation of Cultural Heritage Sites*. 16th General Assembly, Quebec. Paris: International Council on Monuments and Sites.

ICOMOS UK. 2001. *To be a Pilgrim: Meeting the Needs of Visitors to Cathedrals and Churches in the United Kingdom*. London: ICOMOS UK. Io, M. U. & Hallo, L. 2011. Tour guides' interpretation of the Historic Centre of Macao as a World Cultural Heritage Site. *Journal of Tourism and Cultural Change*, 9 (2), 140–152.

Jameson Jr, J. H. 2008. Presenting archaeology to the public, then and now. In: G. Fairclough, R. Harrison, J. H. Jameson Jr & J. Schofield, eds. *The Heritage Reader*. Abingdon: Routledge, 427–456.

Junker, U. 2020. How to get to Easter Island and leave it a better place. https://www.theisla nderonline.com.au/story/6650809/why-easter-island-wants-fewer-visitors-and-better-ones/ (accessed 27 April 2020).

Kalman, H. 2014. *Heritage Planning. Principles and Process*. New York: Routledge.

Keios and Thinking Consulting. 2021. *Sustainable Tourism and Visitor Economy Development Plan for the Bethlehem Urban Area. Report to State of Palestine Ministry of Local Government and the World Bank Group*. Rome: Keios Development Consulting.

Kohl, J. 2003. Post-revolution interpretation. *Legacy*, Nov/Dec, 1–3.

Kourouthanassis, P., Boletsis, C., Bardaki, C. & Chasanidouc, D. 2015. Tourist responses to mobile augmented reality travel guides: the role of emotions on adoption behaviour. *Pervasive and Mobile Computing*, 18, 71–87.

Light, D. & Prentice, R. 1994. Market-based product development in heritage tourism. *Tourism Management*, 15 (1), 27–36.

Lockwood, C. 1999. A Day in the Life of Westminster Abbey. https://www.chicagotribune.com/news/ct-xpm-1999-12-05-9912050410-story.html (accessed 16 April 2021).

Machin, A. 2016. *Making Sense of Tourism. 1: The Beckoning Horizon.* Halifax: Westwood Start.

Marcotte, P. & Bourdeau, L. 2006. Tourists' knowledge of the UNESCO designation of World Heritage sites: the case of visitors to Quebec City. *International Journal of Arts Management*, 8 (2), 4–13.

Masters, D. & Carter, J. 1999. *What Have We Got And Is It Any Good? A Practical Guide on How to Survey and Assess Heritage Interpretation.* Inverness: Highland Interpretive Strategy Project.

Matthews, J. P. 2020. Protecting the archaeological past in the face of tourism demand. In: D. J. Timothy & L. G. Tahan, eds. *Archaeology and Tourism. Touring the Past.* Bristol: Channel View Publications, 152–166.

Mazel, A. 2017. Valuing rock art: a view from Northumberland in North East England. *International Journal of Heritage Studies*, 23 (5), 421–433.

Milano, C., Cheer, J. M. & Novelli, M. 2019. Overtourism: an evolving problem. In: C. Milano, J. M. Cheer, & M. Novelli, eds. *Overtourism. Excesses, Discontents and Measures in Travel and Tourism.* Wallingford: CABI, 1–17.

Milgram, P. & Kishino, F. 1994. A taxonomy of mixed reality visual displays. *IEICE Transactions on Information Systems*, 77 (12), 1321–1329.

Moffat, A. 2009. *The Wall. Rome's Greatest Frontier.* Edinburgh: Birlinn Limited.

Mohammed-Amin, R. K., Levy, R. M. & Boyd, J. E. 2012. *Mobile Augmented Reality for Interpretation of Archaeological Sites.* Nara, Japan: ACM.

Morgan, N. & Pritchard, A. 1998. *Tourism, Promotion and Power, Creating Images; Creating Identities.* Chichester: John Wiley and Sons.

Moro, S., Rita, P., Ramos, P. & Esmerado, J. 2019. Analysing recent agumented and virtual reality developments in tourism. *Journal of Hospitality and Tourism Technology*, 10 (2), 571–586.

Moscardo, G. 1996. Mindful visitors: heritage and tourism. *Annals of Tourism Research*, 23 (2), 376–397.

Moscardo, G. 1998. Interpretation and sustainable tourism: functions, examples and principles. *Journal of Tourism Studies*, 9 (1), 2–13.

Moser, S. et al. 2002. Transforming archaeology through practice: strategies for collaborative archaeology and the Community Archaeology Project at Quseir, Egypt. *World Archaeology*, 34 (2), 220–248.

Moss, S. 2009. Edutainment. In: S. Moss, ed. *The Entertainment Industry. An Introduction.* Wallingford: CABI, 248–260.

Okan, Z. 2003. Edutainment: is learning at risk?. *British Journal of Educational Technology*, 34 (3), 255–264.

Ong, C. E., Ryan, C. & McIntosh, A. 2014. Power-knowledge and tour-guide training: capitalistic domination, utopian visions and the creation and negotiation of UNESCO's Homo Turismos in Macao. *Annals of Tourism Research*, 48, 221–234.

Orbaşli, A. 2008. *Architectural Conservation.* Oxford: Blackwell Science Ltd.

Palma, V., Spallone, R. & Vitali, M. 2019Augmented Turin Baroque Atria: AR experiences for enhancing cultural heritage. In: *International Archives of the Photogrammetry, Remote Sensing and Spatial Information Sciences*, 557–564.

Park, H. Y. 2014. *Heritage Tourism.* Abingdon: Routledge.

Pedersen, A. 2002. *Managing Tourism at World Heritage Sites. A Practical Manual for World Heritage Site Managers.* Paris: UNESCO World Heritage Centre.

Pendelbury, J., Short, M. & While, A. 2009. Urban World Heritage Sites and the problem of authenticity. *Cities*, 26, 349–358.

Richter, L. K. 2005. The politics of heritage tourism development. Emerging issues for the new millennium. In: G. Corsane, ed. *Heritage, Museums and Galleries. An Introductory Reader.* Abingdon: Routledge, 257–271.

Rodger, J. 2007. *World Heritage Site Branding – The Blaenavon Experience.* Oxford: Archaeopress, 13–16.

Salazar, N. B. 2005. Tourism and glocalization: 'local' tour guiding. *Annals of Tourism Research*, 32 (3), 628–646.

Shackel, P. A. & Palus, M. 2006. Remembering an industrial landscape. *International Journal of Historical Archaeology*, 10 (1), 49–71.

Shackley, M. 1998. The cultural landscape of Rap Naui (Easter Island, Chile). In: M. Shackley, ed. *Visitor Management: Case Studies from World Heritage Sites.* Oxford: Butterworth-Heinemann, 66–81.

Shackley, M. 2000. Introduction – World Cultural Heritage Sites. In: M. Shackley, ed. *Visitor Management. Case Studies from World Heritage Sites.* Oxford: Butterworth-Heinemann, 1–9.

Silberman, N. A. 2009. The ICOMOS Ename Charter (2008) and the practice of heritage stewardship. *CRM: The Journal of Heritage Stewardship*, 10, 7–15.

Skeates, R. 2000. *Debating the Archaeological Heritage.* London: Duckworth.

Smith, L. 2006. *Uses of Heritage.* Abingdon: Routledge.

Staiff, R. 2014. *Re-imagining Heritage Interpretation. Enchanting the Past-Future.* Abingdon: Routledge.

Stanco, F. et al. 2012. Augmented perception of the past. The case of Hellenistic Syracuse. *Journal of Multimedia*, 7 (2), 211–216.

Statista. 2021. Number of smartphone users from 2016 to 2026. https://www.statista.com/ statistics/330695/number-of-smartphone-users-worldwide/ (accessed 13 August 2021).

Stewart, E. J., Hayward, B. M., Devlin, P. J. & Kirby, V. G. 1998. The 'place' of interpretation: a new approach to the evaluation of interpretation. *Tourism Management*, 19 (3), 257–266.

Stone, P. G. 2014. The Hadrian's Wall major study and 3rd management plan. In: P. G. Stone & D. Brough, eds. *Managing, Using, and Interpreting Hadrian's Wall as Heritage.* New York: Springer, 63–77.

Su, X. & Teo, P. 2009. *The Politics of Tourism in China.* London: Routledge.

Symonds, M. 2021. *Hadrian's Wall. Creating Division.* London: Bloomsbury.

Tilden, F. 2007. *Interpreting our Heritage.* 4th ed. Chapel Hill: University of North Carolina Press.

Timothy, D. J. & Tahan, L. G. 2020. Understanding perspectives on archaeology and tourism. In: D. J. Timothy & L. G. Tahan, eds. *Archaeology and Tourism. Touring the Past.* Bristol: Channel View Publications, 205–233.

Tourism Development International. 2019. *Integrated Tourism Master Plan for Borobudur – Yogyakarta – Prambanan.* Dublin: Tourism Development International.

Trepal, D., Scarlett, S. F. & Lafreniere, D. 2019. Heritage making through community archaeology and the spatial humanities. *Journal of Community Archaeology and Heritage*, 6 (4), 238–256.

Tussyadiah, I. P., Jung, T. H. & tom Dieck, M. C. 2018. Embodiement of wearable augmented reality technology in tourism experiences. *Journal of Travel Research*, 57 (5), 597–611.

Tuttiett, L. 2014. The management of Hadrian's Wall 2006–2012. In: P. G. Stone & D. Brough, eds. *Managing, Using, and Interpreting Hadrian's Wall as World Heritage.* New York: Springer, 79–87.

UNESCO. 2018. Decision: 42 COM 7B.85 Galápagos Islands (Ecuador) (N 1bis). https://whc.unesco.org/en/decisions/7314 (accessed 20 April 2021).

UNESCO. 2021. Historic Centre of Warsaw. https://whc.unesco.org/en/list/30 (accessed 12 August 2021).

University of Virginia. 2018. President's Commission on slavery and the university. https://slavery.virginia.edu/ (accessed 9 December 2021).

UNWTO. 1997. *Agenda 21 for the Travel and Tourism Industry*. Madrid: UNWTO.

Uzzell, D. 1989. *Heritage Interpretation. Volume 2: The Visitor Experience*. London: Belhaven Press.

Uzzell, D. & Ballantyne, R. 1998. Heritage that hurts: interpretation in a post modern world. In: D. Uzzell & R. Ballantyne, eds. *Contemporary Issues in Heritage and Environmental Interpretation: Problems and Prospects*. London: Stationery Office, 152–171.

Venditti, C. P. 2020. How to combine virtual and reality in archaeology communication: a brief overview of mixed reality and 'its surroundings'. In: E. Proietti, ed. *Developing Effective Communication Skills in Archaeology*. Hershey, PA: IGI Global, 224–244.

Vlahakis, V. et al. 2002. Archaeoguide: an augmented reality guide for archaeological sites. *IEEE Computer Graphics and Applications*, 22 (5), 52–60.

Vujadinovic, S. et al. 2013. Possibilities for mountain-based adventure tourism: the case of Serbia. *Bulletin of Geography. Socio-Economic Series*, 19, 99–111.

Walker, D. 2011. Towards a beneficial World Heritage: community involvement in the Blaenavon Industrial Landscape. *Museum International*, 631 (1–2), 25–33.

Wallis, J. 2019. *Difficult Histories & Positive Identities*. Windsor: Cumberland Lodge.

Waterton, E. 2013. Heritage tourism and its representations. In: R. Staiff, S. Watson & R. Bushell, eds. *Heritage and Tourism. Place, Encounter, Engagement*. Abingdon: Routledge, 64–84.

Weil, L. et al. 2019. Raising awareness for endangered species using augmented reality. https://core.ac.uk/download/pdf/322382898.pdf (accessed 7 July 2022).

West, S. & Ndlovu, S. 2010. Heritage, landscape and memory. In: T. Benton, ed. *Understanding Heritage and Memory*. Manchester: Manchester University Press, 202–237.

Wilson, A. 2020. 10 virtual tours of the world's most famous landmarks. https://www.theguardian.com/travel/2020/mar/30/10-best-virtual-tour-worlds-most-famous-landmarks?utm_source=dlvr.it&utm_medium=twitter (accessed 1 April 2020).

Winter, R. 2009. The modernities of heritage and tourism: interpretation of an Asian future. *Journal of Heritage Tourism*, 4 (2), 105–115.

Winter, T. 2002. Angkor Meets Tomb Raider setting the scene. *International Journal of Heritage Studies*, 8 (4), 323–336.

Winter, T. 2010. Heritage tourism: the dawn of a new era? In: S. Labadi & C. Long, eds. *Heritage and Globalisation*. Abingdon: Routledge, 117–129.

Woodward, S. C. 2004. Faith and tourism: planning tourism in relation to places of worship. *Tourism & Hospitality Planning & Development*, 1 (2), 173–186.

Woodward, S. C. & Carnegie, E. 2020. Student guides as mediators of institutional heritage and personal experience. In: G. Yildirim, ed. *Cases on Tour Guide Practices for Alternative Tourism*. Hershey, PA: IGI Global, 55–73.

Young, C. 2014. The Need for a Management Plan and the 1st and 2nd Plans. In: P. G. Stone & D. Brough, eds. *Managing, Using, and Interpreting Hadrian's Wall as World Heritage*. New York: Springer, 21–32.

Zollner, M., Keil, J., Wust, H. & Pleticnkx, D. 2009. *An Augmented Reality Presentation System for Remote Cultural Heritage Sites*. Goslar, Germany: Eurographics Association.

11

WORLD HERITAGE AND THE SUSTAINABLE DEVELOPMENT GOALS

11.1 Introduction

The instrumental role of heritage sites as catalysts for supporting, or even stimulating, social and economic development has been understood for decades. For instance, in the mid-1960s UNESCO and the (then) International Fund for Monuments supported the Chilean government's proposals to develop Rapa Nui (also known as Easter Island) as an open-air museum, with the enormous stone figures known as *moai* as its centrepiece. Hundreds of these *moai* can be found around the island and date back to the period between the 11th and 17th centuries when a Polynesian culture flourished here (UNESCO, 2020). In order to encourage tourism based around the island's cultural heritage assets, a major programme of conservation was initiated, the island's administration underwent a programme of capacity building and funding was secured to construct an airport as well as enhance public services (Skeates, 2000). The property was inscribed on the World Heritage List as **Rapa Nui National Park** in 1995 and subsequent years saw a sharp increase in inbound tourism, with arrivals rising from fewer than 20,000 at the turn of the millennium to more than 65,000 by 2013 (Figueroa & Rotarou, 2016a) and to over 100,000 by 2020 (Junker, 2020). Many jobs were supported by the economic activity associated with heritage tourism to the island (Skeates, 2000).

Though the development of heritage tourism in this remote destination has not been without its problems (Shackley, 1998), there is no doubt that it stimulated considerable economic and social benefit before it grew to a scale where environmental problems began to emerge (Figueroa & Rotarou, 2016b). And this is the new challenge for World Heritage – and indeed for heritage in general – to balance the conservation requirements of what are often fragile resources on the one hand with the growing expectation that these properties are ideally placed to help drive broad sustainable development initiatives within and across destinations. Thus, this chapter places World

DOI: 10.4324/9781003044857-12

Heritage within its broadest environmental and societal context, through the consideration of the interaction of World Heritage with sustainability and through the framework established by the 2015 Sustainable Development Goals (SDGs).

11.2 The heritage sector and sustainability

Sustainability was a term used from the 1970s onwards through the concepts of 'limits of growth' developed through (then) complex computational modelling undertaken at MIT to consider the 'limits' of population, food production, industrialisation, pollution, and consumption of non-renewable natural resources. Scientists concluded that if the global economy carried on with 'business as usual' (as it was in the late 1960s/ early 1970s) with no changes to historical growth trends, the limits to growth on earth would become evident by 2072, leading to 'sudden and uncontrollable decline in both population and industrial capacity' (Meadows et al, 1972). The burgeoning environmental movement developing through the 1970s and 1980s considered this concept and the ideas of limits, in time influencing Gro Brundtland, who in 1987 prepared the UN Report *Our Common Future*, which defined sustainable development as 'development that meets the needs of the present without compromising the ability of future generations to meet their own needs' (World Commission on Environment and Development, 1987, p. 31). This definition of sustainable development contains two key concepts: first, the concept of needs, in particular the essential needs of the world's poor, to which overriding priority should be given; and second, the idea of limitations imposed by the state of technology and social organisation on the environment's ability to meet present and future needs.

More than a decade ago, Clark (2008) argued that the heritage sector needs to better understand how heritage can contribute towards wider social, economic and environmental objectives in destinations, identifying a number of areas where the heritage sector as a whole (including WHS) could help governments meet individual sustainable development targets, including:

- Reducing waste, by re-using and repurposing historic buildings thereby reducing the amount of construction waste created;
- Reducing energy use, again through the re-use of older historic buildings and thus preserving the embodied energy contained therein, as well as reducing the amount of energy used in demolition and in constructing new buildings;
- Supporting local economic development, directly through heritage conservation and regeneration projects and also through heritage-based recreation and tourism. Both activities increase spending in local economies, thus supporting jobs in the heritage sector and its suppliers;
- Supporting social development initiatives by, for instance, promoting engagement with heritage places among socially disadvantaged groups, celebrating the intangible heritage of migrant or marginalised communities and encouraging young people to learn about their heritage through formal and informal learning initiatives.

Clark's central argument was that the heritage sector needed to move on from the mindset that informed the Venice Charter of 1964 for instance, that talked about protecting and managing individual sites and buildings. Rather, she contended, heritage managers and other stakeholders need to consider the wider environment within which heritage assets sit – both physically in terms of geographic location, but also in terms of the economic and social environment around them. Yet at the time she was writing, few heritage organisations or site managers appeared to be addressing this in a coherent, strategic fashion, generally relying instead on *ad hoc* projects or short-term initiatives.

Certainly, the opportunity to incorporate sustainable development activities into heritage site management plans appears to be one that has bypassed much of the sector until recently. Reviewing management plans for six UK World Heritage Sites over a decade ago, Landorf (2009) found that only two of the plans (**Cornwall & West Devon Mining Landscapes** and **Saltaire**) contained details of broad-based economic, environmental and social objectives and only one, the plan for Saltaire in West Yorkshire (inscribed 2001) addressed local community attitudes. In her view, 'WHSs are not actively planning and managing the economic and social sustainability dimensions in the same way they are managing the environmental sustainability dimension' (Landorf, 2009, p. 66), giving cause for concern that WHSs run the risk of being isolated from their local economy, with an associated impact on the equitable distribution of benefits of sustainable development based around heritage and cultural tourism. Yet there is evidence from many WHS around the world that there is an increasing interest in the role of heritage in general, and WHS management operations in particular, as positive agents of change (see for instance Vasile, 2019).

It is thus important to consider how heritage, and particularly World Heritage, has contributed and can contribute to the broader context for sustainable development that began, many argue, with the Rio Earth summit in 1992 and whose most recent manifestation is the 2030 Agenda for Sustainable Development, adopted by all UN Member States in 2015. After a short review of global efforts to mainstream sustainability into all aspects of public and private sector activities, but particularly the heritage and the tourism sectors, we examine how heritage site managers and their partners are increasingly becoming active in driving economic and social development and in addressing environmental pressures.

11.3 A short history of global efforts to promote sustainable development

11.3.1 1972 UN Conference on the Environment and Sustainable Development

The first UN Conference on the Environment and Sustainable Development occurred in Stockholm in 1972 with delegates discussing the human impact on the environment and its relationship to economic development. The resulting declaration contained 26 Principles, with Principle 4 stating:

> Man has a special responsibility to safeguard and wisely manage the heritage of wildlife and its habitat, which are now gravely imperilled by a combination of adverse factors. Nature conservation, including wildlife, must therefore receive importance in planning for economic development.
>
> *(United Nations, 1972)*

This is the only mention of heritage in the declaration, which was signed a few months before the World Heritage Convention, confirming that global priorities at the time were more focused on environmental protection as a goal, rather than as a process for stimulating or supporting economic and social development – the mention of economic development at the end of the paragraph implies that conservation should be considered when development plans are being developed but the potential role of conservation as an agent of change is not clearly identified. The implication is that the natural environment is to be protected from economic development rather than be part of it. Of the built heritage, there is no mention.

The challenge facing developing countries in particular were noted in Principle 12, which stated that:

> Resources should be made available to preserve and improve the environment, taking into account the circumstances and particular requirements of developing countries and any costs which may emanate from their incorporating environmental safeguards into their development planning and the need for making available to them, upon their request, additional international technical and financial assistance for this purpose.
>
> *(United Nations, 1972)*

As noted in Chapter 10, a criticism made of some approaches to the presentation and interpretation of World Heritage is that a growing cadre of international heritage specialists have been able to impose a westernised approach to their activities at heritage sites – cultural and natural. In part this has been facilitated by the emergence, over the last five decades, of aid-funded technical projects designed to support heritage tourism development initiatives in the Global South – a by-product perhaps of this 1972 declaration and the activities it encouraged.

11.3.2 1987 Brundtland Report

Throughout the 1970s and 1980s more and more attention was paid by State governments, international agencies and NGOs to the growing tensions between economic development on the one hand, and resource conversation on the other. A key event in the mainstreaming of sustainable development was the publication in 1987 of the Brundtland Report for the World Commission on Environment and Development. This defined sustainability (not sustainable development) as 'development that meets the needs of the present without compromising the ability of future generations to meet their own needs' (World Commission on

Environment and Development, 1987, p. 43). The word 'heritage' appears in this 300 page document just 10 times. One mention is in the context of built and architectural heritage being damaged by acid rain and another refers to the loss of as-yet unstudied species of flora and fauna through biodiversity loss as a threat to our cultural heritage. The oceans as global heritage at risk are mentioned twice and Outer Space and Antarctica are each covered in the same context once. Thus still, in the mid-to-late-1980s, heritage was still being seen generally as a tangible asset that needs to be protected. The only mention of the word heritage that suggests a broader role is in paragraph 2 of the report, which states that: 'We have the power to reconcile human affairs with natural laws and to thrive in the process. In this our cultural and spiritual heritages can reinforce our economic interests and survival imperatives' (World Commission on Environment and Development, 1987, p. 11). This is the first and only mention of the possibility that cultural heritage can be an agent of development, though the use of the word 'reinforce' could be taken to imply that it is an 'add-on' to development activities rather than a key driver.

11.3.3 1992 Rio Earth Summit and Agenda 21

Five years after the Brundtland Report was published, Rio de Janeiro hosted the Earth Summit, yet another global event where sustainable development was debated at length and an action plan – Agenda 21 – was adopted by the 182 UN member states who attended. While there was considerable time and effort spent deliberating on natural resource protection and management, cultural heritage as a topic was on the margins of the debate and cultural heritage properties are mentioned only twice – in Paragraph 36.10 of the Agenda 21 document where they are listed as one of the types of attraction (along with zoos, botanical gardens and museums) as resources that can facilitate the promotion of education, awareness and training around conservation issues; and in Paragraph 7.20, which deals with promoting sustainable human settlement development, where there was a call to improve the urban environment including 'older buildings, historic precincts and other cultural artefacts' (UN Department of Economic and Social Affairs, 1992, n.p.).

11.3.4 1997 UNWTO, WTTC and Earth Council response to Agenda 21

Some years later the UNWTO, working in partnership with the World Travel and Tourism Council (WTTC) and the Earth Council, prepared guidelines on how the travel and tourism industry should respond to Agenda 21 (UNWTO, 1997). Sustainable tourism as a concept was by that point moving into the mainstream (see for instance Wahab & Pigram, 1997; Wallis & Woodward, 1997; Mowforth & Munt, 1998) and growing consumer interest in both heritage tourism and wildlife tourism meant that in emerging destinations in South America, southern Africa and South and East Asia in particular, the industry was ready to embrace the opportunities to use tourism as a tool for promoting and supporting conservation and community devleopment.

11.3.5 1999 Global Code of Ethics for Tourism

The tourism sector continued to consider its broader social responsibilities with the publication in 1999 of the Global Code of Ethics for Tourism (UNWTO, 1999) which aimed, *inter alia*, to promote a more responsible and sustainable approach to tourism, accessible to all and taking into consideration both the positive and negative impacts that can arise in destinations as a result of poorly managed tourism. Of particular relevance even now, since UNWTO continues to promote this Code, are Articles 3 and 4. Article 3 considers the role of tourism in sustainable development and states that:

> All the stakeholders in tourism development should safeguard the natural environment with a view to achieving sound, continuous and sustainable economic growth geared to satisfying equitably the needs and aspirations of present and future generations;
>
> Tourism infrastructure should be designed and tourism activities programmed in such a way as to protect the natural heritage composed of ecosystems and biodiversity and to preserve endangered species of wildlife; the stakeholders in tourism development, and especially professionals, should agree to the imposition of limitations or constraints on their activities when these are exercised in particularly sensitive areas: desert, polar or high mountain regions, coastal areas, tropical forests or wetlands, propitious to the creation of nature reserves or protected areas;
>
> Nature tourism and ecotourism are recognized as being particularly conducive to enriching and enhancing the standing of tourism, provided they respect the natural heritage and local populations and are in keeping with the carrying capacity of the sites.

Thus Article 3 provides considerable support for the wise use of natural World Heritage Sites and would appear to argue that conservation issues should be paramount when managing such resources, with nature-based tourism being recognised as a potential agent of change.

Article 4 is explicitly geared towards cultural heritage in its broadest sense, recognising the importance of culture as a contributor towards enhancing the individual experience. The text of Article 4 is presented in full below:

> Tourism resources belong to the common heritage of mankind; the communities in whose territories they are situated have particular rights and obligations to them;
>
> Tourism policies and activities should be conducted with respect for the artistic, archaeological and cultural heritage, which they should protect and pass on to future generations; particular care should be devoted to preserving and upgrading monuments, shrines and museums as well as archaeological and historic sites which must be widely open to tourist visits; encouragement

should be given to public access to privately-owned cultural property and monuments, with respect for the rights of their owners, as well as to religious buildings, without prejudice to normal needs of worship;

    Financial resources derived from visits to cultural sites and monuments should, at least in part, be used for the upkeep, safeguard, development and embellishment of this heritage;

    Tourism activity should be planned in such a way as to allow traditional cultural products, crafts and folklore to survive and flourish, rather than causing them to degenerate and become standardized.

There are a number of relevant points in here, including the expectation of tourist access to built heritage assets of all kinds, including sacred sites and religious buildings; the expectation that at least some of the income from tourism should be ring-fenced for conservation and management activities at the site in question, and that tourism should be seen as a facilitator for interventions that seek to sustain traditional intangible heritage activities. By stating these points so clearly in the Global Code of Ethics for Tourism, UNWTO was clearly promoting a responsible approach to tourism development that supported but did not supplant conservation works at cultural and archaeolgical heritage sites.

11.3.6 2000 Millennium Declaration and the MDGs

Further progress towards global action, particularly in the field of social action, occurred in September 2000 when member states of the UN unanimously adopted the Millennium Declaration and its eight Millennium Development Goals (MDGs) which were predominantly concerned with social issues such as poverty reduction, gender equality and improved healthcare. A sustainable environment was however the seventh goal agreed upon, continuing the UN's interest in tackling the worst excesses of over-consumption, waste and pollution.

11.3.7 2002 Johannesburg Summit on Sustainable Development and the First International Conference on Responsible Tourism in Destinations in Cape Town

Two years later, in 2002, the Johannesburg Declaration on Sustainable Development confirmed the commitment of the global community to poverty eradication and to environmental conservation and protection (Tribe, 2011). Here for the first time, perhaps explicit attention was paid by state parties to the promotion of sustainable tourism as a tool for protecting and managing the world's natural resource base for economic and social development and for integrating tourism into broader economic development activities at national and destination level. Alongside this World Summit on Sustainable Development, a separate event was held in Cape Town – the First International Conference on Responsible

Tourism in Destinations – where tourism was the specific focus. Led by UNWTO and UNEP, and securing contributions from NGOs, industry representatives and other stakeholders, the event concluded with the announcement of the Cape Town Declaration which stated a need to 'ensure that tourism, the industry and the consumers, makes positive contributions to the conservation of natural and cultural heritage and to the maintenance of the world's diversity' (Goodwin, 2016, p. 36).

Two key points emerged from the Cape Town Declaration and the subsequent rise in interest in Reponsible Tourism (as opposed to sustainable tourism):

- Recognition that the host communities in tourism destinations had the right not to be inconvenienced by tourist developments, as well as the right to benefit from these activities. This is summed up in the mantra regularly used by Goodwin and others when talking about Responsible Tourism – that it is about creating *'better places for people to live in and for people to visit'* (Responsible Tourism Partnership, 2020);
- Recognition too that consumers as well as the industry and the public sector needed to play their part in delivering a more sustainable approach to tourism.

A key outcome from the Cape Town Declaration and the associated emergence of a group of responsible tourism academics and practitioners was the increased integration into tourism planning and management in certain destinations around the world of community-focused initiatives that responded much more than previously to the opportunities for integrating social as well as economic development into mainstream tourism (Goodwin, 2016).

11.3.8 2007 UNWTO Davos Declaration

This event focused particularly on climate change and required the global tourism sector to identify how it could progressively reduce its Greenhouse Gasses (GHG) emissions, particularly in the transportation and accommodation sectors (Tribe, 2011). However, the Declaration also noted the need for destinations, as well as tourism businesses, to adapt to changing climatic conditions, laying the groundwork for national, regional and local tourism development strategies and management plans to identify appropriate mitigation measures to tackle climate change (see also Chapter 6).

11.3.9 2012 Rio+20

Rio+20, or the United Nations Conference on Sustainable Development was held in June 2012 in Rio de Janeiro, Brazil. At the conference, Member States of the UN agreed, *inter alia*, to work on developing a suite of so-called Sustainable Development Goals (SDGs) which would build on the MDGs agreed over a decade earlier.

11.3.10 2015 UN Sustainable Development Summit, New York

The 2030 UN Agenda for Sustainable Development was agreed by all member states at a summit held in New York in September 2015. This agenda and its 17 constituent SDGs were produced in order to provide a framework for action by states parties, business and communities alike towards the delivery of 'peace and prosperity for people and the planet, now and into the future' (United Nations, 2019). There is a recognition that eliminating global poverty and related deprivation must run alongside strategies for reducing inequality, stimulating economic growth and improving health and education all the time while tackling climate change and embracing habitat conservation activities. In other words, this Agenda and its 17 SDGs was developed and promoted as a more coordinated approach to global development than previously seen.

In reality, the SDGs are quite broad-based and generally inter-dependent but taken together cover all areas that the UN feels need to be tackled for the global economy to be pushed back onto a sustainable track. The 17 goals are:

1. No Poverty;
2. Zero Hunger;
3. Good Health and Well-being;
4. Quality Education;
5. Gender Equality;
6. Clean Water and Sanitation;
7. Affordable and Clean Energy;
8. Decent Work and Economic Growth;
9. Industry, Innovation, and Infrastructure;
10. Reducing Inequality;
11. Sustainable Cities and Communities;
12. Responsible Consumption and Production;
13. Climate Action;
14. Life Below Water;
15. Life On Land;
16. Peace, Justice, and Strong Institutions;
17. Partnerships for the Goals.

Interestingly, the word heritage is only specifically mentioned in SDG 11: Sustainable Cities and Communities, when it appears in Target 11.4 with the following wording: '11.4 Strengthen efforts to protect and safeguard the world's cultural and natural heritage' (United Nations, 2020)

This suggests perhaps that heritage is not perceived in some parts of the UN as a major topic for debate, and is of marginal relevance to seeking to help deliver a more equitable and sustainable growth model for the global economy. Nonetheless, tourism of all kinds, including cultural and heritage tourism, is seen by UNWTO and its partners as having a key role to play in helping deliver these goals

(UNWTO, 2018). While tourism is specifically identified in three of the SDGs – Goal 8 on economic growth and jobs; Goal 12 on sustainable production and consumption and Goal 14 on life below water – UNWTO argues that adopting a sustainable or responsible approach to all aspects of tourism can help destinations, including World Heritage Sites, contribute towards meeting the UN's agenda for sustainable development. Below we explore some examples of how heritage organisations and the tourism sector are using WHS to do this.

11.4 WHS as vectors for sustainable development

As indicated above, over the last three decades or so there have been many international initiatives to promote sustainable development, with natural heritage in particular being frequently mentioned as an important component, cultural heritage less-so. Yet it appears that management plans for WHS rarely embrace any kind of coordinated approach to reflecting UN aspirations and priorities for development. Where actions are taken to use WH properties as instruments for economic or social development, this appears to happen on a largely ad-hoc basis and is fragmented. Whether this reflects funding availability, a lack of skills or political will other local issues is beyond the scope of this discussion. However, it is instructive to look at the experience of the UK's WHS as an exemplar of how sustainable development is (or isn't) reflected in management plans (Table 11.1)

A full review was carried out of the most recent plans for 31 of the UK's 32 properties on the list, and also of the plan for **Liverpool – Maritime Mercantile City** which was delisted in 2021 due to the irreversible loss of attributes conveying the outstanding universal value of the property. The management plan for one UK WHS – **Jodrell Bank Observatory** – was not publicly available at the time this book was being prepared. Of the 11 UK properties for which plans have been prepared since 2016, a year after the UN published the SDGs, only one makes any reference to them, suggesting that WHS managers at least in the UK do not see this global initiative as something they can materially contribute to. The honourable exception is the plan for the **Slate Landscape of Northwest Wales** which was inscribed on the list in 2021, and which explicitly mentions the SDGs as one of the overarching contexts for the management plan, with the World Heritage nomination being specifically cited as being key to delivering the aims of the 17 Sustainable Development Goals within the geographic area covered by the inscription.

However, the broader concept of sustainable development is mentioned in 18 plans and every management plan bar one addresses certain aspects of sustainability. Ironically, the plan for the WHS that does not mention sustainability once is for the property that includes the Palace of Westminster, the building in which UK politicians debate and pass legislation on all issues, including economic and social development! These more specific mentions of sustainable actions are mainly around the sustainable management of the property itself, contributions to sustainable tourism, adoption of sustainable transportation policies and sustaining local economies. It appears thus that WHS managers are focused, unsurprisingly perhaps,

TABLE 11.1 Acknowledgement of sustainable development and the SDGs in UK WHS management plans: sites ranked by chronological order of inscription on WH list.

Site	Date inscribed	Period of plan	Mention of SDGs?	Mentions of sustainable development	Mentions of sustainability
Castles and Town Walls of King Edward in Gwynedd	1986	2018–2028	No	3	29
Durham Castle and Cathedral	1986	2017–2023	No	No	8
Giant's Causeway and Causeway Coast	1986	2013–2019	No	2	30
Ironbridge Gorge	1986	2017	No	No	15
St Kilda	1986	2012–2017	No	1	17
Stonehenge, Avebury and Associated Sites	1986	2015	No	No	199
Studley Royal Park including the Ruins of Fountains Abbey	1986	2015–2021	No	4	16
Blenheim Palace	1987	2017	No	1	14
City of Bath	1987	2016–2022	No	No	23
Frontiers of the Roman Empire: Hadrian's Wall	1987	2015–2019	No	2	14
Palace of Westminster, Westminster Abbey & Saint Margaret's Church	1987	2007	No	No	No
Canterbury Cathedral, St Augustine's Abbey & St Martin's Church	1988	2002	No	No	6
Henderson Island	1988	2004–2009	No	No	8
Tower of London	1988	2016	No	No	12
Gough and Inaccessible Islands	1995	2010–2015	No	1	3
Old and New Towns of Edinburgh	1995	2017–2022	No	1	13
Maritime Greenwich	1997	2014	No	No	18
Heart of Neolithic Orkney	1999	2014–2019	No	2	24

Site	Date inscribed	Period of plan	Mention of SDGs?	Mentions of sustainable development	Mentions of sustainability
Blaenavon Industrial Landscape	2000	2011–2016	No	1	27
Historic Town of St George and Related Fortifications, Bermuda	2000	2014	No	No	1
Derwent Valley Mills	2001	2014–2019	No	3	53
Dorset and East Devon Coast	2001	2014–2019	No	2	3
New Lanark	2001	2013–2018	No	No	12
Saltaire	2001	2014	No	No	21
Royal Botanic Gardens, Kew	2003	2014	No	No	56
Liverpool – Maritime Mercantile City[1]	2004	2017–2024	No	10	35
Cornwall and West Devon Mining Landscape	2006	2013–2018	No	1	45
Frontiers of the Roman Empire: Antonine Wall	2008	2014–2019	No	2	24
Pontcysyllte Aqueduct and Canal[2]	2009	2019–2029	No	No	7
The Forth Bridge	2015	2014–2019	No	2	11
Gorham's Cave Complex	2016	2016–2021	No	16	26
The English Lake District	2017	2015–2020	No	16	26
Jodrell Bank Observatory	2019	Plan not publicly available			
The Slate Landscape of Northwest Wales	2021	2020–2030	Yes	30	7

Notes:
[1]Site was delisted at the 44th Session of the World Heritage Committee in 2021.
[2]Draft plan reviewed – final version not available at the time of writing.

on the more local dimension of sustainability rather than seeing their actions as part of a wider, global initiative. Once again, therefore, we see a tension between WHS, on the one hand, being promoted as properties of global significance while on the other hand the approach to managing them being located very much within the local.

11.5 Case studies of using WHS management activities to support the SDGS

Below we explore how some World Heritage Site managers and other stake-holders are seeking to align their conservation, access and management activities with those goals most relevant to World Heritage Site management and usage, namely:

- SDG 1: No Poverty;
- SDG 11: Sustainable Cities and Communities;
- SDG 13: Climate Action.

11.5.1 SDG 1: No Poverty

Cultural and heritage tourism have long been used as vehicles for supporting local economic upliftment through the creation of jobs both directly in the tourism and hospitality sectors, and also indirectly through the supply chains serving the industry. Developing meaningful employment opportunities at a fair wage is a challenge in many destinations, particularly where the buying power of major international tour operators is considerable and the local supply chain is forced to compete on price. Yet there are examples of where appropriate intervention has led to the creation of paid employment at cultural heritage destinations at remuneration levels commensurate with the skills required, and where the income generated from tourism is directed into community development initiatives. One such example can be found in The Gambia, at the **Kunta Kinteh and Related Sites** World Heritage Site (see below).

BOX 11.1 CASE STUDY 11.1: KUNTA KINTEH ISLAND AND RELATED SITES WORLD HERITAGE SITE, THE GAMBIA.

The two villages of Albreda and Juffureh, on the northern bank of the River Gambia, are the key access points to the **Kunta Kinteh Island and Related Sites** WHS (inscribed in 2003 and originally named James Island and Related Sites, until former President Jammeh instigated the name change in 2011 to reflect its African, rather than European, heritage). The property meets Criteria (iii) and (vi), with UNESCO noting that:

> Kunta Kinteh Island and related sites, the villages, remains of European settlements, the forts and the batteries, were directly and tangibly asso-ciated with the beginning and the conclusion of the slave trade, retaining its memory related to the African Diaspora.
>
> *(UNESCO, 2011)*

The Gambia has developed as one of West Africa's most significant destina-tions, with tourism accounting for some 16% of the country's GDP prior to the

COVID-19 pandemic and employing, directly and indirectly, more than 120,000 people (WTTC, 2021).

Tourist interest in the Albreda and Juffureh area emerged after the publication in 1976 of Alex Haley's book *Roots*, in which he traced his ancestry back to the Kinteh clan and their home village of Juffureh. The emergence of the Gambia as a 'winter sun' tourism destination from the 1980s onwards led to the development of one-day so-called 'Roots' excursions from the main tourism hotels on the Senegambia strip, just south of the capital Banjul. Effectively, the 'myth' of Kunta Kinteh provided the impetus for commodification of slave heritage at the two villages, with the later inscription of the property on the WH list raising its profile as a 'legitimate' tourism destination.

Tourists would take a 3–3½ hour boat trip upriver before disembarking at Albreda, visiting that village, walking the 15 minutes on to Juffureh for an appointment with a member of the Kinteh family and a tour of the craft market before boarding their boat for a stop-off at James/Kunta Kinteh island out in the middle of the river (Plate 11.1) and the return trip to Banjul. It should be noted that tourism to the Gambia is very seasonal and concentrated almost entirely between the months of October and March, i.e. outside the rainy season, and when sunshine and warm temperatures can be more or less guaranteed. Thus, opportunities for the host communities to benefit from tourism associated with their heritage were limited to a couple of hours a day, for only a few months of the year. This inevitably led to problems as interest in the excursion grew, problems that were only partially resolved by the introduction in 1996 of the Roots festival, that targeted an African American market, inspired by Haley's novel and keen to engage with their ancestral homelands (Gijanto, 2011).

By the turn of the Millennium around 15,000 international tourists were taking the excursion each year, though by 2008 this had fallen to around 8,000 per annum (Bah, 2011). There were two particular reasons for this, the first being the relatively high proportion of repeat tourism to the Gambia – with a barely changing visitor experience at the WHS there was little incentive for people on a second or even third holiday to the country to visit again. The second was the increasing amount of hassle experienced by tourists, a reflection partly of the limited timeslot within which the host community could sell them goods and services and partly because of the limited employment opportunities in the area. As Ceesay (2018) notes, 'with increased tourism in an economically deprived community came a culture of begging, a proliferation of donation boxes in the villages, and the harassment of tourists' (p. 93). The host communities mainly made money from tourists through donations and selling souvenirs, yet the same souvenirs were also available in the main tourist area at Senegambia so there was no motivation for tourists to buy them during excursions.

To address the problems of a declining quality in the tourist experience, and community dissatisfaction with the presence of outside tour guides in their villages, the Ministry of Tourism & Culture convened a meeting with the two communities, the Governor of the North Bank region, tour operators and ground handlers to discuss how to resolve the situation. Responsibility for planning and delivering a response was delegated to the Gambian Tourism Authority who secured funding for a two-year project from the Travel Foundation, a UK-based charity funded by tour operators and that seeks to develop responsible tourism projects in destinations heavily visited by British package tourists.

The objective of the intervention was to create a high-quality tourist experience based around the site's slavery heritage that benefited the two host communities equitably and in a more transparent manner than had previously been the case. As such, it provides a good example of how cultural heritage initiatives can be used to target poverty reduction in host communities.

Key elements of the project, which were all discussed and agreed with the main European tour operators bringing tourists into the Gambia after having been worked up with the host community, included:

- Replacement of the previous practice whereby tourists gave donations to individuals with a formal entrance fee of D50 (50 Dalassi), payable by all visitors with the funds being held centrally for later dissemination (see below);
- Creation of a Trust with equal representation from both communities, whereby the funds raised from admission fees were distributed equally to both villages to fund community development projects identified by the *alkalo* (village head) and designed to combat some of the social problems associated with poverty in the area;
- Recruitment and training of 16 guides – eight from each village – who were paid a wage and who took over from the ground handler's employees as tourists disembarked at the pier at Albreda. This training covered a wide range of areas including guiding principles, customer care, the reasons for UNESCO WHS status, culture and local history, including the history of the Kingdom of Niumi which existed in the area in pre-colonial times.

PLATE 11.1 Gambian guide and European tourists at Kunta Kinteh Island.
Source: Photograph by Simon Woodward.

In parallel with the above activities, conservation and restoration works occurred at key structures within the WHS including the remains of Fort James on Kunta Kinteh Island, the Maurel Frères building in Juffureh, the ruins of the former Portuguese mission near San Domingo and the former CFAO warehouse on the banks of the River Gambia. These capital projects were all undertaken by the National Centre for Arts & Culture (NCAC), a semi-autonomous organisation charged with preserving, promoting and developing Gambian arts and culture (Ceesay, 2018), with the intention of creating further employment opportunities for local people both during the initial conservation works and also later, once operational.

It is reported that in the early years of implementation the revitalised excursion delivered more than £10,000 per annum to the host communities (Bah, 2011) and that the Travel Foundation project did have some positive impact. However, by the time of the 2013/14 season there was more dissent from communities and tour operators, and in 2015 a further development plan was implemented in partnership with CRAterre, a French NGO with experience of sustainable development in rural Africa. This covered conservation of the built heritage sites, an awareness programme within the local community detailing the value of local resources and enhancements to the visitor experience including development of a visitor centre providing interpretive displays, a retail area and visitor conveniences.

Sadly, even prior to the 2020 COVID-19 pandemic, the volume of international tourism to The Gambia had started to fluctuated considerably because of internal political unrest (Maclean & Jammeh, 2019) as well as external macro-economic factors and demand for the 'Roots' excursion has fallen to fewer than 5,000 guests per season, thereby reducing income to the two villages. As a result, there are now moves to promote overnight accommodation in Albreda developed by a local entrepreneur so that tourist length of stay in the two communities is extended, thereby increasing spend and supporting other heritage-based tourism products that are being developed by local residents such as birdwatching & trips out onto the river on fishing boats (pirogues).

11.5.2 SDG 11: Sustainable Cities and Communities

As discussed earlier, in most of the international conventions that have addressed sustainable development over the last two or three decades, discussions about cultural heritage have tended to be limited to the urban environment and the role of regeneration projects based around the conservation of the built heritage as a tool for uplifting the situation of local residents. The need for such programmes is, in the mind of some commentators, an inevitable outcome of global capitalism and the unequal distribution of wealth. A powerful exposition of this train of thought is provided by Porter (2000) who argues that UNESCO and other international agencies often build support for their heritage conservation programmes around the argument that poverty is in part an impoverished awareness of the value of heritage, and that such organisations moralise too much about the need for communities to address conservation themselves without acknowledging the broader structural inequalities that lead to poverty. In effect, the paradigm that has emerged is one that 'situates the impoverished inhabitants as active creators of this decay' (Porter, 2000, p. 211). She also notes the irony that 'poverty is the source of urban decay, at the same time that treatment of this urban decay provides a means for alleviating poverty' (2000, p. 210). Similar challenges have been noted, for instance, by Nobre (2002) who considered the contentious approach to regeneration in **Salvador da Bahia** (inscribed 1985) and by Chaplain (2002) who explored regeneration and sustainability issues around colonial-built heritage, but in the **Historic Centre of Macao** (inscribed 2005).

Porter's particular study location was the **Medina of Fez** (inscribed 1981), considered to be one of the most extensive and best conserved historic towns of the Arab-Muslim world with an urban form dating back to the late eighth/ early ninth centuries CE. The inscription notes that 'the unpaved urban space conserves the majority of its original functions and attribute. It not only represents an outstanding architectural, archaeological and urban heritage, but also transmits a life style, skills and a culture that persist and are renewed despite the diverse effects of the evolving modern societies'. The urban fabric has remained relatively homogeneous and intact over the centuries, as the city's role as the capital of Morocco from the late 13th to early 20th centuries brought wealth and prestige and led to the construction of a wide range of high-quality royal, public, religious and private buildings. However, the two parts of the WHS: Fes el Bali (the original settlement) and Fes Jdid ('new' Fez, which dates back to the 13th century), cover a combined area of only around 220ha (540 acres) and are home to upwards of 250,000 people (Bianca, 2000), many of whom have emigrated into the city from the Atlas Mountains in search of better prospects.

As a result, Fes Medina has for some decades been characterised by the World Bank as a pocket of concentrated poverty with consequent international aid projects funding major programmes of infrastructural improvements (sanitation, building rehabilitation and conservation, access improvements etc). However, Porter's research found that certainly the early phases of aid-funded regeneration projects had limited impact even in creating the target number of construction jobs, which had been seen as an obvious means of lifting people out of poverty. She argues that structural and administrative factors at the municipality level were a key reason for its failure to reach targets. Yet some of the decay was, she argues actively encouraged in colonial times to reflect more perfectly its 'medieval' origins, leading her to note that 'heritage management is not the handmaiden to anything .... but rather the very technique, or modus operandi, of intervention and resource appropriation' (Porter, 2000, p. 204). In such initiatives, there is a risk that the well-being of the local community in an impoverished urban area becomes 'elided with the material constitution of its architectural heritage' (2000, p. 204). Because of this, the 'poverty' which regeneration programmes seek to address becomes transferred into a concern of the material heritage, rather than for the communities living in and among these historic structures and thus 'an easy conversion is made whereby the renovation of houses – the material refashioning of decay into preservation – automatically alleviates the socio-economic inequalities of diminished resource access and constricted capabilities' (2000, p. 211).

Notwithstanding such legitimate questioning about why there appears to be a need to help impoverished residents of run-down urban areas that are perceived to have heritage merit, there are nonetheless examples of good practice in working with such communities to not only enhance the materiality of the urban environment, but to help deliver sustainable livelihoods as well. One such example is explored in the case study below of the Al-Darb Al-Ahmar area of Cairo, Egypt.

BOX 11.2 CASE STUDY 11.2: HISTORIC CAIRO (INSCRIBED 1979).

Al-Darb Al-Ahmar is a historic neighbourhood in Cairo, Egypt and forms approximately one third of the World Heritage property of **Historic Cairo**, inscribed on the World Heritage List in 1979 against Criteria (i), (v) and (vi) with the inscription noting its 'absolutely unquestionable historical, archaeological and urban importance'. The area, covering just under a square mile, contains more than 40 monuments built during successive Fatimid, Ayyubid, Mamluk and Ottoman eras. It is located a little bit to the south of the main Tahrir Square. There are notable historic monuments, including Khayrbek and Um al-Sultan Shaaban mosques, and the old Ayyubid City Walls, which were excavated as part of the Al-Azhar Park project. Darb el-Ahmar also hosts several interesting historical markets, trades and crafts. Today, these unique historical assets attract increasing numbers of year-round heritage tourists. However, the State of Conservation Reports for the property prepared between 1993 and 2019 highlight ongoing concerns regarding housing, identity, social cohesion, changes in local population and community, lack of functioning management systems, rain/water table, dilapidated infrastructure and neglect and lack of maintenance. But though its main monuments are not under threat, many houses and smaller buildings are being demolished thus changing the social make-up of the area. Less than two centuries ago, al-Darb al-Ahmar was one of the wealthiest neighbourhoods in Cairo. Today the 100,000 inhabitants of this historic district are among the poorest.

The current projects to revitalise Darb Al Ahmar can be traced back to a visit to a conference in Cairo by the Aga Khan IV in 1984. It was clear that Cairo residents needed more green space, and the funding of Al-Azhar Park, in excess of US$30 million, was a gift to Cairo from the Aga Khan. Al-Azhar Park was created by the Historic Cities Support Programme of the Aga Khan Trust for Culture (AKTC), an entity of the Aga Khan Development Network (AKDN). It finally opened to the public in 2005.

After the grading works for the Al Azhar Park and the discovery of the old city walls, the major portion of the remaining Ayyubid wall has once again emerged over a length of approximately 1,500 m from Bab al-Wazir to al-Azhar Street, forming the boundary between the Darb al-Ahmar district and the Park. The historic importance of the wall with its gates, towers, interior chambers, and galleries led the AKDN to launch a combined physical and social rehabilitation of the Darb Al Ahmar district. It was clear that the park construction, as well as the historic wall conservation could, and should, act as stimuli for the rehabilitation of Darb al Ahmar.

As well as the revitalisation of housing and the restoration of landmark buildings, AKDN programmes also encompassed education, skills training, apprenticeships, job creation and financing. These training programmes were for a broad range of craft skills and not just those associated with building conservation. There was also careful consideration of opportunities for training women in appropriate roles, from craft production up to conservation architecture.

In 2011 a catalogue was produced showcasing the unique arts of Egyptian craftspeople who work in the district of Darb al-Ahmar, called *The Arts of Darb Al Ahmar*. The designers and producers featured in the catalogue received support from the First MicroFinance Foundation in Egypt, either through loans or business support services.

Several years later, The Aga Khan Foundation's 'The Artisans of Al-Darb Al-Ahmar – Life and Work in Historic Cairo' was open from 19 November 2018 to 5 April 2019. The exhibition looked at the neighbourhood of al-Darb al-Ahmar, home to over 1,000 artisanal workshops, highlighting how the work requires great skill and physical exertion and is a rarity around much of the world.

PLATE 11.2 Landscaping outside a mosque, Darb Al Ahmar.
Source: © Seif El Rashidi.

Since 2016, a longstanding project has been working to revitalise a commercial street in the historic district of Darb al-Ahmar and reconnect the local community with their cultural heritage. The project, developed with help from the

Research Station of the Japan Society for the Promotion of Science, consists of three main actions:

1. Awareness-raising and training workshops. An essential aim of the project was to increase the local community's understanding of cultural heritage and identify priorities for community development.
2. The creation of a community centre. Based on the results of the community engagement programme, new uses were proposed for the community centre of Beit Yakan, a restored historical building located on the street. The cultural centre hosts the woodcraft training facilities, which support the income of local craftsmen, and learning facilities for activities like Islamic geometry, Arabic calligraphy, and traditional crafts.
3. The development of local partnerships. To ensure the sustainability of the initiative in the long-term, the Research Station sought partnerships with local actors, including the wood-working guild, local and regional governments, and non-profit organisations. Since 2018, the project's activities have been financed by local stakeholders and partners.

As a consequence, the project implementation team reports that the commercial street of Souq al-Silah has been revitalised, bringing new opportunities for local craftsmen, and reconnecting the community with their tangible and intangible heritage. The new community centre serves as a training facility and a safe public space for women and children. The organisers also report increased knowledge, awareness, and caretaking of the local heritage.[1]

11.5.3 SG 13: Climate Action

Chapter 6 has already considered at some length the impacts of climate change on natural and cultural World Heritage; thus we offer only a few additional comments here. A report into carbon sequestration in the historic environment prepared by Historic England (2020) argues that

> huge amounts of carbon are locked up in existing historic buildings. Continuing to use and re-use these assets can reduce the need for new carbon-generating construction activities, thereby reducing the need for new material extraction and reducing waste production ... By extending the life of our cherished historic assets, we can materially reduce the need for high carbon consuming activities and materials.
>
> *(p.4)*

Refurbishing and retrofitting historic properties, whether residential, civic, commercial or industrial, can thus become an important tool as we seek to arrest climate change which is of course a key challenge around the world.

In urban World Heritage Sites such as the **Urban Historic Centre of Cienfuegos** (Cuba, inscribed 2005); the **Speicherstadt and Kontorhaus District with Chilehaus** in Hamburg, Germany (inscribed 2015) or the **Historic Quarter of the Seaport City of Valparaíso** (inscribed 2003), the sensitive adaption of any former industrial or commercial premises that are being converted into residential usage is particularly important so that the historic character of the property is maintained and so that relevant OUVs are not compromised. The aforementioned Historic England report argues that installing appropriate energy efficient infrastructure into historic properties when they are being renovated is vital, as by extending the life of these structures the carbon captured in the original construction is not lost, something that is particularly relevant in temperate rather than tropical climates. This means sensitive selection of materials for windows, doors and cladding in particular. And even where historic residential properties in tropical zones are being upgraded (and hence there is less need to address energy loss through windows and doors), retaining the original fabric of the original buildings as much as possible will support moves towards carbon sequestration. This is particularly relevant in WHS such as the **Historic Centre of Salvador de Bahia** (Brazil) or the **Colonial Cities of Melaka and George Town** (Malaysia) where development pressures associated with commercial development are putting particular pressure on city planners who need to balance conservation with economic growth (see Smith & Luque-Azcona, 2012 and Giacalone, 2018 for more about Salvador de Bahia and Said et al., 2013 and Khoo & Lim, 2019 for more about George Town).

11.6 Concluding remarks on World Heritage and the SDGs

There is a clear ambition on the part of UNESCO that 'the integration of a sustainable development perspective into the World Heritage Convention will enable all stakeholders involved in its implementation, in particular at national level, to act with social responsibility' (UNESCO, 2015, p. 2). However, much remains to be done to locate World Heritage issues and properties directly with SDG 11, while also making the connection to other SDGs. Indeed, in this respect the World Heritage community can share the same central criticism that is generally levelled at the SDGs – namely the lack of progress being made towards meaningful, widespread action. In 2019 UN Secretary-General António Guterres stated 'It is abundantly clear that a much deeper, faster and more ambitious response is needed to unleash the social and economic transformation needed to achieve our 2030 goals'.[2] It is perhaps the tension at the heart of the World Heritage process and the connection between local, national and international concerns that provides both the greatest opportunities and the greatest challenges in working towards the SDGs.

Notes

1 Naoko Fukami, Japanese Society for the Promotion of Science, Cairo Research Station. January 2021.
2 See https://www.un.org/sustainabledevelopment/progress-report/ (accessed 3 December 2021).

References

Aga Khan Trust for Culture. 2001. *Historic Cities Support Programme. The Azhar Park Project in Cairo and the Conservation and Rehabilitation of Darb Al-Ahmar*. Geneva: Aga Khan Trust for Culture.

Bah, A. 2011. *Improving Destination Management Strategies for Albreda and Jufureh 'Roots' Heritage: A Case Study on Issues, Planning, Administering and Evaluating a Sustainable Community Excursion*. Banjul, The Gambia: Association for Small Scale Enterprises in Tourism.

Bianca, S. 2000. *Urban Form in the Arab World*. London: Thames and Hudson.

Ceesay, B. 2018. Revamping a heritage tourism destination for more sustainable growth. In: E. Moukala & I. Odiaua, eds. *World Heritage for Sustainable Development in Africa*. Paris: UNESCO, 93–98.

Chaplain, I. 2002. Urban regeneration and the sustainability of colonial built heritage: a case study of Macau, China. *WIT Transactions on Ecology and the Environment*, 54. doi:10.2495/URS020351.

Clark, K. 2008. Only connect: sustainable development and cultural heritage. In: G. Fairclough, R. Harrison, J. H. Jameson Jr & J. Schofield, eds. *The Heritage Reader*. Abingdon: Routledge, 82–98.

Figueroa, E. B. & Rotarou, E. S. 2016a. Sustainable development or eco-collapse: lessons. *Sustainability*, 8, 1–26.

Figueroa, E. B. & Rotarou, E. S. 2016b. Tourism as the development driver of Easter Island: the key role of resident perceptions. *Island Studies Journal*, 11 (1), 245–264.

Giacalone, G. 2018. Possible strategies to break the bond between urban requalification and gentrification. *Sociabilidades Urbanas – Revista de Antropologia e Sociologia*, 2 (6), 105–112.

Gijanto, L. 2013. Historic preservation and development in Banjul, The Gambia. *Journal of African Diaspora Archaeology and Heritage*, 2 (1), 93–114.

Gijanto, L. A. 2011. Competing narratives: tensions between diaspora tourism and the Atlantic past in the Gambia. *Journal of Heritage Tourism*, 6 (3), 227–243.

Goodwin, H. 2016. *Responsible Tourism: Using Tourism for Sustainable Development*. 2nd ed. Oxford: Goodfellow.

Historic England. 2020. *There's No Place Like Old Homes. Re-Use and Recycle to Reduce Carbon*. London: Historic England.

Junker, U. 2020. How to get to Easter Island and leave it a better place. https://www.theislanderonline.com.au/story/6650809/why-easter-island-wants-fewer-visitors-and-better-ones/ (accessed 27 April 2020).

Khoo, S. L. & Lim, Y. M. 2019. Dissecting George Town's human capital challenges in built heritage: voices from the stakeholders. *Journal of Cultural Heritage Management and Sustainable Development*, 9 (3), 376–393.

Lafrenz Samuels, K. 2010. Material heritage and poverty reduction. In: S. Labadi & C. Long, eds. *Heritage and Globalisation*. Abingdon: Routledge, 202–217.

Landorf, C. 2009. Managing for sustainable tourism: a review of six cultural World Heritage Sites. *Journal of Sustainable Tourism*, 17 (1), 53–70.

Maclean, R. & Jammeh, S. 2019. Gambia's joy gives way to sinking distrust as Barrow clings to power. https://www.theguardian.com/global-development/2019/sep/23/gambia-joy-gives-way-to-sinking-distrust-adama-barrow-clings-to-power (accessed 14 August 2021).

Meadows, D.H., Meadows, D.H., Randers, J. & Behrens III, W.W. 1972. *The Limits to Growth: A Report to the Club of Rome*. Chelsea, VT: Chelsea Green Publishing

Mowforth, M. & Munt, I. 1998. *Tourism and Sustainability: New Tourism in the Third World*. London: Routledge.

Nobre, E. A. 2002. Urban regeneration experiences in Brazil: Historical preservation, tourism development and gentrification in Salvador da Bahia. *Urban Design International*, 7 (2), 109–124.

Porter, G. D. 2000. The city's many uses: cultural tourism, the sacred monarchy and the preservation of Fez's Medina. *The Journal of North African Studies*, 5 (2), 59–88.

Responsible Tourism Partnership. 2020. *Cape Town Declaration on Responsible Tourism.* https://responsibletourismpartnership.org/cape-town-declaration-on-responsible-tourism/(accessed 30 April 2020).

Said, S. Y., Aksah, H. & Ismail, E. D. 2013. Heritage conservation and regeneration of historic areas in Malaysia. *Procedia-Social and Behavioral Sciences*, 105, 418–428.

Shackley, M. 1998. The cultural landscape of Rap Naui (Easter Island, Chile). In: M. Shackley, ed. *Visitor Management: Case Studies from World Heritage Sites.* Oxford: Butterworth-Heinemann, 66–81.

Skeates, R. 2000. *Debating the Archaeological Heritage.* London: Duckworth.

Smith, H. & Luque-Azcona, E. J. 2012. The historical development of built heritage awareness and conservation policies: a comparison of two World Heritage Sites: Edinburgh and Salvador do Bahia. *GeoJournal*, 77 (3), 399–415.

Tribe, J. 2011. *The Economics of Recreation, Leisure and Tourism.* 4th ed. Abingdon: Routledge.

UN Department of Economic and Social Affairs. 1992. *Earth Summit Agenda 21. The United Nations Programme of Action from Rio.*, New York: United Nations.

UNESCO. 1981. Medina of Fez. Available at: https://whc.unesco.org/en/list/170 (accessed 14 August 2021).

UNESCO. 2011. Kunta Kinteh Island and related sites. https://whc.unesco.org/en/list/761 (accessed 7 April 2020).

UNESCO. 2015. *Policy for the Integration of a Sustainable Development Perspective into the Processes of the World Heritage Convention. WHC-15/20.GA/INF.13.* Paris: UNESCO.

UNESCO. 2020. Rapa Nui National Park. https://whc.unesco.org/en/list/715/ (accessed 27 April 2020).United Nations. 1972. Declaration of the United Nations Conference on the Human Environment. http://www.un-documents.net/unchedec.htm (accessed 28 April 2020).

United Nations. 2019. Why the SDGs matter. https://www.un.org/sustainabledevelopment/why-the-sdgs-matter/ (accessed 30 April 2020).

United Nations. 2020. Sustainable Development Goals. https://sustainabledevelopment.un.org/sdgs (accessed 3 April 2020).

UNWTO. 1997. *Agenda 21 for the Travel and Tourism Industry.* Madrid: UNWTO.

UNWTO. 1999. *Global Code of Ethics for Tourism.* Madrid: UNWTO.

UNWTO. 2018. *Tourism and the Sustainable Development Goals. Good Practices in the Americas*, Madrid: World Tourism Organization.

Vasile, V. 2019. *Caring and Sharing: The Cultural Heritage Environment as an Agent for Change.* Berlin: Springer International Publishing.

Wahab, S. & Pigram, J. J., eds. 1997. *Tourism, Development and Growth: The Challenge of Sustainability.* London: Routledge.

Wallis, J. & Woodward, S. 1997. Improving the environmental performance of Scotland's hospitality sector. *Managing Leisure*, 1 (2), 94–109.

World Commission on Environment and Development. 1987. *Our Common Future.* Oxford: Oxford University Press.

WTTC. 2021. *Gambia. 2021 Annual Research: Key Highlights.* London: WTTC.

12

WHAT OF THE FUTURE?

12.1 Introduction

The global coronavirus pandemic that started in Wuhan, China in late 2019 had a fundamental impact across every aspect of society, and none more so than on international tourism. From a record figure of 1.5 billion trips in 2019,[1] international tourism trips fell to around 500,000 million international trips, a figure not seen since the 1990s.[2] Almost every global tourism destination suffered massive falls in the number of international tourists arriving on their shores which inevitably led to a parallel decline in visitor activity at those World Heritage properties that were able to remain open to visitors.

One should not forget that a key strategy to manage the pandemic by national governments was to lock down their economies and society for weeks and sometimes months at a time, proscribing all bar essential trips out of the home (generally only for essential shopping and leisure purposes). This raised the parallel challenges for WHS managers used to receiving visitors – on the one hand, they were often obliged to close their doors as part of the broader effort to reduce the spread of the virus while on the other hand even those that were able to remain open found few people were available to visit because domestic tourism was also curtailed as tourist accommodation and hospitality businesses also ceased to operate. Thus, revenue streams from visitors were interrupted or even severed completely; the absence of tourism and its associated disturbance benefited fragile environments and staff normally employed on managing visitors were either furloughed or redeployed to other functions while at the same time conservation and related management responsibilities remained on 'to-do' lists. UNESCO reported that more than 50 countries closed or partially closed all or some of their World Heritage Sites during the first wave of infections in early 2020 (Markham, 2021) and in some instances there was an increase in vandalism, theft and poaching, all of which had the potential to compromise a property's Outstanding Universal Value.

DOI: 10.4324/9781003044857-13

A review of how a selection of World Heritage properties around the world responded to the challenge of a fundamental shift in visitor engagement with their assets provides an interesting starting point to consider the future for World Heritage. Several World Heritage managers contacted by the authors advised us that the pause in operations associated with public health measures to combat the spread of coronavirus offered them the opportunity not only to review their progress against established management plan objectives, but also to reflect on what may need to change in a post-COVID world in terms of how properties are funded, managed and promoted. Thus although most properties prepare, action and update detailed management plans (see Chapter 2), the fundamental shift in the international and domestic tourism landscapes resulting from the coronavirus pandemic has encouraged World Heritage managers and other stakeholders (e.g. States parties, heritage and environment ministries, Destination Management Organisations) to consider, perhaps more creatively than previously, what the future is for World Heritage from a local, national and international perspective.

Of course, at the same time that individual sites were responding to the challenges of the pandemic, broader issues surrounding World Heritage continued to be debated across the heritage community. The politics behind World Heritage listing was tackled in a key text by Lynn Meskell (2018) while the ideas of Caitlin DeSilvey (2017) regarding 'curated decay' have initiated debates about conservation, notions of authenticity and integrity and the balance between culture and nature. The need to acknowledge the slave heritage of many historic properties in the UK (Fowler, 2020) reflected the wider Black Lives Matter movement emanating from the USA and calls attention to how particular heritages remain unrecognised and unreported and aligns with wider needs to decolonise professional practices and academic disciplines. With these all set to the background of the climate and ecological emergency declared by a range of States parties in 2018.

Themes we explore in this final chapter thus include:

- the broader agenda for heritage protection in the face of revised government funding priorities;
- the future of World Heritage through efforts to remixing the colonial legacy of institutions and places, and how shifting narratives might (re)engage local residents and host communities with their World Heritage, as consumers and as managers;
- addressing the various environmental, social and economic challenges that have led to more than 50 properties being placed on the List of World Heritage in Danger;[3]
- utilising emerging technologies to manage, present and interpret World Heritage, in situ and remotely.

We conclude with some thoughts on whether or not World Heritage as a concept will continue to hold its appeal in the years and decades to come.

12.2 The future of heritage protection

States parties to the World Heritage Convention are required to protect national heritage, the duty is stated through Article 4 of the Convention – and the recommended mechanisms for this are stated within Article 5:

- to adopt a general policy which aims to give the cultural and natural heritage a function in the life of the community and to integrate the protection of that heritage into comprehensive planning programmes;
- to set up within its territories, where such services do not exist, one or more services for the protection, conservation and presentation of the cultural and natural heritage with an appropriate staff and possessing the means to discharge their functions;
- to develop scientific and technical studies and research and to work out such operating methods as will make the State capable of counteracting the dangers that threaten its cultural or natural heritage;
- to take the appropriate legal, scientific, technical, administrative and financial measures necessary for the identification, protection, conservation, presentation and rehabilitation of this heritage; and
- to foster the establishment or development of national or regional centres for training in the protection, conservation and presentation of the cultural and natural heritage and to encourage scientific research in this field (Article 5 World Heritage Convention).

Unfortunately, the protection of national heritage at a States party level is not always consistent – as we have seen, for example, through the listing of properties on the List of World Heritage in Danger, and on three occasions through their removal from the World Heritage list. The reasons for this lack of consistency is complex and tied into economic pressures (for example, the development and retention of national heritage infrastructure, policy and processes is often not the highest government priority) and where national systems do exist economic benefits of development are seen to outweigh benefits from natural and cultural heritage – for example, the pressure to develop and granting of permission to develop in designated landscape areas associated with mineral extraction, or major infrastructure impacts (roads, rail, air and port development), and projects with specific impacts within World Heritage property boundaries and their associated buffer zones (such as tall buildings etc). In most cases the national rhetoric is that heritage is seen as vital within national identity, economic and cultural development but despite this in practice heritage is threatened by change.

The challenge is to work towards the sustainable management of change (which is embedded within States party planning and within World Heritage ideas such as HUL). We now have (at least in theory) a well-developed approach to assessing significance and threat (for example through processes of heritage impact assessment), and discussion focuses on the nuanced debate between benefit, impact, justification and mitigation of impact with the notion of natural and heritage capital as important in how value and benefit is considered. It is perhaps within the discussion of the climate and ecological crisis and the developing dialogue of carbon sequestration and embodied carbon that 21st-century values for cultural and natural heritage are emerging – and clearly World Heritage properties can play an important role within this debate.

12.3 Decolonising heritage and shifting narratives

As we have examined, the development of ideas of conservation and heritage embedded within the World Heritage process (and critiqued through examination of the notion of OUV and representative heritage) is tied to ideas of colonialism. If we follow the same powerful argument as Satia (2020) that history is part of the colonial package – then the re-evaluation of the conservation and heritage practices that surround the historical discipline is vital. Examining colonial legacies within local, national and international heritage is critical to the evolution of the World Heritage processes over the next decades.

Within a World Heritage context further work is urgent to examine how the colonial experience must be identified as having OUV. One of the very first World Heritage properties, the **Island of Gorée** in Senegal was inscribed in 1978. The inscription associated with Criteria (vi) notes:

> The Island of Gorée is an exceptional testimony to one of the greatest tragedies in the history of human societies: the slave trade. The various elements of this 'memory island' – fortresses, buildings, streets, squares, etc. – recount, each in its own way, the history of Gorée which, from the 15th to the 19th century, was the largest slave-trading centre of the African coast.

The site is of exceptional significance to diaspora communities and formed an axis within the UNESCO Slave Route Project initiated in 1994 which was instigated to break the silence surrounding the history of slavery.[4]

But in the years since 1978 (and 1994 with the initiatives to work towards a more representative World Heritage) we have seen the World Heritage process become entangled within politics that has to some extent clouded the potential of World Heritage to examine and acknowledge this colonial past.

Decolonising conservation and heritage policy and practices requires the recognition of indigenous communities (for example as already well established in Canada, New Zealand and Australia) as well as the re-examination of institutions, established practices and concepts. In some cases, this is already underway, for example through work to examine the colonial legacy of the collections of the **Royal Botanic Gardens** at Kew, London.[5] But the re-examination of these institutions has also met intense criticism from particular right-wing historical perspectives within the divisive culture wars (for example the reception of the work at Kew and within the UK through the work of the National Trust – itself responsible for elements of nine of the UK's World Heritage properties – **Stonehenge and Avebury, Bath, Jurassic Coast, Lake District, Welsh Slate Landscape, Giants Causeway, Cornwall, Hadrian's Wall and Fountains Abbey**). Decolonising heritage thus means identifying and acknowledging the extent and consequences of the discipline's colonial legacy.

Another critical (but less contested) issue that needs to be addressed is how World Heritage Properties can better evolve with shifting narratives – for example how the inscription and understanding of OUV can be revised in light of new scientific or archaeological perspectives or as new interpretations challenge the established views on places. This develops from the re-examination of meanings and values of places (as above in relation to decolonisation), and in relation to how the language that is used through inscription tends to focus on superlative overviews (itself vital given the requirements to express OUV within the World Heritage Convention). Here a more nuanced understanding of OUV might emerge from debates around value – moving away from architectural or historical significance, rarity of species or landscapes to better capture the values and significance people assign to places. This is challenging on a local and national level – and comes to the heart of the criticisms of the World Heritage processes about who makes decisions and the value of external, expert opinion in contrast to local perspectives on place.

Connected to this rethinking of heritage and one of the consequences of the long series of local lockdowns during the COVID-19 pandemic has been the re-engagement of local communities with their heritage (see the Krakow case study and also the work of the Saltaire LockDown Archive[6]). This organic response (made easier through sharing images and information through social media platforms) to the series of national lockdowns develops from more long-standing initiatives and aspirations to refocus heritage locally rather than for outsiders (for example through the types of investment made for World Heritage properties and initiatives embedded within World Heritage Management Plans). Tensions still remain between local communities and external pressures – tourism as an obvious example, but also through the study, perception and value assigned to heritage sites – where debate has questioned the need for external experts and how best to rebalance indigenous and local knowledge. The example from the Okavango Delta World Heritage Site, Botswana (Keitumetse & Pampiri, 2016) reveals ways in which 'dormant' cultural values are central to local communities in landscapes otherwise perceived (and protected) for their natural heritage values.

BOX 12.1 CASE STUDY 12.1: KRAKÓW.

The **Historic Centre of Kraków**, a former capital of Poland, was inscribed on the World Heritage list in 1978 as 'one of the most outstanding examples of European urban planning, characterised by the harmonious development and accumulation of features representing all architectural styles from the early Romanesque to the Modernist periods' (UNESCO, 2021). The WHS encompasses an area of around 150 ha, containing numerous churches and monasteries, public buildings, palaces and townhouses and the remains of the medieval city walls. It was one of the first 12 sites inscribed on the World Heritage List in 1978 and at the time was considered 'the most valuable historic urban complex in Poland' (Siwek, 2017a, p. 70). The historic fabric of Kraków was, however, threatened particularly by acid rain associated with the emissions from Poland's heavy industry (Siwek, 2017b).

Over the last 40 years the Civic Committee for the Restoration of Kraków Heritage (Społeczny Komitet Odnowy Zabytków Krakowa) and its partners have used ring-fenced state funds to support and co-finance conservation works on hundreds of buildings across the city centre (Glinska-Holcer & Biesiada, 2017). The political transformation associated with the demise of the former Socialist state in 1989 and the consequent restoration of private property rights meant that private property owners were also encouraged to fund conservation activities, with more than 230 applicants being given subsidies worth almost PLN 25 million (equivalent to more than €5.5 million) in the period 2006–2016 (Glinska-Holcer & Biesiada, 2017). Particular attention has been paid to the conservation and restoration of building facades, so important to the city's image as a multi-period heritage destination.

The opening of Poland's borders after the country's accession into the EU allowed Kraków to emerge as one of Europe's leading city-break destinations, with visitor numbers reaching a peak of more than 14 million in 2019, including 3 million international tourists (Walas & Kruczek, 2020). This massive growth in tourism offered property owners the chance to generate income from letting out rooms through online booking platforms such as Airbnb but these pressures led to the gradual depopulation of the historic city centre, with its established community of academics, artists and others moving to surrounding areas (Siwek, 2017a) and the emergence of some considerable local resident dissatisfaction with the high levels of overtourism experienced in central Kraków for much of the year (Szromek, et al., 2020).

The conversion of some historic structures into hotels, guest houses and catering establishments had the benefit of making them theoretically more accessible to the public. However, the ultimate outcome of the growth in tourism over a 20-year period came at the cost of the loss of local engagement as Kraków residents essentially abandoned the city centre and the World Heritage Site to tourism (Siwek, 2017b). Some opportunities have been identified in recent years to divert some tourist activity away from this historic core to neighbouring parts of the city through the development of creative tourism (Pawlusinski & Kubal, 2018) and so-called 'off the beaten track' tourism (Matoga & Pawlowska, 2018) though the appeal of the historic city centre and its night time economy has remained a strong draw, particularly for short-stay international tourists (see, for instance, Thurnell-Read, 2012; Szromek, et al., 2020).

The COVID-19 pandemic led to an almost immediate and total cessation of activity in Kraków's tourism economy in the spring of 2020 with severe consequences for the city's many tourism businesses and the 29,000 residents

dependent on tourism for employment (Walas & Kruczek, 2020). The City Council's response was to use this enforced 'pause' as an opportunity to address a
number of policy objectives that, when achieved, would help the city recover from
some of the negative impacts of tourism that had emerged in the previous decade
or so. The adoption by the authorities in Kraków of the principles of Responsible
Tourism (see, for example, Goodwin, 2016) has allowed the main stakeholders to
identify how best to re-position the city as a destination that is 'a better place to
live in, and a better place to visit' (Piaskowski, 2020).

The sense of estrangement that many residents had for the historic core and
the World Heritage Site was tackled by a promotional campaign encouraging
locals to take their allowed daily exercise either by walking in the streets of the
old town, or by joining in with the exercise classes that were being held in city
parks rather than inside gyms and fitness clubs. The motto for the campaign
was 'I'm lucky to live where others can only come for a while' and was intended to re-awaken civic pride in the World Heritage Site, something that recent
research had demonstrated was declining among locals who felt excluded from
it by the presence of large numbers of tourists (Szromek et al., 2020).

As well as providing financial support for local tourism businesses suffering
from the loss of tourist income, the City Council and the Civic Committee for
the Restoration of Kraków Heritage continued to fund building conservation
works across the World Heritage Site throughout 2020 (Piaskowski, 2020).
Appropriate social distancing measures were introduced to ensure that work
teams remained safe and the work programme that had been planned for the
year was implemented as usual. The Council also used the 'breathing space'
allowed by the drop in tourism activity to identify a suite of new instruments for
managing heritage tourism across the city as well as extending its protection
activities into new districts including Nowa Huta, the Socialist Realist city located on the eastern edge of Kraków, and the Jewish quarter of Kazimierz (this
latter location lying within the boundary of the World Heritage Site).

Research undertaken with tourism entrepreneurs early on during the pandemic found that most expected individual city-break tourism to recover
quickest with group travel (including educational parties), the MICE sector and
religious tourism taking longer to return (Walas & Kruczek, 2020). It is the hope
of the Municipality of Kraków and its partners that when these independent
domestic and international tourists return to the city, they will still be able to
experience its Outstanding Universal Value, but that they will also take the time
to get to know other parts of the city thus spreading both the experience but
also the benefits of tourism. The pandemic crisis has accelerated reflection on
the resilience of tourism and culture. The efforts undertaken by the city before
the pandemic to coordinate the management of the world heritage area and to
improve the quality of life of the inhabitants of the old town have been inten-
sified and are bearing visible results. The Integrated Centre for the Management of Cultural Heritage was set up to – among others – coordinate cultural
events, protect the local cultural landscape, preserve endangered professions or

carry out a revitalisation programme. The programme is based on involving various stakeholders, initiating creative solutions to enhance the quality of tourism and harmonising the different, sometimes conflicting expectations of users of the old town.

Among many initiatives implemented by Kraków in response to the pandemic, PLAYKRAKOW.COM it is also worth mentioning, Poland's first city TV VOD platform for culture and heritage sectors – a dedicated fund to support film productions. A portal introducing and presenting Polish culture not only to stay-at-home Cracovians, but also to Poland and the general public dispersed around the world.

12.4 External challenges for World Heritage Sites

The implications of the climate and ecological emergency for the long-term future of the World Heritage List is dependent on the speed and type of adaptation that is undertaken (and we see this negotiated painfully slowly through the COP processes). Should climate change be limited to within 1.5 degrees, the speed of required change will by necessity impact international and domestic tourism behaviours, and World Heritage Site managers will be faced with the challenges of conservation as well as the impacts on local economies of changed tourism patterns (both of these factors are considered in Historic Environment Scotland's extensive work at the Heart of Neolithic Orkney World Heritage Site, for example: see Day et al, 2019). Of course, the impacts of zero action, or of adapting too slowly and making the shift to decarbonise the world's economies over a longer period of time, will result in more significant impacts to cultural and natural heritage sites. In which case the scale of impacts will (as examined in Chapter 6) accelerate and images of destruction once seen as unusual will become a more established and consequently less challenged norm. As with the needs to re-examine our colonial legacies, the debates around scientific consensus and political action or inaction relating to the climate and ecological emergency are polarised.

What is important within the discussion of adaptation is to use heritage to empower creativity rather than see heritage as limiting change. While heritage has been threatened by infrastructure projects, we need better ways to enable adaptation within World Heritage Sites and at different scales: for example, on the siting of wind farms in protected landscapes, or use of PV panels on historic buildings, or replacement of historic glazing on properties within World Heritage properties.

External challenges also relate to ongoing conflict. For instance, the impacts of ongoing conflict within Yemen whose three cultural World Heritage properties **Zabid** (with conservation needs predating the impacts of the current conflict) **Sana'a** and **Shibam** are all on the List of World Heritage in Danger. Similarly, the ongoing conflict in the Tigray region in Ethiopia is impacting the World Heritage property of **the Rock Hewn Churches of Lalibela** shows the entanglement of heritage within national identity and politics. While the climate crisis is not the singular cause of conflict – the social consequences of the climate crisis, their adverse effects on people and the resulting politicisation of threats and ethnic differences make conflict more likely. As we have seen, ethnic or national politics can be focused on heritage and this makes World Heritage vulnerable within all conflict.

Climate change impacts on the natural and cultural environment are already impacting how people live and engage in their locality and have changed patterns of resource use – in turn impacting cultural and natural heritage. The movement of people as climate refugees focuses discussion on contentious ideas of national identity (where heritage is central), but there are more complex understandings of people and places that will develop – but for which there is a significant amount of work to be done. For example the interconnection between people and seascapes through the Kiribati islands (designated as the **Phoenix Islands Protected Area** WHS), or through the Sundarbans – which is represented by two World Heritage Sites (**The Sundarbans,** Bangladesh and **Sundarbans National Park**, India) requires rethinking of cultural and natural dichotomies and their adaptation in light of the joint tensions of decolonisation and climate crisis – work that is starting through imaginative and creative rethinking of place by writers such as Amitiv Ghosh (2016, 2021).

12.5 Utilising new technologies to manage, present and interpret World Heritage

In her seminal 1977 book, *On Photography*, the American writer and activist Susan Sontag argued that the development of the portable camera in the late 19th and early 20th centuries had 'democratised' the capturing of images, allowing anyone with access to a camera the opportunity to record and share their own way of seeing a place or person. The Kodak company in particular is noted for promoting photography as an essential component of middle-class family life (Urry & Larson, 2011).

From a tourism perspective, a photograph not only provides the individual with a tangible memory that can be consumed well after the journey (Urry & Larson, 2011) but just as importantly, when these images are shared, they support the construction of what Robinson & Picard (2009) refer to as 'place myths', or 'imaginative geographies of the world' (p. 7). In other words, certain iconic views or images become associated with a destination to the extent that visitors wish to take their own photograph of the same view, to record their presence and to effectively justify their presence. Again, in the words of Robinson & Picard, 'the holiday photograph evidences not just the tourist site but the tourist him/herself, in a form of expressive self-creation' (2009, p. 1)

The introduction of digital photography in the late 1990s created new tourism behaviours – it became possible to take many, many more images than previously was the case when using conventional film. And when photography converged with mobile telephony and the internet from the mid-2000s onwards, the *practice* of photography was transformed still further for a number of reasons (Urry & Larson, 2011):

- images became instantly consumable;
- they could be shared worldwide, instantaneously;
- the screen became more important than the viewfinder, to both the producer and the recipient of the image.

Sharing images online became easier still with the introduction of social media platforms such as Facebook, WhatsApp and Instagram to the extent that billions of images are now uploaded onto social media daily.[7] So, the early democratisation of image-making that Sontag talked about in the late 1970s has been strengthened still further by the presence of smartphones that include both a camera and social media connectivity.

It has been demonstrated that how people select the photographs they upload on social media is linked to how they wish to manage their own image (Lo & McKercher, 2015), but that one side effect is that these shared images also play a vital role in shaping general destination images and making travel decisions (White, 2010; Pabel & Prideaux, 2016). By allocating specific hashtags to images, the person sharing the image is thus able, to some extent, to control how far that image spreads as people search for particular topics. This has implications for public awareness and understanding of World Heritage Sites just as much as for any other type of destination. A recent review of 680 million Instagram posts for more than 500 World Heritage Sites found that people were far more likely to share images of world heritage cities than of either industrial heritage properties or prehistoric sites, with the authors suggesting that the number of images uploaded on a platform for a destination can be used as a proxy for its popularity (Falk & Hagsten, 2021). The implication is that the more images of a site are shared by tourists, the greater the level of public awareness of that place and hence the increased likelihood that people viewing the image may wish to visit that place themselves at some time. Crucially, this means that property managers effectively lose control of how their sites are portrayed across the globe.

Of course, it isn't just tourists themselves using social media platforms to share images of places and sites. Destination Management Organisations (DMOs) have increasingly seen the benefit of communicating with existing and potential visitors through different platforms (Uskali et al., 2017; Kumpu et al., 2021) and of course UNESCO itself is active in promoting World Heritage issues on YouTube, Facebook, Twitter and Instagram, although at the time of writing there was no official UNESCO World Heritage presence on the most recent breakthrough platform, TikTok. The contribution that social media can make to raising awareness of World Heritage properties and the threats some of them may be facing is an increasingly important area of practice and research. For instance, some of the findings of a major research project investigating the impact of climate change on the coastal archaeology of **Neolithic Orkney** were communicated on a daily basis during COP26 via a TikTok account managed by the lead researcher, Nicole Burton of the University of Bradford, with the user name @the_archaeologist. Viewing data and user responses to the various messages are being analysed at the time of preparing this book with the hope that they will reveal the most effective approach to communicating this important message to teenagers and young adults who represent the core user group of this platform.[8]

Ensuring that the correct platforms are used to target different market segments/ interest groups is key to successful and effective communication, as is creating engaging and relevant content that moves the viewer to respond which is something not always achieved, as a recent review of the social media presence of UNESCO's Marine World Heritage Sites has found (Kenterelidou & Galatsopoulou, 2021).

Social media platforms and mobile phone technology can also be used as management tools. A recent example of how social media has been used in a 'citizen science' project to monitor and report on threats to a World Heritage property comes from **Bisotun** in Iran (inscribed in 2006 against Criteria (ii) and (iii)), where the local community were encouraged to use Instagram and WhatsApp to report problems across the 35,000 ha of the site and surrounding buffer zone (Nasrolahi et al., 2021). This project reported some success though also identified problems including the inability to always accurately identify the precise location of the reported issue and as a result will be building a project-specific mobile phone app to improve the quality of information provided by respondents. At **Mount Kenya National Park/Natural Forest** World Heritage Site in Kenya (inscribed 2013), plant identification software converted into a mobile phone app has been developed to allow people living in and near the area, and also tourists, to increase the volume of plant occurrence records available for analysis of species distributions within the park. Introduced in 2019, the project has already provided a considerable amount of new information about the distribution of certain species across the protected area (Bonnet et al., 2020).

One further technological development worthy of mention is the drone. These also make use of digital cameras to screen live images back to a viewer on the ground. They are increasingly being used to facilitate visual inspections of buildings and monuments and to identify signs of damage or other threats to natural heritage. They offer a cost-effective alternative to in-person survey, and when combined with other remote sensing approaches (air-borne or satellite imagery) help in the identification and monitoring of sites. The complexity here is ensuring new technologies are democratic with data shared with site managers and other relevant bodies in Open Access formats to avoid data or digital exclusion.

In short, the emergence in the last ten years or so of social media platforms as vehicles for sharing content about World Heritage properties has transformed both their marketing but also potentially their management. As the rate of technological change continues to increase, new applications and platforms will undoubtedly emerge and future World Heritage managers will need to respond to new ICT-based opportunities that may offer new, innovative ways of sharing and using user-generated media content (not just photographs, but film, sound recordings, text etc) for both marketing and management purposes.

12.6 Concluding remarks

Regardless of the academic critique of World Heritage and the problems associated with the World Heritage processes, the World Heritage concept remains remarkably resilient and provides a space for the imaginative rethinking of natural and cultural heritage in the 21st century and the entanglements between people and places at a local, national and international level. The experience of the authors in their teaching gives insight into these imaginative responses to the World Heritage concept – for example, in a fictional future World Heritage list students are keen to consider the potential OUV of recent sites such as Chernobyl as a symbol of destruction and re-wilding after the world's most devastating nuclear disaster, the potential for a transnational serial nomination of the Disney parks in the US, France, Japan and China as representative of new forms of leisure within designed landscapes, and a multitude of variations on these themes from global brands (from the Golden Arches of McDonalds to blue and yellow boxes of IKEA) (it should be noted these are not without precedent, seen for example through the Fray Bentos Industrial Landscape World Heritage Site in Uruguay). Others have pondered how OUV might be demonstrated on the range of sites impacted by the Climate Crisis – do the sites of devastating wildfire, melting permafrost or glacial retreat around the world represent OUV? Or those sites that represent our ecological crisis – perhaps the sites where species have become endangered and extinct? Or what about existing Industrial Heritage World Heritage Sites? Should their OUV be reconsidered not as the cradle of the industrial civilisation but as the start of the devastation resulting in the climate and ecological crisis? In response to the global COVID-19 pandemic, should those locations where the disease was first identified or vaccines developed and administered be celebrated for their OUV? World Heritage thus provides these imaginative spaces to think through how we are connected locally, nationally and internationally.

The next decades will reveal what the limits of reimagining of Outstanding Universal Value are, if the total number of World Heritage Sites should be capped and what re-imagined tourism (in response to the climate crisis and COVID pandemic) will do in relation to revenue and world heritage activity. The 80/20 principle could perhaps be applied in many ways – perhaps 80% of the World Heritage list demonstrates that initial desire to 'safeguard humanities heritage … ' and the ever-growing 20% represent the tensions around international, national and local politics – and perhaps 80% of the World Heritage list sites quietly continue as World Heritage properties without the management, conservation or political controversies we have highlighted here (demonstrated by the other 20%). Either way, World Heritage provides ideas and practices we can analyse so that we can do things better and where we can experiment with new concepts of heritage.

Our motivation in writing this much-delayed overview of our engagement with World Heritage remains the same – the World Heritage concept captures our own and our students' imaginations and we have both been fortunate to engage with World Heritage Sites in different ways – our work has been entangled (and in very different ways) with this now, half-century old concept. If being 50 is the new 40 (or 30), the Middle Ages of the World Heritage convention show the joint battles of middle age – critique and innovation.

Notes

1 See https://www.unwto.org/world-tourism-barometer-n18-january-2020 (accessed 21 January 2021).
2 See https://www.statista.com/chart/21793/international-tourist-arrivals-worldwide/ (accessed 21 January 2021).
3 Fifty-two at the time of writing in early 2022. See http://whc.unesco.org/en/danger/ (accessed 5 February 2022).
4 See https://en.unesco.org/themes/fostering-rights-inclusion/slave-route (accessed 5 February 2022).
5 See https://www.kew.org/read-and-watch/time-to-re-examine-the-history-of-botanical-collections (accessed 5 February 2022).
6 See https://saltairefestival.co.uk/saltaire-festival-lockdown-archive/ (accessed 5 February 2022).
7 See https://theconversation.com/3-2-billion-images-and-720-000-hours-of-video-are-shared-online-daily-can-you-sort-real-from-fake-148630 (accessed 10 December 2021).
8 See https://wallaroomedia.com/blog/social-media/tiktok-statistics/ (accessed 10 December 2021).

References

Bonnet, P. et al. 2020. How citizen scientists contribute to monitor protected areas thanks to automatic plant identification tools. *Ecological Solutions and Evidence*, 1 (2), 12023.

Day, J, Heron, S, Markham, A, Downes, J, Gibson, J and Hyslop, E. 2019. *Climate Risk Assessment for Heart of Neolithic Orkney World Heritage property: An application of the Climate Vulnerability Index*. Edinburgh: Historic Environment Scotland.

DeSilvey, C. 2017. *Curated Decay: Heritage beyond Saving*. Minneapolis: University of Minnesota Press.

Falk, M. T. & Hagsten, E. 2021. Visitor flows to World Heritage Sites in the era of Instagram. *Journal of Sustainable Tourism*, 29 (10), 1547–1564.

Fowler, C. 2020. *Green Unpleasant Land. Creative Responses to Rural England's Colonial Connections*. Leeds: Peepal Tree Press Ltd.

Ghosh, A. 2016. *The Great Derangement: Climate Change and the Unthinkable*. Chicago: University of Chicago Press.

Ghosh, A. 2021. *The Nutmeg's Curse: Parables for a Planet in Crisis*. Chicago: University of Chicago Press.

Glinska-Holcer, E. & Biesiada, D. 2017. How the City of Krakow takes care of monuments. In: M. Rozbicka & D. Lipska, eds. *Heritage in Poland*. Warsaw: National Heritage Board of Poland, 169–171.

Goodwin, H. 2016. *Responsible Tourism: Using tourism for sustainable development. 2nd ed.* Oxford: Goodfellow.

Keitumetse, S & Pampiri, M. 2016. Community cultural identity in nature-tourism gateway areas: Maun Village, Okavango Delta World Heritage Site, Botswana, *Journal of Community Archaeology & Heritage*, 3 (2). 99–117.

Kenterelidou, C. & Galatsopoulou, F. 2021. Sustainable biocultural heritage management and communication: the case of digital narrative for UNESCO Marine World Heritage of Outstanding Univesal Value. *Sustainability*, 13 (3), 1449.

Kumpu, J., Pesonen, J. & Heinonen, J. 2021. *Measuring the value of Social Media Marketing from a Destination Marketing Organization Perspective.* Cham, Switzerland: Springer, 365–377.

Lo, I. S. & McKercher, B. 2015. Ideal image in process: online tourist photography and impression management. *Annals of Tourism Research*, 52, 104–116.

Markham, A. 2021. Climate change, World Heritage, COVID-19 and tourism. *World Heritage*, October, 100, 36–44.

Matoga, L. & Pawlowska, A. 2018. Off-the-beaten-track tourism: a new trend in the tourism development in historical European cities. A case study of the city of Krakow, Poland. *Current Issues in Tourism*, 21 (14), 1644–1669.

Meskell, L. 2018. *A Future in Ruins. UNESCO, World Heritage, and the Dream of Peace.* New York: Oxford University Press.

Nasrolahi, A., Gena, C., Messina, V. & Ejraei, S. 2021. *Participatory Monitoring in Cultural Heritage Conservation. Case Study: The Landscape Zone of the Bisotun World Heritage Site.* New York: ACM, 186–188.

Pabel, A. & Prideaux, B. 2016. Social media use in pre-trip planning by tourists visiting a small regional leisure destination. *Journal of Vacation Marketing*, 22 (4), 335–348.

Pawlusinski, R. & Kubal, M. 2018. A new take on an old structure? Creative and slow tourism in Krakow (Poland). *Journal of Tourism and Cultural Change*, 16 (3), 265–285.

Piaskowski, R. 2020. Impact of COVID-19 on the Krakow WHS. Personal communication, 14 December.

Robinson, M. & Picard, D. 2009. *The Framed World. Tourism, Tourists and Photography.* London: Ashgate.

Satia, P. 2020. *Time's Monster: History, Conscience and Britain's Empire.* London: Allen Lane.

Siwek, A. 2017a. Between preservation and the challenges of today. *World Heritage*, 84, (July), 40–43.

Siwek, A. 2017b. Historic Centre of Krakow (1978). In: M. Rozbicka & D. Lipska, eds. *Heritage in Poland.* Warsaw: National Heritage Board of Poland, 69–74.

Sontag, S. 1977. *On Photography.* London: Allen Lane.

Szromek, A. R., Kruczek, Z. & Walas, B. 2020. The attitude of tourist destination residents towards the effect of overtourism – Krakow case study. *Sustainability*, 12 (228), 1–17.

Thurnell-Read, T. 2012. Tourism place and space. British stag tourism in Poland. *Annals of Tourism Research*, 39 (2), 801–819.

UNESCO. 2021. Historic Centre of Krakow. https://whc.unesco.org/en/list/29/ (accessed 15 February 2021).

Urry, J. & Larson, J. 2011. *The Tourist Gaze 3.0.* 3rd ed. London: Sage.

Uskali, A., Koca, B. & Sonmez, S. 2017. How 'social' are destinations? Examining European DMO social media usage. *Journal of Destination Marketing and Management*, 6 (2), 136–149.

Walas, B. & Kruczek, Z. 2020. The Impact of COVID-19 on tourism in Krakow in the eyes of tourism entrepreneurs. *Studia Periegetica*, 2 (30), 79–95.

White, L. 2010. Facebook, friends and photos: a snapshot into social networking for generating travel ideas. In: N. Sharda, ed. *Tourism Informatics: Visual Travel Recommender Systems, Social Communities, and User Interface.* Hershey, PA: IGI Global, 115–129.

INDEX

Printed in the United States
by Baker & Taylor Publisher Services